THE THIRD PERSON OF THE TRINITY

PROCEEDINGS OF THE LOS ANGELES THEOLOGY CONFERENCE

This is the eighth volume in a series published by Zondervan Academic. It is the proceedings of the Los Angeles Theology Conference held under the auspices of Biola University in January 2020. The conference attempts to do several things. First, it provides a regional forum in which scholars, students, and clergy can come together to discuss and reflect on central doctrinal claims of the Christian faith. It is also an ecumenical endeavor. Bringing together theologians from a number of different schools and confessions, the LATC seeks to foster serious engagement with Scripture and tradition in a spirit of collegial dialogue (and disagreement), looking to retrieve the best of the Christian past in order to forge theology for the future. Finally, each volume in the series focuses on a central topic in dogmatic theology. It is hoped that this endeavor will continue to fructify contemporary systematic theology and foster a greater understanding of the historic Christian faith among the members of its different communions.

CHRISTOLOGY,
ANCIENT AND MODERN:
Explorations in Constructive
Dogmatics, *2013*

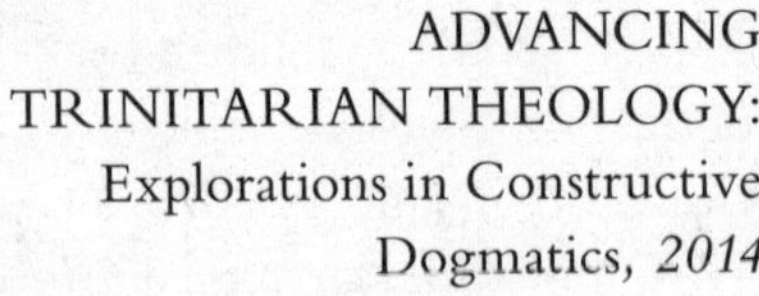

ADVANCING
TRINITARIAN THEOLOGY:
Explorations in Constructive
Dogmatics, *2014*

LOCATING ATONEMENT:
Explorations in Constructive
Dogmatics, *2015*

*THE VOICE OF GOD IN
THE TEXT OF SCRIPTURE*:
Explorations in Constructive
Dogmatics, *2016*

THE TASK OF DOGMATICS:
Explorations in Theological
Method, 2017

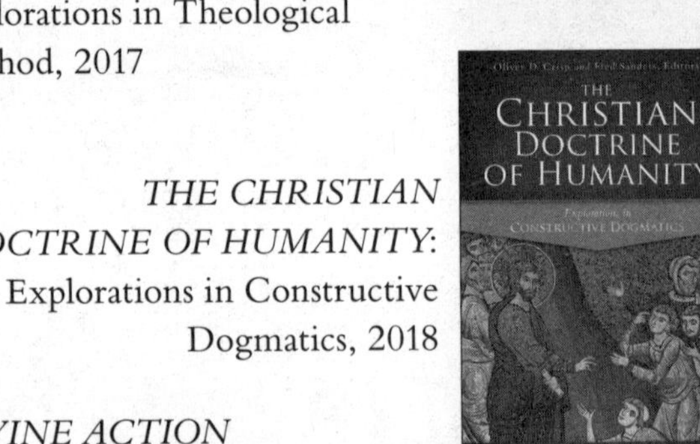

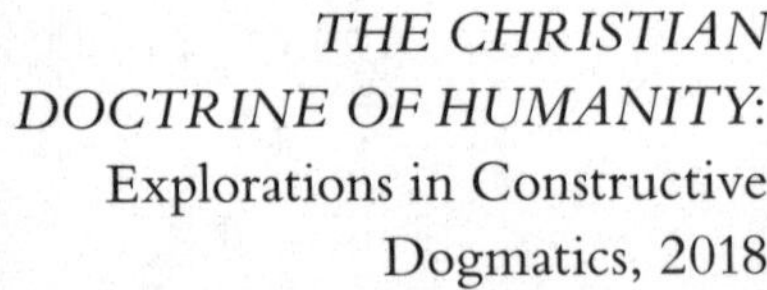

*THE CHRISTIAN
DOCTRINE OF HUMANITY*:
Explorations in Constructive
Dogmatics, 2018

*DIVINE ACTION
AND PROVIDENCE*:
Explorations in Constructive
Dogmatics, 2019

Oliver D. Crisp *and* Fred Sanders, Editors

THE THIRD PERSON OF THE TRINITY

Explorations in CONSTRUCTIVE DOGMATICS

CONTRIBUTORS

Esther E. Acolatse, Daniel Castelo, Lucy Peppiatt, Ephraim Radner, Fred Sanders

ZONDERVAN ACADEMIC

The Third Person of the Trinity

Requests for information should be addressed to:
Zondervan, *3900 Sparks Dr. SE, Grand Rapids, Michigan 49546*

Zondervan titles may be purchased in bulk for educational, business, fundraising, or sales promotional use. For information, please email SpecialMarkets@Zondervan.com.

ISBN 978-0-310-10691-3 (softcover)

ISBN 978-0-310-10692-0 (ebook)

Cover Design: Mark Veldheer
Cover photo: © Peter Godong / UIG / Bridgeman Images

Printed in the United States of America

---

20 21 22 23 24 25 26 27 28 29 30 /LSC/ 15 14 13 12 11 10 9 8 7 6 5 4 3 2 1

In memoriam,
Revd. Dr. David Efird

"Behold an Israelite indeed, in whom is no guile!"
—John 1:47

CONTENTS

ACKNOWLEDGMENTS

THE EDITORS WOULD LIKE TO THANK Professor Clinton E. Arnold as dean of Talbot School of Theology and the faculty and administration of Biola University for their support for the Eighth Los Angeles Theology Conference (LATC) in January of 2020, out of which these published proceedings grew. We are also grateful for the generous administrative support provided by Oscar Merlo, director of Biola's Center for the Study of the Work and Ministry of the Holy Spirit Today and in particular the assistance of Jenny Baik and Luisa Ortez, who oversaw the practical running of the event. Once more, we are delighted to record our grateful thanks to our editor and colleague, Katya Covrett. Almost incredibly, after all these years she is still an editor extraordinaire.

CONTRIBUTORS

Esther E. Acolatse—is associate professor of pastoral theology and intercultural studies at Knox College in the University of Toronto, Canada. She holds a BA (Hons) from the University of Ghana, an MTS from Harvard University, and a PhD from Princeton Theological Seminary.

Daniel Castelo—is professor of systematic and constructive theology at Seattle Pacific University. He earned his BA from Lee University, his MDiv from Church of God Theological Seminary, and his PhD from Duke University.

Joshua Cockayne—is lecturer in analytic theology in the Logos Institute, School of Divinity, University of St Andrews, Scotland. He earned his BA, MA, and PhD degrees in philosophy from the University of York and is currently training for ordained ministry in the Scottish Episcopal Church.

Leon Harris—is assistant professor of theology, Talbot School of Theology, Biola University. He earned his BS degree from Biola University, MDiv and ThM degrees from Talbot School of Theology, and PhD in systematic theology from the University of Aberdeen.

Daniel Lee Hill—is assistant professor of theology at Dallas Theological Seminary. He holds a BA degree from Hampton University, a ThM from Dallas Theological Seminary, and a PhD from Wheaton College.

Kimberley Kroll—is a doctoral candidate in divinity in the Logos Institute, University of St. Andrews. She holds a BA in philosophy and English from Queens College, City University of New York, an MDiv from Grace Theological Seminary, and an MA in Philosophy from Biola University.

Joanna Leidenhag—is lecturer in theology, School of Divinity, University of St. Andrews. She holds an MA in modern history and theology from the University of St Andrews, an MA in theological studies from

Princeton Theological Seminary, and a PhD in divinity from New College, University of Edinburgh.

Joshua M. McNall—is church relations ambassador and assistant professor of pastoral theology in the School of Ministry and Christian Thought, Oklahoma Wesleyan University. He earned his BA from Oklahoma Wesleyan University, his MA in theology from Gordon-Conwell Theological Seminary, and a PhD from the University of Manchester.

Lucy Peppiatt—is principal of Westminster Theological Centre in the UK, where she also teaches systematic theology. She earned a BA in English literature from the University of Birmingham, a BD from the University of London, an MA in systematic theology from King's College, London, and a PhD in Systematic Theology from the University of Otago.

Ephraim Radner—is professor of historical theology at Wycliffe College in the University of Toronto, Canada. He holds a BA from Dartmouth College, an MDiv from Yale Divinity School, and a PhD from Yale University.

Fred Sanders—is professor of theology, Torrey Honors Institute, Biola University. He holds a BA in fine art from Murray State University, an MDiv from Asbury Theological Seminary, and a PhD from the Graduate Theological Union in Berkeley, California.

Jerome Van Kuiken—is dean and associate professor of Christian thought in the School of Ministry and Christian Thought, Oklahoma Wesleyan University. He holds a BA in religion from Kentucky Mountain Bible College, an MDiv from Wesley Biblical Seminary, and a PhD in theology from the University of Manchester.

Adonis Vidu—is professor of theology at Gordon-Conwell Theological Seminary. He holds a BA from Emmanuel Bible Institute in Romania, an MPhil from Babeș-Bolyai University in Romania, and a PhD from the University of Nottingham.

Sameer Yadav—is associate professor of religious studies, Westmont College. He holds a BA in Philosophy from Boise State University, an STM degree from Yale Divinity School, and a ThD from Duke University Divinity School.

INTRODUCTION

We believe in the Holy Spirit, the Lord, the giver of life,
who proceeds from the Father [and the Son].
With the Father and the Son he is worshiped and glorified.
He has spoken through the Prophets.
—NICENE CREED (AD 381)

"THIRD ARTICLE THEOLOGY" refers to the theological content of the third article of the Nicene Creed, the symbol of the great ecumenical council of AD 381. The fathers of the Second Ecumenical Council, held at the imperial city of Constantinople in AD 381, amended and expanded the symbol of the Council of Nicaea in AD 325 so as to bequeath to the church, among other things, a clear presentation of the dogma of the Holy Trinity. From the point of view of subsequent church history, one of the chief additions to this later symbol was the expanded article on the Holy Spirit. He is confessed as the Lord, the giver of life, who proceeds from the Father, and who is worshiped and glorified with the Father and Son: three divine persons, one indivisible Godhead. He is also the one who inspired the prophets of old. As is well known, later ecumenical disputes about the third article of the creed were a contributing factor in the great division of Christendom into East and West in the Great Schism of AD 1054. The Western church unilaterally added to the creedal statement about the procession of the Spirit the clause, "and the Son" (in Latin, *filioque*). Although this was supposed to be a way of clarifying the different ways in which the divine persons proceed so as to safeguard the distinction of divine persons, the Eastern churches took it as an imposition that was never agreed upon ecumenically. The rest, as they say, is history. The *filioque controversy*, as it has become known, is still with us today, and books, essays, and articles—as well as constructive proposals for the resolution of this ecumenical running sore!—are still rolling off the presses. Although the vitriol that this dispute engendered has been neutralised over the centuries, and although there has been real ecumenical progress in discussion of this thorny issue, it remains one of the great unresolved theological sources of division in the church.

This collection of essays from the Eighth Los Angeles Theology Conference, held under the auspices of Talbot School of Theology at Biola University, focuses on third article theology. We had wanted to have a conference on this theme for some years. But we lacked a clear unifying theme that would help bring together different theological contributions in a way that did not end up with a rather scattered set of reflections and interrogations of what is one of the most divisive of Christian dogmas. How were we to achieve the goal of a conference that did not add to this division? One thing was clear to us: another collection of essays focused entirely on the *filioque* controversy was probably not what was needed. So how could the conference keep the irenic temper of previous LA Theology Conferences, which were ecumenical in tone and yet sought to resource and fructify contemporary systematic theology through consideration of the vital dogmatic topic? The answer we landed upon was to focus on *the Holy Spirit as the third person of the divine Trinity*. Once this much was clear, the rest followed. Third article theology should be about the identification and articulation of the procession of the third person of the Godhead, whom we confess to be the Lord and giver of life, the one who proceeds from the Father, who is glorified with the Father and the Son, who inspires the prophets. Surely a collection of essays exploring facets of this great article of the creed would be a welcome addition to the literature that focuses on the divinity and personhood of the Holy Spirit in the Godhead rather than on the division that confessing the third article has sometimes brought about in the life of the church. The results of this process of deliberation, as well as the conference that was consequent upon them, are now in your hands.

The discussion kicks off with Fred Sanders in the first chapter. Beginning with the Bible's way of naming the third person, he explores the perennial challenges of articulating a pneumatology that takes into account all the things that need to be held together. He argues that the foundation of pneumatology lies in the twin doctrines of the eternal processions (within the Godhead) and the temporal missions (in the world). When a theology of the revealed divine names is developed in constant conceptual dependence on a theology of missions and processions, pneumatology finds its proper place within Christian theology.

In chapter 2, Adonis Vidu takes up the question of how the missions of the Son and Spirit are ordered to each other. Epistemically, he moves from the missions to the processions. Historically, this has been the strongest argument for the *filioque* clause of the Nicene Creed, since (it is said) the Spirit is sent by the Son, from the Father. However, he reasons that this view has been based on an understanding of the mission of the Spirit as starting at Pentecost. But if there is a mission of the Spirit already at the conception of Jesus, then the Son is sent through the Holy Spirit, not the Spirit through the Son. Vidu argues that operations, which are common and appropriated, must be more carefully distinguished from missions, which are proper to the person sent. Thus, while there is an operation of the Spirit at the conception of Christ, he maintains that it is not strictly speaking a mission. The mission of the Spirit follows after the completion of the Son's mission, just as the procession of the Spirit follows after the procession of the Son. Confounding the missions would lead to confounding the processions and thus the persons. Positively, if the mission of the Spirit presupposes the completed mission of the Son, it follows (he maintains) that the former is effected through the humanity of Christ specifically, as the "Spirit of Christ" or the "Spirit of the Son."

In chapter 3, Kimberley Kroll and Joanna Leidenhag consider the problem of thirdness in pneumatology. They argue that this problem sometimes leads to the peculiar and liminal place allotted to the Holy Spirit in theology proper. The first two sections of the chapter outline how this problem of thirdness tends to either depersonalise and abstract pneumatology or assimilate it to other doctrines. To avoid these consequences, they propose that a theologically grounded notion of what and who the Spirit is, is found only when properly constrained by a third question: How? This question of how in relation to the Spirit is often gestured toward by way of the prepositions *through*, *in*, and *by*. Since it is through, in, and by the Spirit that creatures come to participate in Christ and know the Father, Kroll and Leidenhag argue that it is imperative for theologians to wrestle with this *how* question. In the final section of the chapter, they argue that the self-revelation of the Holy Spirit (i.e., *how* the Holy Spirit reveals himself) should inform our understanding of who and what the triune God is.

In chapter 4, "The Mystery of the Immanent Trinity and the Procession of the Spirit," Sameer Yadav explores the *filioque* by arguing for a particular way of identifying the evidential base and inferential structure required for determining the question of single versus dual procession of the Spirit. He also considers the theological stakes of favoring one model over the other.

Yadav advocates a form of mysterianism about the immanent Trinity, in dialogue with some recent, prominent advocates of mysterianism. On his view, even a minimalist approach to the inferential structure of Trinitarian belief must include a commitment to logical coherence. The primary ground and purpose of Trinitarian belief consists in its "grammatical" relation to the Christian experience of salvation and practice of worship. How much is at stake in the doctrinal decision about whether the Spirit proceeds from the Father alone or from the Father and the Son? Yadav argues that decisions made here matter for determining the proper shape of worship as well as for making decisions about the hypostasis of the Spirit.

Chapter 5 takes an epistemic turn, as Daniel Castelo steps back from the content of pneumatology to consider the necessarily pneumatological orientation of Christian God-knowledge. Castelo is concerned not only to locate theological discourse within a responsibly public setting (such as the modern university) but also to approach pneumatology as spiritual illumination, which reveals some of the ways God-knowledge is a particular kind of knowledge. "It is a kind of knowledge made possible by the Spirit pouring out God's love upon our hearts, that very center and core of who we are . . . not so much seized but received, not so much generated but participated in" (p. 81). By attending to the doctrine of the Holy Spirit in a few key scriptural categories, Castelo traces the implications of consistently recognizing the pneumatic character of all Christian God-knowledge.

Chapter 6, coauthored by Jerome Van Kuiken and Joshua M. McNall, asks about the place of the Holy Spirit in Trinitarian theology by canvassing recent proposals to confess a Spirituque doctrine. They define Spirituque as "the idea that the much-debated filioque of intra-Trinitarian relations should be complemented by the notion that the Spirit participates with the Father in the Son's eternal generation so that it may be correct to say (at least in some sense) that the Son's eternal generation involves both the Father and the Spirit" (p. 88). Theologians from a variety of confessional traditions have explored Spirituque as a way of locating the Holy Spirit's person and work in order to overcome a perennial temptation to subordinate pneumatology to Christology. While noting the diverse motivations and goals of the various Spirituque proposals that have circulated, Van Kuiken and McNall offer a cautious but constructive affirmation of the move.

In chapter 7, "Holy Pedagogue, Perfecting Guide: The Holy Spirit's Presence in Creation," Daniel Lee Hill builds a bridge between areas of pneumatology that are not often connected: the Holy Spirit's particular mode of presence to created reality and the work of the Holy Spirit in salvation. Drawing on resources from Basil of Caesarea to Robert Jenson, Hill argues for an understanding of the Spirit's presence as "inscribing creation with its telos, training creation in wisdom, and guiding creation toward its ultimate end: reconciliation in Christ" (p. 106). While acknowledging that cosmological categories like space need to be conceptually purified and refined for theological use, Hill presses them into service in an argument that illuminates the consistently recognizable character of the Holy Spirit's work in a way that distinguishes the orders of creation and redemption without bifurcating them.

In chapter 8, Esther Acolatse explores "The Relational Nature of the Spirit in God and Humans." Her concern is to recognize God's transcendence by tracing the way the Holy Spirit exists in relation to the Father and the Son within the divine life. Acknowledging this inner-divine relationality does not result in distancing God from humans and their spiritual lives; on the contrary, it enables us to recognize that the divine incursions into human spirituality are more than just a naturalized mysticism commonly available to all human subjects. Encounters with the divine Spirit are not merely experiences of our created spirituality but are the kind of things witnessed to by Pentecostal and majority world Christians: a meeting with God the Spirit. In critical dialogue with the work of John Levison, Acolatse extends this analysis to connect the spiritual life of God to the spiritual life of creatures, without collapsing them into each other.

Lucy Peppiatt has previously written on the complex subject of Spirit Christology; in chapter 9 she turns to questions of Christomorphic pneumatology. Although the main point of her essay is to give proper attention to the doctrine of the Holy Spirit, Peppiatt argues forcefully that pneumatology must be developed alongside Christology and never in isolation from it. In fact, from one angle, all the work of the Holy Spirit stands out as the work of the Spirit of Christ, bearing witness to Jesus Christ. To explore how these two doctrines mutually implicate each other, Peppiatt interrogates the kenosis tradition in Christology, showing how theologies of christological kenosis would benefit from the inclusion of pneumatological plerosis: "So on the one hand we have the story of the assumption of humanity by the Son that entails a kenosis. On the other we have the filling of humanity by the divine in the Son in the hypostatic union and importantly for us, by the Spirit at Pentecost, where the Spirit is poured out on all flesh" (p. 158). The result of letting pneumatology be shaped by Christology is not just a clarification and concretizing of the shape of Christology but a better scope and balance for Trinitarian theology overall.

In chapter 10, Joshua Cockayne notes how the Nicene Creed groups belief in the Holy Spirit with belief in the church. To draw out the meaning of this creedal linking of Spirit and church, he draws on recent philosophical work on social ontology. Cockayne finds possible models for thinking about the work of the Spirit in constituting and uniting the church in proposals about group agency. The church is in certain ways like other human groups; though constituted by many individual human agents, it is capable of acting as one group agent. Cockayne notes that the church differs from the examples of social wholes discussed in the literature on social agency though, because its unity comes not from human structure and organisation but from the continued work of Holy Spirit uniting and sustaining it.

Chapter 11, "The Holy Spirit as Liberator: An Exploration of a Black American Pneumatology of Freedom," is a close look at one particular, unique tradition within modern Christian history with the intention of drawing out universally instructive theological insights. Leon Harris examines the work of the Holy Spirit as the deliverer of black Christians from a disruption of their *imago Dei*, who makes possible the (re)creation of their status in Christ. Engaging with select voices from the black American theological tradition, Harris indicates the difference that could be made by a constructive pneumatology within the contemporary black church. Such a pneumatology would help hold together some things that often come apart in theological traditions that are not similarly shaped by the holistic deliverance of the black church: in particular, the deep coherence of spiritual and material liberation is something to which this tradition's pneumatology bears eloquent witness.

Chapter 12 is an extended meditation by Ephraim Radner on the claim that the Holy Spirit teaches us to die faithfully. Radner has diagnosed a consistent modern preoccupation with pressing the category of pneumatology into service as a way of escape from creatureliness, making the Spirit serve as a contrast to the world of created existence and struggle. It is against this background that he insists on the Spirit as teaching faithful death rather than enabling an escapist transcending of death. The latter would in fact be a refusal to be creatures who learn from their maker how to exist in "our unsolicited births and our inescapable deaths" (p. 207). Radner introduces as a case study the life and work of the little-known Jewish Christian theologian Ulrich Simon (1913–97). Simon wrote about tragedy and history, but Radner is more interested in showing the way this theological writing arose from his life of contingent vulnerability. Simon's theological life enables the insight that "the Holy Spirit is the very divine condition for a reality that places death and faith as the limit of creaturely existence," Radner says (p. 198). This final chapter, "Running Away from Sorrow: Pneumatology and Some Modern Discontents," is an evocative and inconclusive conclusion for a volume on the person and work of the Holy Spirit.

With our Orthodox and Roman Catholic sisters and brothers we confess the third article in its ecumenical form. With our sisters and brothers in the churches of the Reformation, we echo the creed as it is refracted down the centuries in the particular confessions of these different communions. With our Anabaptist, Baptist, and Free Church sisters and brothers, we confess the Lordship of the Holy Spirit. With our charismatic, Pentecostal, and third-wave sisters and brothers we confess to hearing the voice of the Spirit in the churches today, the same Spirit who inspired the prophets of old. With all those who confess the name of Christ and who hope for the gracious susurrations of the Holy Spirit, we offer these essays as a contribution to the ongoing dogmatic conversation about third article theology and about the presence of the person and work of the Holy Spirit in the life of the body of Christ today. May these essays extend discussion of the doctrine of the person and work of the Holy Spirit today, *ad maiorem dei gloriam*.

Oliver D. Crisp and Fred Sanders, April 2020

CHAPTER 1

THE SPIRIT WHO IS FROM GOD

The Pneumatology of Procession and Mission

FRED SANDERS

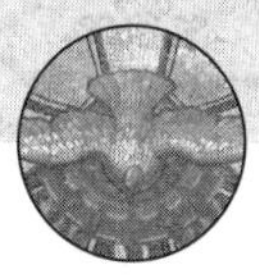

THIS CHAPTER IS AN ESSAY in triangulation, locating the doctrine of the Holy Spirit by inference from other doctrines and with reference to those other doctrinal loci. Such an indirect strategy is necessary because of some peculiarities of pneumatology. While the doctrine of the Spirit is not obscure in itself, its exposition is beset with certain ambiguities that resist a more straightforward method. These pneumatological ambiguities become theologically troublesome especially in relation to the doctrines that border it: the Trinity, Christology, and the relation of God to creation. These contiguous doctrines generally have clearer boundaries. They have histories in which they have been more elaborately formulated. As a result, they can draw attention away from pneumatology. Instead, this chapter attempts to borrow clarity from these surrounding doctrines for the consolidation of pneumatology. It takes three steps toward placing pneumatology within a comprehensive doctrine of God. First, it analyzes the pattern of biblical naming of the Holy Spirit; second, it relates pneumatology to the doctrine of divine processions and missions, which is fundamental for classical Trinitarian theology; and third, it explores the fruitfulness of using the less biblically obvious category of gift as a description of the third person of the Trinity. The Holy Spirit is God and is from God; by triangulation, this chapter undertakes to specify the meaning of both sides of this statement.

NAMING THE THIRD PERSON OF THE TRINITY

To speak about the third person of the Trinity is not yet to invoke any name. The phrase "third person of the Trinity" is not so much a name, nor even an identifying description, as it is a kind of doctrinal map locating this one by triangulation from other plottable doctrinal points: it directs us to find the Spirit in the Trinitarian taxis at location three. It says something like, "Go to the Father, follow the way of procession, and when you get to the Son, you are not quite there yet; make a left turn and proceed to the terminus of Pneumatology Lane." The phrase "third person of the Trinity" is also fairly obviously an invocation of a set of theologoumena honored by long usage but not found in the words of Scripture. The key words *Trinity*, *person*, and even *third* are not given to us in the very words of scriptural revelation. These words are offered as conceptual paraphrases that give an account of the overall meaning of what Scripture says on these topics. One disadvantage of using this elaborate theological terminology of "third person of the Trinity" is that it could lead to abstraction and distraction. In order to avoid these pitfalls, we need to make careful use of the phrase and handle it intentionally, as a schematic way of saying what Scripture says, while regularly taking recourse to the way Scripture actually speaks. But using this elaborate terminology also has distinct advantages. One advantage is that it conjures for our minds the overall doctrinal matrix within which we are speaking of this person, while also picking out precisely the Spirit in distinction from the Father and the Son. One of the constant duties of pneumatology is picking out the Holy Spirit within the Trinity without lifting the Holy Spirit from that Trinitarian matrix. We want to be able to ponder this one in particular, but not this one in isolation. The phrase *third person of the Trinity* does this rather abstractly and schematically, but it does locate the Spirit.

Let us now follow Scripture in actually naming the third person of the Trinity. Scripture names the third person of the Trinity in many ways, and Christian theology has the task of responding appropriately to this biblical pattern of naming in a way that is both responsive to God's word, confessing the identity of the Spirit, and responsible to theology's office of teaching, following "the pattern of the sound words" (2 Tim 1:13) that we have heard from the apostles and prophets.[1] Serving the Lord and serving the church in this way, the theological work of pneumatology is a particular mode of conceptually guarding "the good deposit" entrusted

1. Unless indicated otherwise, Scripture quotations in this chapter come from the ESV.

to us, which Paul tells Timothy is something that must itself be done "by the Holy Spirit who dwells within us" (2 Tim 1:14). There is something reflexive or self-involving if we apply this phrase *by the Holy Spirit* to pneumatological study. All theology, as a catechetical guarding of the good deposit by a disciplined following of the pattern of sound teaching, must take place "by the Holy Spirit who dwells in us," but the doctrinal locus of pneumatology is uniquely a field of doctrinal work simultaneously *by* the Spirit and *about* the Spirit. At its most instructive, Christian pneumatology serves as a foregrounding of what has always already been going on as the pervasive background of all theology and can catalyze the deepest moments of insight and awareness. But great care is required because exercises in pneumatology, at their least instructive, can become doctrinally diffuse, saying nothing much in particular; or vacuous, holding open a place to receive some content at a later time; or distracting, inviting the mind to pursue any number of other subjects in quest of the long-awaited definitive treatment. Theologians confront this danger when they direct attention to the Holy Spirit; they might come away with a lot of good ideas, each of which is interesting, promising, and in itself perfectly correct, but move in so many directions that it no longer feels like one doctrine. In other words, one of the desiderata for responsible pneumatology is that once it is done, it should stay done. A well-ordered and well-functioning doctrine of the Holy Spirit should secure a solid and permanent basis for all the things we need to say in the full scope of the doctrine. The Spirit blows where it wills, but pneumatology ought to stay put.

The biblical pattern of naming, I suggest, provides a foundation for a stable pneumatology. That pattern establishes a relation between God and God's Spirit, which is precisely what was selected for further development by the central traditions of Christian theology. Viewed thus as an expansion of a biblical pattern of naming, the ancient patristic notion of the procession of the Spirit protects against pneumatological chaos. The pneumatology of the early church developed and articulated these concepts in part with this goal of stability in mind; especially the line of Alexandrian thinkers from Origen through Didymus the Blind, Athanasius, and Cyril were attentive to the way the doctrine of eternal procession served as a grounding or integrating concept for the vast and disparate array of ways the Scripture speaks of the Holy Spirit. This first phase of the argument will not be carried out in the mode of commentary on patristic arguments, though. Instead, it will be a brief demonstration on the grounds of the matter itself, which is the pattern of words used by Holy Scripture in naming the Spirit.

In one sense, the difficulty we encounter in expressing pneumatology could be called the Bible's fault. The Holy Spirit's self-revelation and self-naming in inspired Scripture is diverse. In the Old Testament we meet references to the Spirit of God, but already there is diversity and plurality in the divine names used: we hear of the Spirit of Elohim and the Spirit of Yahweh, even the Spirit of Adonai and of the Most High. By Isaiah 11, this Spirit is the Spirit of wisdom and understanding, the Spirit of counsel and might, the Spirit of knowledge and the fear of the Lord. Elsewhere, the pattern of naming splits off even more, so that no sooner do we learn that the Spirit indwells the temple than we have to learn that the glory also indwells, and that spirit and glory are, if not synonyms, at least acceptable parallelisms. And so begins the proliferation of new nouns that can serve as ciphers of the Spirit: holiness, glory, power, cloud, presence. In poetic parallelisms, all of these can point to the Spirit without invoking the expected name. In the thicket of these many Old Testament names, the most constant element sometimes seems to be the word *of*. In fact, there lies the real biblical root of the doctrine of procession. The fundamental pattern in the Spirit's self-naming is ofness. The ofness is also complex, of course: sometimes it signifies identity (the Spirit of God is God); sometimes it signifies distinction (not just God, but the Spirit of God). Other divine self-descriptions follow this logic, including a range of self-descriptions that we have no reason to think of as especially pneumatological: both the face of God and the name of God are used with the same tension, signifying God yet also signifying something from God. We might say, in these instances, that God is on both sides of the *of*: God of God, to use the Nicene idiom. In a phrase like Spirit of God, the word *Spirit* sometimes functions adjectivally, meaning "divine Spirit." "Spirit of holiness," on this construal, signifies "Holy Spirit," a name not prominent in the Old Testament and not especially hypostatized when it does occur.[2] *Of* can function generatively (what comes from God) or genitively (belonging to God, characterizing God). However we interpret of, the ofness is a primal element of the biblical revelation.

What the New Testament adds is a certain consolidation, but not a straightforward linguistic one. It is true that the New Testament writings promote the term *Holy Spirit* to the dignity and function of a proper name, above all in the baptismal formula "in the name of the Father and of the Son and of the Holy Spirit" (Matt 28:19). Here is an apostolic, or even a

2. In the Old Testament, the adjective *holy* and the noun *spirit* are only combined in Ps 51:11 and Isa 63:10.

dominical, way of thinking and speaking of what goes by so many names in the Old Testament. But while there is a definite consolidation of pneumatological reference, it is not exactly a consolidation of names. In fact, the New Testament actually expands our catalog of names, and does so more or less predictably, on the threefold lines suggested by the baptismal formula: Spirit of the Father, Spirit of the Son, Spirit of Jesus, Spirit of Christ, Spirit of adoption, and so on. The New Testament consolidation, in other words, is not a consolidation of names but of sending, because central to New Testament pneumatology is the fact that the Spirit is sent.

We are about to turn our attention from revealed names to the revelation of the Spirit's sending. Before we do so, let us clarify why our way forward through a theology of names is, if not exactly blocked, at least not a clear enough road to proceed straightforwardly. As we have seen, "Father, Son, and Holy Spirit" is in every way imaginable a venerable formula, and the way it assigns a name to the third person of the Trinity is eminently useful for clear theological discourse. Nevertheless, this form of words does not provide everything we might wish for as we take up the project of pneumatology. Consider these three observations about what the name *Holy Spirit* in the baptismal triad does and does not provide. First, Holy Spirit as the name of the third person in a doctrinal formula is not distinct. *Holy* is common to the divine being, and so is *spirit*. But combined, somehow they become the name that picks out the third person. Second, Holy Spirit is not a relational name. Father implies Son and vice versa, but Holy Spirit does not imply any correlative terms. Father and Son are relational realities with relational names; Holy Spirit is a relational reality without a relational name. Father and Son are family words, but Holy Spirit is not. Greek and Latin traditions, as we will see, have offered two different ways of making the Spirit's name serve these relational ends: in Greek, speaking of Spirit as breath, and in Latin speaking of Spirit as gift. Third, Holy Spirit is not a necessarily personal name; it is not obviously about somebody rather than something. The whole matrix of New Testament language about the Spirit seems to pick up on this aspect of the name and speaks of the Spirit as poured out or given.

None of the difficulties listed here are insurmountable; they merely require both a careful handling of the Bible's manifold ways of speaking and a willingness for theologians to specify what is meant by the variety of occurrences of the name Holy Spirit. One good example of a theologian who gladly takes on this task is Herman Witsius, whose exposition of the Apostles' Creed alerted readers to the variety of ways to construe the word *Spirit* as it occurs in Scripture:

> The term *Spirit*, when used with respect to God, is taken either *essentially*, or *personally*, or *metonymically*. It is taken *essentially*, when it is ascribed to God, in reference to the essence common to all the persons;—personally, when it is attributed to some one person, whether the second or the third;—*metonymically*, when it denotes certain effects or gifts.[3]

The guidance Witsius provides does not come from digging deeper into the historical or grammatical context of each appearance of the word *Spirit*. It comes rather from his commitment to bring the overall context of Scripture, read cumulatively and canonically, to bear on any individual occurrence of the word. He moves from whole to part, considering the full witness of Scripture to the revelation of the triune God and then offering a rough taxonomy of possible meanings of any occurrence of the word under investigation. In doing so, he takes in more than just the analysis of revealed names. He also takes in the salvation-historical matrix of divine actions within which these names are given. That is to say, the main reason he is unconfused by the ambiguity of the word *Spirit* is that he has already taken his bearings from the economy of salvation, in particular from the epochal event of the Father and Son sending the Spirit.

A theology of revealed names must arise from—or ride along on the momentum of—economic-soteriological analysis. The central tradition of pneumatology has widely recognized this but has rarely made it explicit, partly because it has always pursued pneumatology comprehensively and organically in a way that does not bifurcate names and sending. Especially if we attend to patristic exegetical writings, we find extensive development of the recognition that the Spirit is sent from God and a confident tracing of this sending back into the eternal being of God by recognition of an eternal procession. In short confessional formulas, the theology of names often comes to the fore, and especially in pneumatology the narrative about the Spirit's sending is somewhat backgrounded and implicit. But read sympathetically, the Nicene fathers and those in their tradition work out their name theology and even their precise terminology on the basis of a mission-and-procession theology. This explains why, in the *Fifth Theological Oration* (Oration 31, "On the Holy Spirit"), Gregory Nazianzus was able to rest the whole doctrinal and hermeneutical complex of pneumatology on a single

3. Herman Witsius, *Sacred Dissertations on What Is Commonly Called the Apostles' Creed* (Edinburgh: Fullarton, 1823), 2:304. An even more detailed account can be found earlier in this Protestant Scholastic tradition in Petrus van Mastricht, *Theoretical-Practical Theology*, vol. 2, *Faith in the Triune God* (Grand Rapids: Reformation Heritage, 2019), 571–72.

statement of Jesus containing a single key word from John 15:26: *proceeds*. The Holy Spirit is "the Spirit of truth, who proceeds from the Father."[4] In conflict with opponents who deny the deity of the Spirit, Gregory elevates the word *who proceeds* (Gk. *ekporeuetai*) to the status of a technical term for the eternal relation of origin by which the Spirit eternally is from God. Nazianzus recognizes that this saying of Jesus includes two elements. Jesus refers to the time "when the Helper comes, whom I will send to you from the Father, the Spirit of truth, who proceeds from the Father." Nazianzus installs the distinction between missions and processions at the comma between "I will send to you from the Father" and "the Spirit of truth who proceeds from the Father." He offers this as an interpretation of Scripture, in a hermeneutical synthesis of the full biblical witness to the Spirit. This is how classical Trinitarian theology wove together the theology of revealed names and the theology of divine missions.

MISSION AND PROCESSION

With consideration of the mission of the Spirit, pneumatology falls into line with Christology because Christ and the Spirit are co-sent in the New Testament. The two sendings are brought into relation in the argument of Galatians 4:4–6: "When the fullness of time had come, God sent forth his Son . . . and sent the Spirit of his Son into our hearts, crying 'Abba, Father!'" The logic that establishes eternal generation applies in parallel fashion to the eternal procession of the Spirit. The God who sent a Son must have always had a Son, and the God who sent a Spirit must have always had a Spirit. These two temporal missions reveal eternal processions, indicating an eternal fromness in the life and being of God. These processions in the divine life can be called the internal works of God that simply are God. They are goings-forth that are first of all internally realized, and as such, fully realized, fully perfect, and satisfied in all their dynamics. By grace they open up to temporal sendings. This is the classic doctrine of the Trinitarian processions and missions, and it is the most important conceptual tool for confessing the identity of the Spirit as God. But before pursuing its pneumatological implications further, we should attend to the way it demarcates the eternal, always-already-perfectly-accomplished life of God proper and the free, gracious actions into which God enters.

4. Gregory of Nazianzus, Oration 31, in *On God and Christ: The Five Theological Orations and Two Letters to Cledonius*, trans. Lionel Wickham (Crestwood: St. Vladimir's Seminary Press, 2002), 122.

Very loosely, the distinction being recognized here is between the inner life and the outer actions of God. We can expound it more fully by refusing for a moment to expound the dynamic in terms of missions and processions, instead speaking initially in a slightly more abstract way. We can speak of the actions of God, internal and external. Employing the concept of *action* to talk about what God does, we will say that God is the source of all sorts of things in the world. But then if we turn around and ask about what God is doing when considered apart from these doings in the world, we have a choice to make. One option is to say that in the divine life there is no action, only being. We could then describe being as something very alive, as something greater than action, while carefully avoiding the word *action* because we want to save it for what God does with the world. You can go pretty far with this option. Question: What's God doing when he's not doing anything? Answer: Being, but in a divine way. Apophatic silence descends, perhaps a bit prematurely, before the flash of insight that is supposed to give us a glimpse of what we are talking about by choosing this language.

But another, less standoffish option is to apply the category of action to the divine life in itself and then to specify what those actions in the life of God are. And this is the path that mainstream Trinitarian theology in fact pursued. Building on what Augustine called *opera* and the Cappadocians called *energeia*, Latin-language theology developed a distinction between the inward acts of the Trinity and the outward acts. What are the inward acts of the Trinity? They are generation and procession, concepts that had long been fundamental to Trinitarianism but that now came under the general conceptual framework of *actions* in God. Theologians in the classic tradition of Trinitarian doctrine have found it easy to confess that the external actions of the Trinity are undivided. One reason is that they started from a clear confession that the internal actions of the Trinity were not undivided. Or, to put it less double-negatively, the internal actions of the Trinity are distinct and distinguishable as real relations that stand in relative opposition to each other. This relative opposition is crucial because the key thing about these actions is that each of them has a person of the Trinity at each end. The Father begets or generates the Son, which puts Father and Son at opposite ends of the relation. The Spirit proceeds from the Father ("at least from the Father," we can ecumenically agree, prescinding for now from *filioque* questions), putting Spirit and Father over against each other within the divine life. This polarity, or opposing relation, is why the inward works are not called undivided: they mark the distinctions among the persons. The formula used by the Council of Florence in 1439 is what has become the classic statement of the principle: *In Deo omnia sunt unum, ubi non obviat relationis opposition*, "In God all things are one except where there is opposition of relation."[5]

In the second volume of Wolfhart Pannenberg's *Systematic Theology*, he advocates using the category of action. He uses it, in fact, to distinguish between internal and external actions of God. One advantage he points out is that it helps conceptualize divine aseity: the notion of internal actions is "a great gain for the actual understanding of God that God should be thought of as active." Pannenberg asks,

> Does there not have to be a world of creatures, or a relation to it, if God is to be thought of as active? Christian doctrine denies this by describing the trinitarian relations between Father, Son, and Spirit as themselves actions. To these divine actions in the creation of the world are added as actions of a different kind, as outward actions.[6]

Pannenberg calls for a high wall of distinction between internal and external actions:

> The acts of the trinitarian persons in their mutual relations must be sharply differentiated from their common outward actions. This differentiation finds support in the rule that posits and antithesis between the inseparable unity of the trinitarian persons in their outward action relative to the world and the distinctiveness of their inner activities relative to one another, which is the basis of the personal distinctions of Father, Son, and Spirit.[7]

In other words, external acts of the Trinity are undivided because the internal acts of the Trinity are distinct relative to one another. Because this is true, we can recognize that "God does not need the world in order to be active. He is in himself the living God in the mutual relations of Father, Son, and Spirit. He is, of course, active in a new way in the creation of the world."[8] The internal actions of the Trinity thus help us conceive of God

5. Eastern Orthodox readers may understandably be suspicious of the declarations of the *filioquist* Council of Florence, but the principle of relations of opposition can also be traced in older, Greek sources like Gregory of Nazianzus and John of Damascus.

6. Wolfhart Pannenberg, *Systematic Theology*, vol. 2 (Grand Rapids: Eerdmans, 1994), 1.

7. Pannenberg, *Systematic Theology*, 2:3.

8. Pannenberg, *Systematic Theology*, 2:5.

in himself as the living and active God, not a God waiting for a created, historical stage on which to be living and active. They enable a confession of dynamism as part of the divine life, as a form that aseity takes. And they do this in an orderly way without illegitimately manufacturing any new content for Trinitarian theology. The content provided by the category of action continues to be what it has always been: the generation of the Son and the procession of the Spirit. Anchoring the livingness and activity of God in eternal generation and eternal spiration, the older theology had the conceptual space to declare the external works of the Trinity undivided.

By contrast, any theology that denies or downplays the eternal generation of the Son is likely to need the historical manifestation of the incarnate Son to carry all the meaning and significance; and any theology which downplays the eternal procession of the Spirit is likely to require the historical manifestation of the Spirit to function as an exhaustive and fully satisfying pneumatology. A theologian with a weak grasp of the internal actions of the Trinity is a theologian who will need to make too much of the separateness of the external actions. Such theology is bound to exploit the external actions for more than they can contain and is under considerable pressure to read them as the actions of three different agents doing three distinct things. In extreme cases, for example Moltmann at his most drastic,[9] the events in the history of salvation may turn out to be the actual ground of the distinctions among the persons of the Trinity. There is an understandable desire to recognize the cross of Christ as the place where all the action is. But to fail to recognize that the action was in the being of God before it was among us is to give away too much. As Karl Barth asked Moltmann in a 1964 letter, "Would it not be wise to accept the doctrine of the immanent trinity of God?"[10]

For pneumatology in particular, exclusive preoccupation with external actions at the expense of internal actions has a disfiguring effect. The underlying reason for this has to do, once again, with the biblical revelation, which does not identify a single, central way of working for the Spirit but instead offers a baffling diversity of works of the Spirit. Theologians and exegetes have long recognized this. Consider this telling sentence from Basil of Caesarea's fourth-century treatise *On the Holy Spirit*:

---

9. "The economic Trinity not only reveals the immanent Trinity; it also has a retroactive effect on it." Moltmann, *The Trinity and the Kingdom: The Doctrine of God* (Minneapolis: Fortress, 1993), 160.

10. Karl Barth, *Letters 1961–1968*, ed. Jurgen Fangmeier and Hinrich Stoevesandt, trans. and ed. by Geoffrey W. Bromiley (Grand Rapids: Eerdmans, 1981), 175.

> Through the Holy Spirit comes our restoration to Paradise, our ascension to the Kingdom of heaven, our adoption as God's sons, our freedom to call God our Father, our becoming partakers of the grace of Christ, being called children of light, sharing in eternal glory, and in a word, our inheritance of the fullness of blessing, both in this world and the world to come.[11]

It is a magnificent collocation of what the Holy Spirit does for believers and is redolent of the whole sweep of the biblical witness. Some of Basil's phrases are obviously from a single passage of Scripture, while others evoke a journey of biblical theology from Genesis ("Paradise") to Revelation ("the world to come"). In context, the sentence is part of Basil's book-length argument for the deity of the Holy Spirit, and it is a key passage for that argument. These great benefits of receiving the Spirit are of such a character that they could not be given to us by any person who was not God. That is implicit in the fact that Basil links the Spirit's work to the Trinitarian work of salvation. "Through the Holy Spirit comes our . . . adoption as God's sons, our freedom to call God our Father, our becoming partakers of the grace of Christ." The Spirit makes good to us the work of the Father and the Son; therefore he too is God.

But formally, the main thing to notice about this list is that it is a list. There is something about the work of the Holy Spirit that makes theologians start making lists. There is a manifoldness, an overflowing fullness, a profusion of specificities, and a diffusion of bounties that makes pneumatology take the form of lists. At the systematic level, often the real constructive challenge for pneumatology is not so much filling out the list of the many works of the Spirit but finding a way to comprehend them all under one organizing and summarizing category or notion. Many of the most edifying discussions of pneumatology are strong on the listing and weak on the gathering.[12] Think of what a contrast that is with the work of Christ: though there are infinite facets to the work of Christ, and his work can be contemplated under various illuminating headings (office, status, moment, object, etc.), it is always obvious that these are various ways of getting at the one work of Christ. Not so with the Spirit. Accounts of his work tend more toward sprawl and diffuseness. This phenomenon probably accounts for some of the unsettledness we experience in pneumatology,

11. Basil of Caesarea, *On the Holy Spirit* (Crestwood: St. Vladimir's Seminary Press, 1980), 59.

12. This applies, I think, even to Abraham Kuyper's great treatise *The Work of the Holy Spirit* (New York: Funk and Wagnalls, 1900).

the way every book on the Holy Spirit seems in some ways to be starting the project all over from the beginning again. The character of the revelation tends toward wonderful, glorious listhood.

When we speak of missions revealing processions, we are not speaking of any sending. Not all sendings reveal eternal processions. God sends prophets, apostles, servants, angels, and all manner of other emissaries. But when God the Father sends the Son and the Spirit, we meet God in sendings that have infinite depth behind them: self-sendings in which God sends God; sendings in which God is God with us. This is the economic Trinity, in which we see that the *of* in the locution "Spirit of God" goes all the way back into the depths of God. For a doctrine of God to be in earnest, it must take this step, seeing the processions behind the missions or, in modern idiom, confessing in the economic Trinity the revelation and presence of the immanent Trinity.

GIVING OF THE GIFT

We have observed the fact that much of the biblical revelation of the Spirit tends toward a diffuseness but needs to be understood against a more unified background, the background of its eternal depth in the one procession of the Spirit within the eternal life of God. The history of theology is a history of trying to find faithful ways of foregrounding this deep scriptural background, making the scriptural background functional or operational for confessing the theology of the Holy Spirit. In the history of the doctrine, a few proposals have been especially influential. Chief among these is Augustine's strategy of pressing the biblical notion of gift into service as a useable name for the third person of the Trinity. Augustine is keenly aware of the terminological ambiguity we have been examining: *Spirit* is a word for God but somehow also the word for the third person of the triune God. He puzzles over this repeatedly, including in the fifth book of his *De Trinitate*. When Jesus affirms to the Samaritan woman in John 4:24 that "God is Spirit," Augustine notes that it seems to be a reference to the Father (who seeks worshipers), to the Holy Spirit (symbolized by the water Jesus will provide), and to God as a whole, that is, to the divine nature or the Holy Trinity.[13] By what standard can the theological reader make these distinctions? Augustine's solution moves on two lines simultaneously. First, he draws in an argument from the nature of the Holy Spirit's place

13. Augustine, *On the Trinity*, 5.11.12.

in the economy of salvation, broadly considered: the Spirit is given by the Father and the Son. And second, on the basis of this giving, Augustine lifts up the word *gift* and presses it into service as a name, a name that is inherently relational.

In an essay on pneumatology, Robert Louis Wilken expounded the logic of this Augustinian move by noting how pneumatological naming is shaped by the unique role of the Holy Spirit in the economy of salvation. The distinctiveness of the doctrine of the Holy Spirit depends on the way it arises from recognition of the Spirit's work in salvation history. Wilken's orienting question is whether Pentecost can be considered a peer of Easter, noting that "in some ways the history of the feast of Pentecost can serve as a metaphor for the development of the Christian doctrine of the Holy Spirit."[14] That development, as we have already mentioned, is different from Christology. The doctrines about Christ practically jumped off the pages of Scripture and into orthodox theological confession as compared with the way the biblical witness about the Holy Spirit gradually emerged without often being the focus of conciliar attention. Comparatively speaking, the history of Christology is the striking appearance of the solar disc of sunrise pushing back the darkness, while pneumatology is the slow dawning of an overcast day that imperceptibly turns the night into morning. Putting the contrast differently, christological progress always turned on confronting a heretical teaching in order to refute it and defend the truth, a truth which became clearer in the course of conflict. Progress in pneumatology, on the other hand, was always marked by a process of culling Scriptures and exploring relationships among passages. In pneumatology, Wilken says, "the Fathers are less engaged in defending something than in searching for something. Only gradually and after they peered intently at the murkiness before them, does the goal of their quest come clear."[15]

Within this gradual process, one of the key clarifying moments was when a particular Latin theological tradition pressed the word *gift* into pneumatological usage. Wilken points to Hilary of Poitiers as the first theologian to speak confidently about the Holy Spirit in terms of the many biblical passages in which it is "the distinctive characteristic of the Spirit, that he is given, received, and possessed." Drawing on this pattern, Hilary

14. Robert Louis Wilken, "Is Pentecost a Peer of Easter? Scripture, Liturgy, and the Proprium of the Holy Spirit," in *Trinity, Time, and Church: A Response to the Theology of Robert W. Jenson*, ed. Colin E. Gunton (Grand Rapids: Eerdmans, 2000), 158–77, at 150–60. Wilken's chapter title draws on the clever phrasing and theological proposals of Robert Jenson.

15. Wilken, "Is Pentecost a Peer of Easter?," 163.

calls him the *donum fidelium*, the "gift to the faithful."[16] *Gift*, in other words, is shorthand for being given, received, and possessed. Hilary noticed something distinctive about the biblical language for the Holy Spirit, namely, that a field of biblical terms associated with the Spirit depict being given and poured out, on the one hand, and being received or indwelling, on the other. That is, the gift is seen not only from the perspective of the giver but also from that of the recipient. The gift enters the life of the recipient and becomes his own, which in turn relates the recipient to the giver. Gift, as presented in the Scriptures, has built into it overtones of reciprocity and mutuality.[17]

Though the gradual progress continued, the next leap forward seems to be Augustine's decision to trace the characteristic giftness of the Spirit back from the church's experience into the immanent being of God. It is Augustine who, agreeing that the Spirit is the gift to mankind in the history of salvation, thinks to ask the question, "Was he already gift before there was anyone to give him to?" (*De Trinitate* 5.15.6). As Wilken paraphrases the question, "Does the term 'gift' as a designation of the Holy Spirit only apply to the economy?"[18] The pneumatological move here is parallel to the christological. If Christ is the Son of God for us, he must have been the eternal Son of God; and if the Spirit is gift to us, he must have always had the character of gift. But whose gift to whom? In the absence of creatures, the exchange would have to be between the Father and the Son. Yet it is just here, at the move to the eternal inner life of the Trinity, that gift seems too impersonal a term to serve well.

At this point, it begins to matter that Hilary did not simply use proof texts to identify Spirit with gift but worked with the thrust and logic of a wide range of texts to derive an account of the Spirit's characteristic role as marked by reciprocity and mutuality. Augustine took this approach one step further by annexing to this gift-reciprocity-mutuality cluster the word *love*. In order to distinguish the proprium, the distinctive character of the third person as manifested in the economy, we must think in terms of a gift of self-involving love that creates communion. "Augustine wants to say not only that the gift of the Holy Spirit creates a communion between God and the believer but also that the Spirit is the 'communion' between Father and Son."[19] And that, finally, is why the third person is specially

16. Wilken, "Is Pentecost a Peer of Easter?," 165.
17. Wilken, "Is Pentecost a Peer of Easter?," 166.
18. Augustine, *De Trinitate*, 5.15.6, cited in Wilken, "Is Pentecost a Peer of Easter?," 167.
19. Wilken, "Is Pentecost a Peer of Easter?," 172.

called Holy Spirit, even though the other two persons are holy and spirits, and God in general (the one triune God) is holy and spirit. As Augustine says, "He is properly called the Holy Spirit . . . with good reason. Because he is common to them both, he is called properly what they are called in common."[20]

This particular Latin pneumatological tradition that reached its ripe formulation in Augustine is a powerful integrative proposal. It is perceptive in its recognition of the giving, mutuality, and reciprocity effected by the third person of the Trinity in the economy of salvation. It is also perceptive in taking the next step of asking what divine reality lies behind the history of salvation: a *who* question about a person of the Trinity cannot be fully answered without taking recourse to the eternal Trinity, to God in himself without any necessary reference to us and our salvation. As for the decisive step of transposing this insight about the gift into the eternal being of God, it functions properly for pneumatology as long as we keep in mind that it is intended as a heuristic help for making sense of what Scripture says, and that it is carefully designed to solve certain problems we would encounter if we tried to do pneumatology by working exclusively with the data of the revealed names. It leverages the Spirit's mission to make the most of the insights delivered by the names. Yet other developments from other theological trajectories are also possible. In fact, a prominent development in the tradition of Greek-language theology addresses many of the same problems and finds strikingly parallel solutions. The tradition that stretches from Irenaeus to John of Damascus plays on the Greek word *pneuma* and emphasizes its underlying breath imagery. Just as word and breath both come out of the one who speaks, the Son and Spirit have their eternal origin in the Father, and both carry out among us a characteristic extension of their way of being in the eternal life of God. This Greek tradition has different opportunities and shortcomings than the Latin tradition. But both traditions take up biblical material and invest it with deeper significance than is evident in Scripture itself; both press key biblical terms into use for purposes that they do not serve in any explicit biblical argument. Above all, they are alternative strategies for doing exactly the same thing: anchoring the theology of the revealed names to a mission-procession theology and making explicit the inherent relationality of the Spirit who is God and who is in God. In both cases, and perhaps in other less influential threads of Christian tradition, the presupposition is that the biblical revelation is

20. Augustine, *De Trinitate*, 15.19.37, cited in Wilken, "Is Pentecost a Peer of Easter?," 172.

perfect, but we need to develop it carefully if we are to speak responsibly in the doctrine of the Spirit. A broadly Nicene pneumatology, one that understands itself to be not improving on the form of words given in Scripture but rather offering conceptual paraphrases that equip us to grasp what we are reading, is a pneumatology that establishes the big picture and keeps the most important things in the foreground.

THIRDNESS AND THE SPIRIT WHO WAS ALWAYS ALREADY THERE

In concluding this discussion of the third person of the Trinity, we can offer a brief justification for treating the third person third; a defense, really, and in that sense an apology, of getting around to the Spirit last. It seems to me that speaking third of the Spirit is not a problem; it is, in fact, a long and healthy tradition in Christian theology. It is a tradition in which the main lines of the Christian confession are established first without a focus on the Holy Spirit. But when, in a later move, reflection on the Spirit is added to those main lines, a world of greater depth opens up, and the full glory of Trinitarian soteriology shines forth. Nothing changes, but everything is better when pneumatology is explicated at last. A few key examples demonstrate this.

Consider the Creed of Nicaea, which in 325 labored to say the right thing about the relation of the Son to the Father. At the end of the creed, having elaborately affirmed that they believe in the Son, the fathers of Nicaea added the unimpressive phrase, "and in the Holy Spirit." Fifty-six turbulent years later when this creed was retrieved and expanded at Constantinople 381, this paltry third article blossomed forth into the confession we recite in the Nicene Creed today: I believe in the Holy Spirit, the Lord and giver of life, who proceeds from the Father, who is worshiped and glorified together with the Father and the Son, who spoke through the prophets. What happened when the Creed of Nicaea, with minimal explicit pneumatology, added the rich pneumatology of 381? Trinitarianism came into its own. The whole statement of faith became richer, fuller, and deeper. It is worth noting that the creed of 325 did not omit all mention of the Spirit. It said little rather than much, but it did say something. The tradition we are considering is one that initially says little about the Spirit but then later says much.

Second, a parallel development can be seen in one of the greatest pro-Nicene fathers, Athanasius of Alexandria. Most of his theology is a relentless hammering home of the Nicene recognition of the full deity of the Son, consubstantial with the Father. He only occasionally mentions the Holy Spirit, and never as a focus of attention in his own right. Athanasius had message discipline, and the message was, Arianism is false. But then, at the request of Serapion of Thmuis, Athanasius wrote a series of letters explaining the person and work of the Holy Spirit, which amount to a brief treatise so powerful and integrated that it is hard to believe Athanasius had held all that understanding about the Spirit subliminally in his mind throughout the Arian crisis. What happens when the christological Athanasius extends his attention to explicit discussion of the Holy Spirit? His work achieves a rounded Trinitarian contour that is a wonder to behold. Perhaps contour is the wrong metaphor; the shape and form of Athanasian theology do not change, but drawing out the pneumatological depths transfigures everything he says.

Third, the structure of Calvin's *Institutes* shows a similar dynamic. For various reasons, Calvin postpones much discussion of the Spirit until book 3, when he asks how the salvation that the Father has worked out in Christ can become ours. His answer is faith, but then he climbs high into the mysterious workings of the Spirit and expounds a practical pneumatology of magisterial power.

Rather than tracing out this tradition in later examples, I want to reach back to the sources and suggest, reverently, that Holy Scripture follows a similar pattern in several places. The gospel of Matthew reaches a first climax in chapter 11, when Jesus says that nobody knows the Father except the Son and vice versa, and then reaches a rounded conclusion in chapter 28, when the risen Christ extends that formula to include the third person, the Holy Spirit, whose work he left implicit in chapter 11. John's gospel likewise expends considerable energy on the dyadic relation of the Word to God and then of the Father to the Son before turning sustained attention to the Holy Spirit around chapter 14 and especially 16. In Romans, Paul works out the righteousness of God and the propitiation in Christ before turning his attention fully to the Spirit in chapter 8, in which Romans reaches a doxological and kerygmatic highpoint. To end with the broadest possible gesture at the structure of the entire economy of salvation, the Spirit, who is never absent but often anonymous in the early phases of God's work, is conspicuous precisely at the fulfillment of God's promises, when his name and character and distinctive work come into their own and become a matter of proclamation and teaching.

The point is that while it is wrong to neglect the Holy Spirit, it is also wrong to belabor pneumatology in a distracting way or to attempt to lay a pneumatological foundation in the first moves of systematic theology.

There is a wise tradition of establishing the main lines of theology before drawing out the implicit pneumatological realities that have undeniably been at work all along. At least in the order of instruction, this seems to be a prudent way of working for pilgrim theologians instructing the church. Late in Thomas Goodwin's book *The Knowledge of God the Father and his Son Jesus Christ*, he admits that the whole project has a dyadic, if not to say binitarian, ring: "There is a third person in the Godhead, the Spirit of God the Father, and of Christ; who in my handling the point will fall in, and appear to be that only true God, as well as these other two named."[21] As it turned out, the Spirit did in fact "fall in" to Goodwin's later handling, not only in that book but especially when, in a later book, he developed an extended pneumatology. If the Spirit had not fallen in, we would judge Goodwin's dyadic start differently in retrospect. But Goodwin was able to make his implicit pneumatology explicit. We should recognize that this sort of move, from an undeveloped pneumatology to a strong and elaborate one in a subsequent movement, happens all the time in Christian theology, and it is commendable.

The only reason it works at all, however, is that the Spirit who we recognize third was also there from the beginning as the very condition of confessing truth about the Father and the Son. In 1 Corinthians 2:12 Paul says, "Now we have received not the spirit of the world, but the Spirit who is from God, that we might understand the things freely given us by God." Here Paul recognizes the constitutive role the Holy Spirit is always already playing in theology and points to the divine initiative in the Spirit playing that role: we have received the Spirit so that we can understand what God has given. God has given something and has also given the understanding of it. He has given that understanding as an abiding principle of our spiritual understanding.

In a beautiful passage, John Henry Newman appealed to this pneumatological emergence to account for the strange way that Christian theologians talk. They have before them a reality to which they are attempting to do justice, and their propositions, proofs, decisions, and arguments must be understood as attempts to account for that reality. Newman puts it this way:

> Though the Christian mind reasons out a series of dogmatic statements, one from another, this it has ever done, and always must do, not from those

21. Goodwin, *The Knowledge of God the Father and his Son Jesus Christ*, vol. 4 of *The Words of Thomas Goodwin* (Edinburgh: Nichol, 1862), 351.

> statements taken in themselves, as logical propositions, but as illustrated and (as I may say) inhabited by that sacred impression which is prior to them, which acts as a regulating principle, ever present, upon the reasoning, and without which no one has any warrant to reason at all. Such sentences as "the Word was God" or "the Only-begotten Son who is in the bosom of the Father," or "the Word was made flesh," or "the Holy Ghost which proceedeth from the Father," are not a mere letter which we may handle by the rules of art at our own will, but august tokens of most simple, ineffable, adorable facts, embraced, enshrined, according to its measure, in the believing mind. For though the development of an idea is a deduction of proposition from proposition, these propositions are ever formed in and round the idea itself (so to speak), and are in fact one and all only aspects of it. Moreover, this will account both for the mode of arguing from particular texts or single words of Scripture, practised by the early Fathers, and for their fearless decision in practising it; for the great Object of Faith on which they lived both enabled them to appropriate to itself particular passages of Scripture, and became a safeguard against heretical deductions from them. Also, it will account for the charge of weak reasoning, commonly brought against those Fathers; for never do we seem so illogical to others, as when we are arguing under the continual influence of impressions to which they are insensible.[22]

This is the Christian mind, the angle of approach from which pneumatology makes sense, and makes sense of Scripture. In pneumatology, the mind "inhabited by that sacred impression . . . which acts as a regulating principle, ever present" is both the presupposition of all statements and the object of them.

And this is why Paul prays, in Ephesians 1:17, that God would give to Christians "a spirit of wisdom and revelation" (NRSV), that is, that they would be subject to the work of the Spirit. Pneumatology is the doctrine in which the prayer for illumination becomes the subject.

We could call this gift of "a spirit of wisdom and revelation" an invisible mission of the Holy Spirit, a sending of the Spirit to illumine our understandings to know the deep things of God, which only the Spirit knows properly and by nature. John Webster calls this divine operation the work

22. See Andrew Louth's odd little book *Discerning the Mystery* (Oxford: Oxford University Press, 1983), 146–47. Louth's footnote places this quote in Newman's *Sermons, Chiefly on the Theory of Religious Belief, Preached Before the University of Oxford* (London: Parker, 1843), 335–36.

of illumination and glosses the language of Ephesians 1:17 in his description of it: "What sets in motion creaturely apprehension of the gospel is God himself: the inner glory of God in its outward splendor, the inner wisdom of the Spirit who knows God's depths and is in himself infinitely wise, and who communicates this to creatures."[23] He describes the same pneumatological illumination in these terms: "God so orders rational creatures that there is a creaturely coordinate to this omnipotent and omnipresent divine radiance. We are not simply bathed in light; it does not simply shine over us or upon us. Rather, it illuminates and so creates in creatures an active intelligent relation to itself."[24] That is the condition and goal of the doctrine about the third person of the Trinity: even today may our Christian minds receive this Spirit of wisdom and revelation in the knowledge of God.

---

23. John Webster, "Illumination," in *The Domain of the Word: Scripture and Theological Reason* (London: Bloomsbury, 2012), 61.

24. Webster, "Illumination," 57.

CHAPTER 2

FILIOQUE AND THE ORDER OF THE DIVINE MISSIONS

ADONIS VIDU

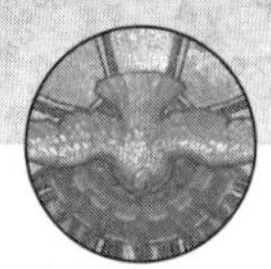

THE QUESTION OF THE ORDER of the divine missions is of great dogmatic significance.[1] The order between the missions bears on the very nature of the missions themselves. It is not merely an idle question, of priority for the sake of priority. In the context of Protestant theology, the theology of the divine missions has often fallen into the background. One may speculate about the cause, given the obvious deference shown in Protestant dogmatics to classical Trinitarianism. It may have something to do with the concentration of soteriological debates upon the binary of forensic/ontological nature of salvation. An approach to soteriology through the doctrine of the divine missions segues much too easily to an ontological approach to salvation. But we should not be detained with these questions at this point.

It is beyond doubt, however, that the doctrine of the divine missions is directly related to how one conceives the saving activity of the Trinity. The missions reveal a Trinitarian origin and end to the divine action, which is the flip side of its unified character correctly specified by the axiom *opera trinitatis ad extra sunt indivisa*. Not only is the Trinitarian substructure of the divine operation indicated, but the manner of humanity's return

1. I am grateful for the comments and suggestions received, especially from Joanna Leidenhag, Lucy Peppiatt, Luke Stamps, Adam Johnson, James Arcadi, and others.

to the Trinity is equally specified.[2] That is, both objective and subjective soteriology will bear the fruit of these theological decisions. Legge puts it adequately: "As the divine missions make present in a new way and reveal the Trinitarian processions, they are likewise the vectors of our return to the Triune God."[3]

Some of these implications will become evident as this paper progresses, but the task of the paper is to focus on the purely Trinitarian question of the order of the christological and pneumatological missions. I intend to argue in favor of a traditional Western account of the two missions in response to recent critiques from within and without the *filioque* tradition. I will present three objections (organized into two classes) to this christological priority. In response to one class of objections, I will invoke the distinction between divine operations and missions. Finally, in response to the second class of objections, and by utilizing the same distinction, I will demonstrate how the mission of the Spirit is an outcome of the Son's mission. The Spirit's mission to humanity results from the logically prior incorporation of the human nature of Jesus Christ into the Trinitarian processions.

All of us are likely familiar with the traditional account of this ordering. The first mission is that of the Son, in the fullness of time (Gal 4:4). The Son is sent by the Father. The Father is not sent; he sends the Son and the Spirit. Upon the completion of his mission, more specifically upon his ascension, Christ sends his Spirit (from the Father), or the Father sends his Spirit (in the name of Jesus). Whether the Father or the Son together with the Father is sending the Spirit, the Pentecostal outpouring appears to presuppose the completion of the Son's mission (John 7:39: "The Spirit was not yet given because Jesus wasn't yet glorified").

---

2. I am assuming as legitimate the procedure of grounding the return of creatures to God (*reditus*) in the divine processions. According to this model, salvation is in its deepest meaning and terminus an incorporation into the divine existence. David Coffey has objected to this approach on account of its understanding of the Spirit as the divine love ("A Proper Mission of the Holy Spirit," *Theological Studies* 47 [1986]: 227–50; *Grace: The Gift of the Holy Spirit* [Sydney: Faith and Culture, 1979]). Since this model starts in the unity of essence and not in the distinction of persons (as does the Orthodox critique as well), it is incapable of grounding the return of human persons to God through a distinct mission of the Holy Spirit. To be sure, Coffey's "bestowal model" continues to tether the Spirit to Christ, as the love that Christ returns to the Father. The Crowe/Lonergan argument should also be mentioned, viz., the reversal of the order of the processions by the order of the missions: what is last in processions is first in missions. Cf. Frederick E. Crowe, "Son of God, Holy Spirit, and World Religions," in Frederick E. Crowe, *Appropriating the Lonergan Idea*, ed. Michael Vertin (Toronto: University of Toronto Press, 2006). Crowe cites Lonergan as the inspiration for this reversal in the order of the divine missions, referring to the latter's *Method in Theology* (New York: Seabury, 1972). For a more detailed discussion, see Robert M. Doran, *The Trinity in History: A Theology of the Divine Missions*, vol. 1, *Missions and Processions* (Toronto: University of Toronto Press, 2012), esp. chapter 4.

3. Dominic Legge, *The Trinitarian Christology of Thomas Aquinas* (Oxford: Oxford University Press, 2017), 120.

This classical Trinitarian ordering of the missions has come under criticism in contemporary theology. The typical worry of Eastern Christians has been that the *filioque* is turning the Spirit into a mere afterthought, undermining his dignity as the only divine person that has no fruition. Yet it needs to be observed that, as a whole, the Eastern position also favors prioritizing the mission of the Son. So it is possible in principle to reject the *filioque* and retain the priority of the Son's mission. Orthodox theologians will refuse, however, to draw conclusions about the processions from the manner of the Spirit's mission.[4]

The more recent objections, however, challenge the very ordering of the missions. Thus it is no longer an undisputed fact that the mission of the Son is prior to the mission of the Spirit. Remarkably, some of these objections come from within the *filioque* tradition.

OBJECTIONS

Three kinds of objections to the priority of the Son's mission may be enumerated: (a) objections from the work of the Spirit in Old Testament saints; (b) objections from the work of the Spirit in non-Christian religions; (c) objections from the work of the Spirit in the life of Jesus.

For the purposes of this paper we can lump the first two groups together. Not that they are entirely the same, yet both of these groups of people seem to show evidence of a work of the Spirit in a way that does not appear to be mediated (or accompanied) by an explicit faith in Jesus Christ.

The Old Testament saints surely possessed the Holy Spirit insofar as they were empowered by him. We need not dwell in detail over the cases of the judges (Judg 6:34; 14:6), Saul (1 Sam 11:6), David (1 Sam 16:13), prophets (2 Chron 15:1), and indeed others (Exod 31:3). But this work of the Spirit clearly comes prior to the mission of the Son, even if in the arc of redemptive history it anticipates the latter.

With regards to non-Christian religions, we can see an increasing willingness to speak about a "universal gift of the Spirit" given to other

4. Other considerations are in play here from an Orthodox perspective, perhaps chief among which being the idea that the Spirit has not given himself to us hypostatically. For that reason the Orthodox tradition hesitates to infer a procession from the mission of the Spirit. Gregory of Cyprus, for instance, concedes that the grace of the Holy Spirit comes through Christ, but what is thereby given is not the hypostasis of the Spirit or a created gift but rather the exterior manifestation of the Spirit, his energies (*Tome of 1285*). Palamas also admits that, as energy, the Holy Spirit is the Spirit of Christ and comes from Christ (*Apodictic Treatise* 1.9, ed. B. Bobrinskoy, in *Palama Syngrammata*, ed. P. Chrēstou [Thessalonikē, 1962]).

religions. In Roman Catholic theology Vatican II inaugurates such a trajectory, culminating in Pope Francis II claiming that "the pluralism and the diversity of religions, color, sex, race and language are willed by God in His wisdom, through which He created human beings."[5] In Evangelical theology, Amos Yong's pneumatological theology of other religions has suggested that there is a work of the Spirit in and through other religions.[6]

There is much to discuss in relation to the controversial suggestion about a work of the Spirit in other religions. I propose to focus on a single issue. If there is a mission of the Spirit that does not presuppose faith in Jesus Christ, this seems to conflict with both Catholic dogma and the Reformational *sola fide*. In what way is such a work of the Spirit related to Christ? In what way are we to understand the Spirit as the Spirit of Christ?

Karl Rahner's explanation is most elegant. We need to think of the Christ event not as an *efficient* cause of the Spirit but as a *final* cause. In "Jesus Christ in the Non-Christian Religions," Rahner writes, "Christ is present and efficacious in the non-Christian believer (and therefore in the non-Christian religions) through his Spirit."[7] He assumes the Pauline language that the Spirit is the Spirit of Christ (e.g., Gal 4:6) and explains that what Christ does in his mission cannot be an efficient cause of the sending of the Spirit since that would make one of the divine missions dependent upon some created aspect.[8] God does not need to enable himself to send the Spirit through the human work of Christ.

He goes on to say, "This Spirit is always, everywhere, and from the outset the entelechy, the determining principle, of the history of revelation and salvation; and its communication and acceptance, by its very nature, never takes place in a merely abstract, transcendental form," and "The universal efficacy of the Spirit is directed from the very beginning to the zenith of its historical mediation, which the Christ event."[9]

---

5. Pope Francis and Ahmad Al-Tayyeb, "A Document on Human Fraternity for World Peace and Living Together," February 4, 2019, http://www.vatican.va/content/francesco/en/travels/2019/outside/documents/papa-francesco_20190204_documento-fratellanza-umana.html.

6. Cf. Yong, *Discerning the Spirit(s): A Pentecostal-Charismatic Contribution to Christian Theology of Religions* (Sheffield: Sheffield Academic Press, 2000); Yong, *Beyond the Impasse: Toward a Pneumatological Theology of Religions* (Eugene, OR: Wipf & Stock, 2014).

7. Karl Rahner, "Jesus Christ in the Non-Christian Religions," in *Theological Investigations*, vol. 17, *Jesus, Man and the Church*, trans. Margaret Kohl (London : Darton, Longman and Todd, 1981), 43.

8. Rahner's logic is echoed by Bernard Lonergan's clarification about the role played by the created effects in a mission, which are exclusively *consequent*, as opposed to *antecedent*. While I agree with this assumption, the operation of Christ's humanity need not be construed as *enabling* God to send the Spirit but rather as the desired modality through which he freely chooses to dispense him. Cf. Bernard Lonergan, *The Triune God: Systematics* (Toronto: University of Toronto Press, 2009), 443.

9. Rahner, "Jesus Christ in the Non-Christian Religions," 46.

There is much more than needs to be said about Rahner's broader stance, in particular his understanding of nature and grace and his transcendental anthropology, among others, to do full justice to his position. Quite simply, he sees the Spirit as the cause of the incarnation and the cross. The incarnation is not something taking place from above, but rather it can be understood as an emergence from the very openness of humanity toward transcendence, under the supervenient guidance of the Spirit. This leads to a different understanding of saving faith as "the seeking *memoria* of the absolute bringer of salvation,"[10] which is compatible with other "savior figures" when understood as anticipations of the one true Savior, Jesus Christ.

Rahner's proposal raises many questions. Perhaps chief among these is the one concerning the benefit of an explicit faith in Jesus Christ. If the universal gift of the Holy Spirit is already inclusive of other religions, how should we understand the missionary mandate of the church? This brings to the fore the integral relation between the two missions. If, as he states in a paper dealing explicitly with this question ("Anonymous Christianity and the Missionary Task of the Church"), grace "has been present all along and belongs to the enduring existential modalities of man," it appears that Christian conversion is merely the extension of this implicit existential modality into explicit recognition, leading to a "more radical dimension of responsibility" and "a greater chance of this Christianity interiorly bestowed by grace being brought to its fullness in all dimensions."[11]

Christianity, then, must be understood simply as the fruition of an implicit potentiality already present in creation—through grace, to be sure—but this means that the content of the Christ event has a merely epistemological value and has no ontological implications for the state of the believer. If, that is, the non-Christian believer already has a saving "searching memory" of Christ, her coming to know and profess an explicit faith in Christ makes no difference ontologically to her condition, for she already has the Spirit. This is not to deny the significance of this explicit recognition of an internal movement toward Christ, but it seems seriously to deflate the New Testament's description of the benefits of being "in Christ" (e.g., Rom 8:1).

The final objection against the priority of the mission of the Son invokes the reality of a mission of the Spirit in the life of Jesus. Several theologians,

10. Rahner, "Jesus Christ in the Non-Christian Religions," 46.

11. Rahner, "Anonymous Christianity and the Missionary Task of the Church," in *Theological Investigations*, vol. 12, *Confrontations*, trans. David Bourke (London: Darton, Longman and Todd, 1974), 170, 177.

including Rahner, have called attention to the fact that the incarnation of the Son takes place through the Holy Spirit. The events leading up to the birth of Christ betray the Spirit's prevenience: John the Baptist is full of the Spirit from his birth; Mary conceives from the Holy Spirit (Matt 1:18). Additionally, the beginning of Jesus's ministry is under the tutelage of the Spirit, from his baptism, to his wilderness temptations, to the commencement of his ministry itself (Luke 4:18), and so on.

Kathryn Tanner surmises that the two missions are therefore interweaving and intermingled. "Rather than a simple one-way relationship from the Son to the Spirit in other words, the complex back and forth of their mutual interdependency is drawn out" by the narratives.[12] She stresses the gradual deification of Christ's humanity, such that only at the end of Christ's life is he "genuinely full of the Spirit."[13] The Spirit establishes Jesus's sonship; he unites the Son and Father "in bringing about and sustaining the conformity of wills between the one and the other."[14] This means that the more the Spirit is evident in Christ, the more his divine sonship is evident, such that they become "increasingly manifest together."[15]

In this intermingling, the Son only gives to the Spirit his "shape," Tanner argues; he does not provide the power in the same way that the Spirit provides it for the Son. "The Son sends the Spirit to us from the Father, but not as the Father does. The Spirit has already been sent from the Father as a condition of the Son's own incarnation and mission; and therefore the Son cannot be sending the Spirit in the way the Father does."[16]

There is a clear priority of the Spirit's mission for Tanner since the Spirit must already be sent in order to form the humanity of Christ and to constitute his sonship. While she wants to preserve the mutual dependence of the two missions, the priority clearly belongs to the Spirit's mission, and the contribution of the Son's mission to that of the Spirit is minimally regarded as one of "shaping."

The idea that the Spirit is already at work in the conception of Christ is certainly important. Yet to say that the Spirit constitutes the very sonship of Christ is problematic. One reason for this is that no traditional account of the processions distributes the Spirit as active in the procession of the Son.[17]

---

12. Kathryn Tanner, *Christ Is Key* (New York: Cambridge University Press, 2010), 163.
13. Tanner, *Christ Is Key*, 171.
14. Tanner, *Christ Is Key*, 166.
15. Tanner, *Christ Is Key*, 169.
16. Tanner, *Christ Is Key*, 174.
17. One contemporary version of this *Spirituque* can be found in Thomas Weinandy, *The Father's Spirit of Sonship: Reconceiving the Trinity* (Eugene, OR: Wipf & Stock, 1995). For a very instructive

On the other hand, to say that the Spirit is the one through whom Christ *realizes or expresses* his sonship in human form is totally different. The former claim is problematic because it undermines the sole possession of the human nature by the Son. It is because humanity is assumed by the Son that we can speak about the Son of God in human form. Tanner's assertion seems to imply the incarnation of two persons: the Son and the Spirit in one human nature.

The reason is that in order for the Spirit to have a mission, a created effect must either already exist (as in the case of the indwelling) or be created simultaneously with the mission. The first option, however, has Nestorian implications for Christology unless the human nature already subsists in the Son, in which case the Son's mission would retain priority. The second option implies the incarnation of the Spirit, since the created effect is brought about by its union with the Holy Spirit as well. Once we recognize that the human nature of Christ only subsists from its union with the Son, the priority of the Son's mission follows. Whatever must be ascribed to the Spirit will then be in the order of operation (and therefore only by appropriation[18]). That is to say, the participation of the Spirit to the various stages of the incarnate life of the Son will be in the form of operations whose agency belongs to the whole Trinity, including the Son.

If the Spirit sanctifies and empowers the humanity of Christ, it does so not from a position of hypostatic union with it. Only the Son receives the human nature into hypostatic union with himself. The Spirit does not give himself to us hypostatically, except, as Lossky, Staniloae, and other orthodox theologians recognize, in the hypostasis of the Son.[19]

It would thus seem that each of the two classes of objections leads to problematic positions: the first (from the work of the Spirit in Old Testament saints and non-Christian religions) undermines the uniqueness

discussion, the reader may be referred to Jerome Van Kuiken and Joshua M. McNall's chapter in the present volume.

18. The procedure of appropriation stipulates that a particular attribute or operation belongs to the Trinity as a whole, yet it can be taken to indicate or manifest one of the persons in particular. For additional material on appropriation, see Emery, *The Trinity: An Introduction to Catholic Doctrine on the Triune God* (Washington, DC: Catholic University of America, 2011), 161–68; Neil Ormerod, *The Trinity: Retrieving the Western Tradition* (Milwaukee, WI: Marquette University Press, 2005), 99–124; for a critical account, see Catherine M. LaCugna, *God for Us: The Trinity and Christian Life* (New York: Harper One, 1993), 99–100, 164–67.

19. Dumitru Stăniloae, "The Procession of the Holy Spirit from the Father and His Relation to the Son, as the Basis of Our Deification and Adoption," in *Spirit of God, Spirit of Christ: Ecumenical Reflections on the* Filioque *Controversy*, ed. Lukas Vischer (London: SPCK; Geneva: World Council of Churches, 1981); Vladimir Lossky, *The Mystical Theology of the Eastern Church* (Crestwood, NY: St. Vladimir's Seminary Press, 1976), 159.

and significance of the person and work of Christ in bringing about a supernatural relation with the Holy Spirit, or deification; the second class of objection (from the work of the Spirit in Christ) appears to imply a double incarnation—of the Spirit and of the Son in the same human nature.

Here is the key question then: Can we do justice to the presence and work of the Spirit in the life of Jesus without undermining the unique and real subject of the incarnation, the Son?

DISTINGUISHING OPERATIONS FROM MISSIONS

What has emerged from the foregoing presentation is that greater precision is needed about the ways the Spirit might be present or at work, such that it is possible to speak about a real contribution the Spirit makes to the incarnation of the Son without weakening the subsistence of the human nature in the Son alone. If such a distinction is possible, then perhaps one can also distinguish between a presence of the Spirit in the Old Testament saints and the Spirit's presence in Christian believers, or between the presence and work of the Spirit in non-Christian religions and the presence of the Spirit in the church.

As it happens, classical Trinitarianism already employs such a distinction. It is the distinction between operation and mission. I submit that this distinction can serve a number of related purposes: first, it can allow an *operation* of the Spirit in non-Christian religions, including Old Testament anticipations of Christ, whilst reserving an ontologically distinct *indwelling* of the Spirit in those who profess explicit faith in Christ; further, it can account for the Pauline language of "Spirit of Christ," which indicates a Christoformation of the Pentecostal Spirit.

Briefly stated, an operation can be defined as the production of an (created) effect in the world; a mission can be defined as a union between a divine person and such a created effect.[20] A mission entails an operation;

20. The metaphysical description of this union cannot be attempted here. While appeals to the notion of cause are inevitable, it is not clear which kind of causality is entailed. Aquinas, for example, denies that God can enter composition with creatures, and therefore formal and material causes (which are intrinsic to the effect) are ruled out. Other theologians have complained that an appeal to efficient and final causation leaves the terms of the union extrinsic to each other. There is a tradition—from Petavius, through Scheeben, and Rahner—of speaking of the union in terms of a quasi-formal causality (Scheeben, *The Mysteries of Christianity* [New York: Herder and Herder, 2006], 167ff; Rahner, "Some Implications of the Scholastic Concept of Uncreated Grace," in *Theological Investigations*, vol. 1, *God, Christ, Mary and Grace*, trans. Cornelius Ernst, OP [Baltimore, MD: Helicon, 1961]), which has met significant opposition from, e.g., W. Hill, "Uncreated Grace-A Critique of Karl Rahner," *The Thomist* 27 (1963): 333–56.

an operation does not imply a mission. Aquinas understands a mission to involve the extension of a procession to a created effect.[21] This is a more developed view of a mission compared to that of Augustine, but fundamentally continuous with it. It should be pointed out that a mission bears two fundamental dimensions: epistemological and ontological. On the one hand, the missions reveal the persons distinctly. On the other hand, they bring about a relation of union between God and the creature, which is a relation that is real in the creature yet logical in God.

Most missions comport both dimensions, but the so-called symbolic missions do not.[22] The baptismal dove, for example, epistemically reveals, or rather indicates, the Spirit, and yet the Spirit is not ontologically united or incarnate in the dove. No attempt has been made to theologically conceive of the dove as the pneumatic equivalent of the hypostatic union. For this reason, this mission has been regarded as symbolic: the dove *symbolizes* the Spirit; it *is not* the Spirit.

One must speak of a proper sense of a mission, where both dimensions are present, epistemological and ontological, and which captures the reality that in such a mission the eternal procession truly extends to a creature in a relation of union with it. As Gilles Emery explains, "The Spirit is not given if he is only known symbolically, without the reception of the grace that sanctifies."[23] In a mission, one part of the created world is drawn by the Trinity to be united specifically with one of the divine persons. In the mission of the Son, the created effect is the human nature of Christ; in the case of the indwelling of the Holy Spirit, it is human persons themselves.

This distinction explains the uniqueness of the relation between God and humanity inaugurated through Jesus Christ and the Pentecostal Spirit. The indwelling of the Spirit is qualitatively different from the operation of the Spirit upon Old Testament saints and, by implication, upon non-Christians. The radical novelty of this relation to the Spirit is anticipated by the prophets (Ezek 11:19; 36:25–28; 37:1–14; Jer 31:31–34; Joel 3:1–5).

It should also be noted that in the tradition of classical Trinitarianism, the operations and missions do not indicate a change in God, but in the creature.[24] In a mission a real union takes place with the divine person,

21. Aquinas, *Summa Theologica*, trans. Fathers of the English Dominican Province (Westminster, MD: Christian Classics, 1981), I, q. 43, a. 2, ad. 3.

22. Cf. Aquinas, *Summa Theologica*, I, q. 43, a. 7, ad. 4.

23. Gilles Emery, *The Trinitarian Theology of St. Thomas Aquinas* (Oxford: Oxford University Press, 2007), 393.

24. Aquinas, *Summa Theologica*, I, q. 43, a. 2, ad. 2.

according to the nature of the receiving effect. Incidentally, it is precisely because such a union takes place (symbolic missions notwithstanding) that a manifestation of the triune person is possible. Otherwise, in an operation the persons are indistinguishable from one another, given that they are a single cause. Augustine was right to understand a mission in terms of the manifestation of a particular person.[25]

This means that all the divine persons are involved in Old Testament history. But since no created effect had been united (either hypostatically, or by grace) with one of the divine persons, the persons have not been properly manifested and are not said to have missions. The persons produce the effects together, but these effects, not being united to any particular person, do not manifest it hypostatically.[26] It does not mean that the persons were not active, only that they do not manifest themselves as such by union with a particular created reality. Only in light of their full revelation (because of their missions) can we retroactively "spot" the persons in the Old Testament.

Together with the Augustinian tradition, I would claim that there are no divine missions prior to the coming of Christ, while there are certainly inseparable triune operations in which the Spirit can be glimpsed retroactively. This answers objection (a). The work of the Spirit in the conception of Jesus Christ is one work attributed to the Spirit by appropriation. Since created reality is united not to the Spirit as such but to the Son, there is no mission of the third person in the conception of Christ. The mission is the Son's. Yet the Son's mission does not take place without the operation of the whole Trinity (proper mission presupposes inseparable operation), including, by a special appropriation, the Holy Spirit. This answers objection (c). As for the second objection, about a mission of the Spirit in other religions, we will turn to our final section.

THE SPIRIT HAD NOT BEEN GIVEN BECAUSE JESUS WAS NOT YET GLORIFIED

By distinguishing between missions and operations, the logical correlation between the two missions can be more clearly discerned. It is an undisputed fact that the outpouring of the Spirit is connected to the completion of the

---

25. Augustine, *The Trinity* (New York: New City Press, 1991), IV.28, 30.

26. By hypostatic manifestation I mean a revelation of a person in their hypostatic character, and not simply an indication of their reality.

Son's mission. Until Christ was glorified, he could not be sent. The completion of Christ's missions entails certain operations: going to the cross, overcoming temptation, obeying the Father, and so on.

But Christ completes these actions through a human nature that already subsists in the person of the Word. The union between the human nature and the word is the presupposition, not the conclusion, of these acts of obedience. These acts presuppose the reality of a mission of the Son. The eternal Son manifests his love of the Father on the human plane. This manifestation is the consequence of the fact that he is eternally the Son, in loving communion with the Father.

It is precisely this love of Christ for the Father, completed and perfected in his human obedience in the face of ultimate suffering, that mirrors on the human plane the shared love between the Son and the Father, which (in this Augustinian-Thomistic tradition) is the Holy Spirit. The third person emerges on a human plane *from within the very humanity of Christ*,[27] which loves all and obeys all. It is the river of living water which spills out *e latere Christi* (from the side of Christ). The Spirit is not simply bestowed upon Christ as an extrinsic reward for his obedience, a favorite theme of some Reformed theologians. Rather, he flows from Christ, having overfilled him. Thus the ultimate benefit of Christ's mission is the formation (on the human plane) of the Pentecostal Spirit.

It must be said, then, that Christ does not receive the Spirit in the same manner believers do. This is one of those aspects of Christology where imitability by the Christians is not a desideratum. In virtue of the unique relation of hypostatic union, from which the humanity of Christ subsists in the Son, *and* in virtue of the perichoresis of the divine persons, the human nature of Christ already possesses the fullness of the Spirit. Thus the Spirit cannot be said to be bestowed upon it extrinsically. Axiomatically, this undercuts many attempts at Spirit Christology. The Spirit's relation to Christ and to other human beings is asymmetrical in important ways. Christ has the Spirit because his humanity exists as possessed by the Word.

But by the same logic could we not say that the Father is equally present in Christ? Here too, however, the relationship between the persons is asymmetrical, in a *filioque* paradigm, for the Spirit comes from the Son and the Father while the Father does not come from the Son. The point

27. On this topic, see my "Ascension and Pentecost: A View from the Divine Missions," in *Being Saved: Explorations in Human Salvation*, ed. Marc Cortez, Joshua Farris, S. Mark Hamilton (London: SCM, 2018).

is that when the human nature is received into the Trinitarian relations in the person of the Son, it automatically finds itself oriented in specific ways to the other two persons: to the Father as receptivity and to the Spirit as productivity—yet only in virtue of the first orientation to the Father.[28] The human nature is oriented to the Spirit as productivity, only because logically it is first oriented as receptivity to the Father.[29] Christ's human nature is slotted into a particular Trinitarian taxis where it is attached to the Son. But in this particular Western paradigm, the Son does not receive the Spirit immanently. Neither, then, does the Son receive the Spirit economically.

And yet the life of the incarnate Son is full of the Spirit, one might even say increasingly full. Such a plenitude of the Spirit is achieved in the life of Jesus not by way of an extrinsic pouring, as is the Christian experience of the Spirit, but by an intrinsic upwelling, from the depths of the being of Christ. The Spirit is intrinsic to Christ in virtue of the hypostatic union, yet much like his beatific vision, it is in the depths of his personality and needs to work itself out in Christ's concrete existence. Granted that the Spirit can be understood as the shared love between the Father and the Son, Christ already possesses that love at an ontological level. David Coffey has called this Christ's basic or transcendental love of God.[30] It is a love that does not immediately manifest itself volitionally and concretely. It is like the attachment a baby has to his mother prior to consciousness, knowledge, and concrete actions. Christ's growth in wisdom and stature can then be understood as the actualization through human knowledge of his beatific vision. Similarly, his learning obedience can be understood as the actualization—as man—of his immanent receptivity (being from another). Conversely, his growing love for the Father can be understood as the actualization on a human plane of his natural, ontological shared love with the Father. Immanently he already shares in this love and thus spirates the Spirit with the Father. Economically, this eternal love, while present in the depths of his being, will be in the process of manifestation and actualization precisely as man.

The *filioque* is mirrored on the human plane in the fact that Christ has to return his love to the Father. The return that requires no time in the immanent Trinity is played out on the scene of human history, in the

---

28. For more on this see Legge, *Trinitarian Christology*, 112ff.

29. It should be noted that Christ is not said to *obey* the Spirit, even as he is *led* (ἤγετο) by the Spirit (Mark 1:12, Matt 4:1).

30. Coffey, "'Incarnation' of the Holy Spirit," *Theological Studies* 45 (1984): 476.

midst of the drama of human sin and godforsakenness. By thus mirroring the *filioque*, humanity is drawn to participate in the divine processions. It acquires the mode of existence of the Son (hypostatic union), and it spirates the Holy Spirit.

If we understand the Pentecostal Spirit as the human love of the Son for the Father, the experience of the earliest Christians of the Spirit precisely as the Spirit of the Son (Rom 8:9; Gal 4:6; Phil 1:19) makes sense. It is because the outpoured Spirit has been Christoformed—the Spirit of Christ, or the Spirit of the Son.

Tanner's point that Christ *shapes* the Spirit for us and yet does not provide the power for the Spirit in the same way the Spirit provides the power for Christ (by being active in his conception) must be rejected here. To say that the Spirit provides the power for Christ economically indicates that the Spirit provides the power for Christ immanently.[31] Economically, Christ does not send the Spirit, according to Tanner, because the Spirit has already been sent as the power for the Son's mission. This indicates a merely occasionalist correlation of the work of Christ and the work of the Spirit. The Spirit is shaped by Christ in the sense that it is only in and through the Christ event that we receive the Spirit, and yet that Christ event in itself makes no constitutive contribution to the Spirit we receive.

Tanner appeals to Stăniloae's point that just as immanently the Spirit *rests* on Christ, so economically the Spirit is only given to us through the one on whom he rests. Stăniloae and Lossky are careful to distinguish the incarnation, whereby the Son provides his person to human nature, from the mission of the Spirit, whereby the latter provides his divinity to human persons.[32] This is a laudable distinction between the respective missions. It is consonant with an account of salvation as deification, with which I am largely sympathetic. Yet there are some fundamental difficulties that such an account will have to address.

When Eastern Orthodoxy speaks of the Spirit's communication of his divinity to human persons in deification, it fails to account for the fact that the believer does not merely receive "divinity," or the divine energies, but also the person of the Spirit. In the believer, a mission of the Spirit

31. This is not because everything economic must have an immanent correlate, but the missions must be understood as our inclusion in the actual processions. Remember that the persons do not change, only the created effect does. A divine person is only said to have a mission of a created reality enters into a relation with a procession. So if the effect is not modified according to the immanent existence of the persons, these may not be said to be sent.

32. Lossky, *Mystical Theology*, 167.

(and the Son) indicates a union between the believer and the distinct persons of the Trinity, not simply a union to the inseparable, natural, and uncreated energies of God. Ironically, this tradition, which insists so much on the distinct personality and equality of the Spirit, ends up providing a largely impersonal account of the Spirit's mission in terms of the divine energies.

This raises the question even more: In what way is the deifying energy that the believer truly receives connected specifically to a person? If it is merely "shaped" by Christ in the sense that Christ is the locus of this energy, it is not clear how it is related to the person of the Spirit since immanently the Spirit's personhood is given independently of Christ's personhood. If, on the other hand, the Spirit's personhood is constituted by Christ's personhood *ad intra*, then to identify the Pentecostal Spirit with the human love of Christ for the Father supplies us with a notion of the Spirit's mission that does not yield merely natural energies.

It may be retorted that such an account of the Spirit's identity as the shared love between the Father and the Son is precisely impersonal, since the Spirit is defined in nonpersonal categories of love in contrast to the personal names Father and Son. In response it will suffice to point out that the latter names themselves indicate "subsistent relations" within the unity of the divine essence. It is misguided to play off the impersonal designation *love* against the personal names of Father and Son since what is personal in God indicates (at least in this tradition) relations that subsist within the unity of the divine essence.

The fact that in the immanent Trinity the Spirit is tethered to Christ grounds the economic relation between the Spirit and Christ. Further, it consolidates the personal character of the Spirit's mission—as opposed to mere common divine energies. The Spirit is not *merely* the love between the incarnate Son and the Father any more than the Son is *merely* the self-knowledge of the Father. The Spirit is Christoformed economically just as he is filioformed immanently.

This indicates the natural correlation between the two missions. The aim of the missions is to draw humanity to participate in the Trinitarian communion. But this sharing is specifically to be realized in Christ. In Christ the Son we occupy our place in the life of the Trinity as sons and daughters of God. The Holy Spirit, who indwells us, is precisely the Spirit who first filled and now overflows from Christ. For this reason it is impossible to understand the work of the Spirit in other religions as a mission in this weightier sense, for we then have to suppose another entry point into the Trinitarian life, one which does not pass through the Logos.

In that case there would exist an alternative blossoming of humanity not mediated through the humanity of the second Adam.

We must distinguish between the operation by which the Trinity draws us to Christ, the operation by which we are baptized into Christ, and the relation of union by which the Spirit indwells us. The first two are operations; the third is a mission. The missions, it might be said, are the fruition of the operations. The mission of the Son is consequent upon the operation by which the Trinity shapes a human nature for him; the mission of the Spirit is consequent upon the operation by which the Son shapes the Spirit for us, namely his obedience and love. The Old Testament faithful experienced operations of the Spirit (or appropriated to the Spirit, to be more precise); in common grace, non-Christian believers may indeed have a "searching memory" of Christ. But once we understand these as operations, not as proper missions, we can then do justice to the utterly unique and supernatural reality, inaugurated and made possible by God in Christ, of the indwelling of his Holy Spirit—indeed, the Spirit of Christ.

The most natural grounding for this order of the divine missions is the *filioque*. Eastern Orthodoxy rightly admits that the Spirit comes from Christ, but only because it immanently rests on the Son. But this fails to capture the authentic Christoformation of the Spirit; or at least it leaves it without an immanent correlate, in which case it jeopardizes our understanding of salvation as participation in the life of God himself.

CHAPTER 3

ON THE REVELATION OF THE HOLY SPIRIT AND THE PROBLEM OF THIRDNESS

KIMBERLEY KROLL AND JOANNA LEIDENHAG

"GOD IS SPIRIT" (JOHN 4:24), and yet one person of the Godhead is given the amorphous designator *Holy Spirit*.[1] Unlike the recognizable designators *Father* and *Son*, as well as the familiar relation that holds between them, this Holy Spirit in his person and relation to other persons (divine and human) creates what we call the problem of thirdness. The first two sections of this paper will outline how the problem of thirdness leads the theologian adrift into (1) the Charybdis of impersonal abstractions or (2) the mouth of the Scylla where it is swallowed by other (more tangible) doctrine. Whereas (1) attempts to answer the question "What is spirit?" (2) is preoccupied by "Where is the Holy Spirit?" Note that the questions of what and where do not arise in the same way or with the same urgency when considering the first and second persons of the Trinity. The names Father and Son, analogous to a well-known human relation, provide some relief here. The Father and the Son are clearly persons whose identities are understood in an ordered yet equal and loving relation to one another. By contrast, the third person who bears the name Holy Spirit provides no such relief, and so the theologian is thrown back onto the questions "What is

1. Lewis Ayres astutely points out that Holy Spirit "is a combination of terms that surely must also be true of Father and Son," so even this may not be a unique title for the third person of the Trinity. Ayres, "Augustine on the Trinity," in *The Oxford Handbook of the Trinity*, ed. Matthew Levering and Gilles Emery (Oxford: Oxford University Press, 2012), 129.

spirit?" and "Where is spirit?" or, put another way, "How do we fit a third person, the Holy Spirit, into our understanding of the Godhead?"

The two perennial questions of pneumatology, "What and where is the Holy Spirit?" are questions that biblical scholars and systematic theologians must address, but these questions should not exhaust the scope of pneumatology. In this paper we make no attempt to answer the what and where questions of spirit. Instead, we seek merely to highlight how the conclusions one draws regarding the what and where questions function as determinates for one's pneumatology delineating particular restraints, permissions, and contexts for which the doctrine is realised. In this paper, we will argue a theologically grounded notion of what and where the Holy Spirit is can only be found when properly constrained by another question: How? The question of how the Holy Spirit acts is often gestured toward by the prepositions *through*, *in*, and *by*. Since it is through, in, and by the Spirit that creatures come to participate in Christ and know the Father, it is imperative that theologians wrestle with this how question. Thus, in the final section of the paper, we argue that properly navigating the pneumatological sea requires a route delineated by an oft ignored question: How does the mode of revelation of the Holy Spirit inform our understanding of what and who the triune God is?

This is not an attempt to argue for a third article theology as we understand this to be a privileging of pneumatology over, though not necessarily against, traditional dogmatics. Any prioritization of a given doctrine over another can lead to the malformation of one's theological system, such as in overrealised Christologies and eschatologies. Though we seek to address complexities related to the third person and, in a way, grant him more ground on the theological playing field, we also seek to avoid what might be considered an overrealised pneumatology.[2] Instead, the sort of ground we are looking to grant the Spirit is ground most theologians already grant him without second thought; and maybe it is just this lack of second thought that is part of the problem. The Holy Spirit is the one *through* whom we are united to God and being transformed into the image of his Son. But how? Should we think of the Spirit as akin to glue,[3] as a conductor of divine

2. All that is meant by an overrealised pneumatology is something akin to what might be thought of as an overrealised Christology held by some Barthians. That is, the former answer all questions with "through the Spirit" and the latter "through Christ." Both these statements are true in that the Trinitarian operations are inseparable and all things are worked out "in the Spirit" and "in Christ" (and in the Father). Yet this flippancy rids the biblical text of its witness and the distinctions between the divine hypostases revealed through God's acts in creation.

3. Oliver Crisp notes, in holding all things together, the Spirit should be thought of as more

electricity, or something like this? Is he stuck to us or running through us like a current, or is he the current itself? This is a fundamental problem—if not the fundamental problem—of pneumatology: we have no clear picture of what spirit itself is, much less how the concept of spirit should inform and demarcate the uniqueness of the third person of the Godhead. Therefore, the problem of thirdness plus confusion regarding the concept of spirit tends to entail the positing of what we will refer to as "the black box(es) of the Holy Spirit" in lieu of constructive pneumatological doctrine.

A black box is a type of system, device, object, or in this case, divine person that is understood merely through what can be observed via inputs and outputs. That is, the internal workings of a black box (i.e., its characteristics and nature) remain unknown, and thus one infers from the external relations what one might be able to know about the black box itself. Interestingly, the black box of the Holy Spirit seems to be that which holds much—dare we say *all*—of theology together. This is why when theologians are unsure as to how to think of God in relation to *x*, *y*, and *z*, we proclaim victoriously, "It is *through* the Spirit that *x*" or "The Spirit *in* me testifies to *y*" or "It is *by* the Spirit that *z*." These prepositions seem interchangeable, and often two or three are used in a single sentence. Why? Because we have no idea what we mean when we assert these (and other) prepositions when related to spirit. It is this ambiguity around the term *spirit* that steers the theologian to ask the first question: What is spirit?

WHAT IS SPIRIT?

If we start with the immanent Trinity, the ordering of persons in the divine life of the Godhead, then the so-called problem of thirdness is quickly apparent. The Father is the source of the divine life from which the Son and the Spirit eternally proceed. The Son proceeds from the Father such that the Father's name and personhood is constituted as the one who eternally generates the Son, whose person reciprocally is constituted as the one who is generated. These two, then, have their differentiated personhood in relation to one another completed. And yet the personhood of the Spirit cannot be articulated in the same fashion and must be grounded in a different way. Regardless of whether one prefers the Latin or social model of the Trinity and what one thinks of the *filioque* debate (which we shall come to later), the problem of thirdness persists.

---

than glue. But for lack of a better term, this is the one he employs. Crisp, *The Word Enfleshed: Exploring the Person and Work of Christ* (Grand Rapids: Baker Academic, 2016), 161.

Augustine's description of the third person as the Love, the Bond, or the Gift, following from the preexisting and implicitly superior relation between the Father and the Son, exemplifies this problem. For whilst Augustine insists that "there is not subordination of the Gift and no domination of the givers," it remains that the Spirit as Gift and Love is qualitatively and functionally different to the givers and the lovers.[4] As the Father generates the Son, the Holy Spirit is also generated—almost by default—as that which the Father gifts to the Son, namely, the Spirit of the Father. Loving the Father in return, the Holy Spirit then becomes the Spirit of the Son returned to the Father.[5] The thirdness of the Holy Spirit is not beside the Father and the Son as in a threefold repetition but is *of* the Father and the Son, derivative of them and *abstracted* from them into a transferable or shareable substance.[6] Augustine derives this argument from New Testament passages that describe the love within the Trinity (1 John 4:7–16) and the Spirit as love poured out in our hearts (Rom 5:5). Yet there is no discussion of how the love of God is poured into our hearts or how the Spirit reveals or communicates this love. Because the how question has been ignored, the Spirit becomes the relation and the love in both the economy of salvation and the intra-Trinitarian life.

In the legacy of Augustinian thought, the Holy Spirit is not conceived of as a divine person in the same way as the Father and Son, but the Holy Spirit is that which two divine hypostases share and which eternally binds and differentiates their personhood. This Holy Spirit, then, is personalizing, but how are we to affirm that he is a person? This problem does not arise because of a presupposed definition of the term *person* taken from the created world and misguidedly applied to God; there is no definition of *person* working behind the scenes in this problem. The problem is that "What is a divine person?" is answered differently for the Holy Spirit than for the other two members of the Godhead. The Father and the Son are those which have loving familial relations. However, the Holy Spirit is the love that two divine hypostases share. Here we see that love does not constitute the Father or the Son but is the particular relation between the Father and the Son. This implies that unlike the Father and Son, who are *defined* by

4. Augustine, *The Trinity*, trans. Stephen McKenna (Washington, DC: Catholic University of America Press, 1963), 15.19.36.

5. Lewis Ayres, *Augustine and the Trinity* (Cambridge: Cambridge University Press, 2010), ch. 9.

6. The idea that the divine eternal unity is found in a "threefold repetition" that rules out subordination of any one person to the other two is language taken from Karl Barth, *Church Dogmatics*, vol. 1, *The Doctrine of the Word of God*, part 1, trans. G.W. Bromiley, ed. G. W. Bromiley and T. F. Torrance (Edinburgh: T&T Clark, 1975), 350ff.

their relations, the Holy Spirit simply *is* their relation and therefore cannot be the same kind of thing as the Father and the Son.[7] On this schema, the Holy Spirit neither gives nor receives, neither loves nor is loved, neither reveals nor can be revelation. Instead, the Holy Spirit is playing a different, unique, and seemingly lesser role of the Gift, Love, or the Revealedness,[8] which must always be predicated of something greater.

It is telling that in the grammar of Christian theology the Holy Spirit is most closely associated with prepositions such as *in*, *by*, *with*, and *through*, as mentioned earlier. The grammatical function of a preposition is as a connecter of the subject and predicate and then within the predicate as connecter of the action and direct object; prepositions are used to express spatial or temporal *relations* within a semantic construction. This is analogous to how *Holy Spirit* is often instrumentalised in much of Christian theology.[9] Syntactically, the preposition holds everything together in linguistic space just as "the black box of the Spirit" functions as the place-holder for all the mysterious theological moves one makes when working out God in relation to Godself and God in relation to his creation. When the Holy Spirit is made to be merely the "connection" that maintains proper theological structures, the Holy Spirit as black box is understood as (1) *the relation* between the Father and the Son (the so-called divine input) or derivatively as (2) *all the relations* between the Godhead (the input) and God's acts in the world (the so-called external outputs). Thus, whenever God is said to be "in relation" or something creaturely is said to be "in relation" to God, one could just insert the term *spirit* for the relation and avoid thinking about how the Holy Spirit, being God, is in relation. And so,

7. This problem of thirdness (the inconsistent logic of how the divine persons are established in our models of the Trinity) persists even when we remember Aquinas's definition of *all* the Trinitarian persons (and the divine essence) as "subsistent relations." This definition arises from the doctrine of simplicity and functions as an important bulwark against anthropomorphism. However, this doubling up of the language of relation in Trinitarian theology leads to an equivocation. On the one hand, all the Trinitarian persons are relations (or are something nonidentical to human persons). And yet the third person is *the* relation (bond, fellowship, or love) between the Father and Son in a special or unique way. Whereas the first and second persons stand in a reciprocal, *constitutive*, and *complete* relation of Father and Son, the relational status of the third person is something quite different. See Thomas Aquinas, *Summa Theologiae*, cura et studio Instituti Studiorum Medieavalium Ottaviensis, tomus primus (Ottawa: Collége Domincian d'Ottawa, 1941), 1.29.4; 1.30.2; and 1.39.1. Thank you to Adonis Vidu for raising this issue and to Matthew Joss for helping us to clean up some of our overly obtuse language here.

8. This is taken from Karl Barth's efforts to ground the doctrine of the Trinity in the concept of revelation, where the Father is the Revealer, the Son the objective Revelation, and the Spirit the subjective imparter of Revelation, or Revealedness. Barth, *Church Dogmatics*, I/1:332f.

9. An example of this is John V. Taylor's pneumatology, which focuses on the Holy Spirit's role as the "invisible go-between," the "in-between-ness," who "sets up the current of communication" between two subjects, I and Thou. Taylor, *The Go-Between God: The Holy Spirit & The Christian Mission* (London: SCM, 1972), 17.

typically, one seeks to understand the Holy Spirit just as one mechanically approaches understanding the black box, that is, one asks "What is the black box (or spirit)?" and "Where is the black box within the metasystem (or where is the Spirit located within God's relation to the world and the world's relation to God)?" And yet all we look to are the (theologically constructed) internal and (phenomenologically observable) external outputs, attributing these *to be* his person. Without trying to understand *how* he is revealed, which assumes a distinction between the person and mode or act of revelation, the Spirit is reduced to a type of stuff that is "activity" or is "relation"—love, grace, form, power, space, and so on. That is, the Holy Spirit is minimised to mediator between divine persons, or between divine and created persons, and is neither personal nor fully divine. He is mere abstraction.

One might, in attempt to avoid the abstraction of spirit through speculation of the inner life of the Trinity, take a different approach in answering the question "What is spirit?" via an exegetical investigation of the biblical text. However, the biblical text alone does little to elucidate what spirit is because the concept spirit is obscure and can refer to a variety of realities (e.g., an attitude, intention, disposition, desire, energy, the will, a whole person, etc). Further, the terms רוּחַ and/or πνεῦμα are often used as synecdoche for a subject who is thought to have or express the above noted features. The biblical text refers to spirit as breath and wind, suggesting a life-giving force, movement, and an invisible and transcendent power seen only through its effects,[10] and yet it also refers to spirit as water, possibly hinting that spirit should be thought of as a material substance. In John's gospel, spirit is attributed with what looks like agency when spirit is said to teach, lead, and guide. And in Paul, spirit adopts. Given the multiple uses and referents of the term *spirit*, are biblical scholars able to make *spirit* pellucid and offer a more concrete answer to the question "What is spirit?"

Essentially, conversations surrounding the nature of the spirit in biblical scholarship are deeply tied to what a given scholar takes to be the biblical author's cosmological framework.[11] The initial presupposition regarding

10. Anthony C. Thiselton, *The Holy Spirit: In Biblical Teaching, through the Centuries, and Today* (Grand Rapids: Eerdmans, 2013), 18.

11. For example: Volker Rabens, *The Holy Spirit and Ethics: Transformation and Empowering for Religious-Ethical Life*, 2nd ed. (Minneapolis: Fortress, 2016); Troels Edgberg-Pedersen, *Cosmology and the Self in the Apostle Paul: The Material Spirit* (Oxford: Oxford University Press, 2010); Dale B. Martin, *The Corinthian Body* (New Haven, CT: Yale University Press, 1999); Jörg Frey and John Levison, "The Origins of Early Christian Pneumatology: On the Rediscovery and Reshaping of the History of Religions," in *The Holy Spirit, Inspiration, and the Cultures of Antiquity Multidisciplinary Perspectives*, ed. Jörg Frey and John Levison (Boston: de Gruyter, 2014), 1–38.

an author's working cosmology often entails an initial answer to the what question of spirit.[12] However, parsing what one takes to be the right ancient cosmology of a biblical author cannot elucidate the concept of *spirit simpliciter.* The former merely provides an answer regarding what type of stuff spirit is. Yet many of the what questions linger, such as: Is spirit merely a phenomenal experience, an epistemic epiphany or delusion, or an ontological entity? Is there a difference between spirit as the animation of humans and spirit as divine? Is spirit transcendent or immanent? How might spirit, given the sort of stuff it is, effect or be affected by that which is not spirit? Is spirit personal, nonpersonal, or both?

Curiously, we can really only conceptualise a possible ontology of spirit, whether as an ancient author or a modern exegete, in one of three ways—material, supramaterial, or immaterial—because these ways appear to be the only available options given our metaphysical space. Given the diversity of cosmologies present in the biblical text and the plethora of interpretations in contemporary scholarship, attempts to answer the question "What kind of stuff is spirit?" leads scholars to construct highly abstract models in an attempt to explain the inner nature of the black box of spirit.

WHERE IS THE SPIRIT?

Due to the problem of thirdness, the question "Who is the Holy Spirit?" is often made synonymous with the question "Where is the Holy Spirit?" This occurs because who the Holy Spirit is, is derived commonly by way of his relating to the other members of the Godhead or to nondivine persons. Thus who the Spirit is becomes linked to where the Spirit is seen to work, (i.e., in the human person, by Jesus of Nazareth, or through the sacramental actions of the church).[13] Again, the Holy Spirit's personhood becomes secondary

12. We use the term *presupposition* not because biblical scholars assume a cosmology without some sort of supporting *historical* argument, but simply because commitment to a particular cosmology functions hermeneutically as an exegetical lens for how biblical scholars work with and from the text. Further, it is worth noting that biblical scholars, especially those working within *religionsgeschichtliche Schule,* concede that Paul (at least) is doing something new with spirit which cannot easily fit within any of the available ancient cosmologies. As such, the historical context does not do much to illumine the theological moves Paul (and other biblical writers) are making when utilising the term spirit. For further explication on this point, see Volker Rabens, "Physical and Mystical Dimensions of Human Transformation in Philo and Paul," paper presented at Studiorum Novi Testamenti Societas (SNTS) meeting in Athens, Greece, 2018; and Kimberley Kroll, "The Condescension of God: The Nature of the Relation of the Indwelling Holy Spirit" (PhD diss., University of St. Andrews, forthcoming).

13. This can also be seen in Catholicism and Eastern Orthodoxy when the Spirit is given a 'face' via Mariology and the concept of *Hagia Sophia,* respectively.

as he is the Spirit *of* more concrete phenomena: the spirit of humanity, the spirit of Christ, or the spirit of the church. Theologians are inclined to take the identity of the Holy Spirit, as third person of the Godhead, for granted by affirming that the Holy Spirit is God. This is so obviously the correct answer to the who question that one moves on immediately to consider the location of the Spirit in the economy of salvation. When this move is made without attention to the uniqueness of his personhood or the mode of his presence, then any possibility of the Spirit's unique characteristics or distinct contribution to theology is ruled out. The Holy Spirit becomes a general divine presence, a power source to be plugged in at some point, and pneumatology is subsumed under more concrete doctrine or equated with his works (outputs).[14] Because the primary goal of this paper is to highlight where pneumatology has gone adrift, we will follow the tide and limit our discussion to "Where is Spirit?"

By "more concrete doctrine," we are referring to doctrines that are clearer regarding the what question presented in the prior section and thereby make it easier to locate where spirit is. That is, if you ask, "What is incarnation?" or "What is church?" or "What is human?" or "What is creation?" then one can point to the thing itself (inadequate as that is for ontology) and answer, "There it is." This is not the case with spirit; even if spirit is defined as something material, it is never understood as being material in the way that we understand the physical, and thus we never know where to locate it. We cannot get out of this by simply denying that spirit has location or objecting that spirit cannot be bound within space-time. Prolific through the biblical text and theological tradition is the association between spirit and divine presence. The third person of the Trinity is the one who "draws near" and who the psalmist pleads not to be taken from him (Ps 51:11). Such presence or absence comes with implications for authority

14. It is worth taking note that this same problem (i.e., a depersonalisation of one of the members of the Godhead due to that member being overly identified with his works) has been identified as a problem in Christology. That is, due to a concern that Christ was being instrumentalized, seen as *merely* his works (e.g., atonement) and their efficaciousness, without attention being paid to the fullness of His being the second person of the Trinity, theology has seen a shift in trajectory and taken care to be attentive to the person of the Son and not collapse the person of the Son into the works of the Son. This same tendency of collapse is found in pneumatology, though it is (possibly) more complex due the fact that it is not only works but mere *concreta* that Holy Spirit is swallowed up by. For instance, Graham A. Cole makes the comparison to Christology when he enjoins theologians to focus on who rather than what the Holy Spirit is. However, since he makes elusiveness, self-effacement, and divine selflessness the fundamental methodological principles of doing pneumatology, the who question can only be answered by discussing the outputs or works of the Spirit, which thereby collapses pneumatology into other doctrine (in this case, creation, covenant, Christology, and ecclesiology). Cole, *He Who Gives Life: The Doctrine of the Holy Spirit* (Wheaton, IL: Crossway, 2007), 42, 281, 284.

or anointing as well as ethical value or holiness. Therefore, in this section, we will look at ways theologians (affirming some account of the Trinity) answer the question "Where is the Holy Spirit?" that have led to either a stunted or overrealised pneumatology. Although the doctrine of inseparable operations demands that the Spirit must be involved in all of these areas, He can't be contained, nor should his particularity within the triune Godhead be defined primarily as *in relation* to these doctrines. When pneumatology is subsumed by other doctrines, the distinctive, essential contribution that the Spirit makes to the Christian gospel is, in our systematic articulations, lost and forgotten.

SPIRIT AS AGGREGATE OF CHRIST

FILIOQUE

The spark that lit the Great Schism of 1054, separating the Greek-speaking Eastern church from the Latin-speaking Western church, was the question of how to express the relation between the Son and the Spirit in the triune life; this schism continues to stir up embers of dissent even today. Above we described how the place of the third person within the Trinity has been somewhat ambiguous and difficult to conceptualize after the opposed and reciprocal relations between the Father and the Son were first established. The Father is unoriginate; the Son is eternally originating from the Father. This, as is well known, leaves open two possibilities for the Holy Spirit: Does the Holy Spirit, like the Son, originate from the Father alone or from the Father and the Son? If one opts for the latter and accepts that the Holy Spirit proceeds from both Father and the Son (or from the Father and through the Son), then, as Jürgen Moltmann argued, it would seem that "the Holy Spirit is once and for all put in third place in the Trinity, subordinated to the Son."[15] This subordination, which needs not be an implication of the *filioque* within the immanent life of God, is made manifest in the retrospective justification for this additional clause as representative of the divine economy. Such arguments typically emphasize passages where the Holy Spirit is sent by Jesus, under his command and disposal, and give little consideration to passages where the Holy Spirit births, drives, guides, or empowers Jesus's ministry. One might alternatively shift the meaning of the *filioque* clause so that the Holy Spirit comes from the "common origin,"

15. Jürgen Moltmann, *The Spirit of Life: A Universal Affirmation*, trans. Margaret Kohl (London: SCM, 2009), 293.

or shared essence between the Father and the Son, and this route is clearly more promising.[16] However, one must proceed with caution so as not to imply that there is another component to the Godhead, a shared essence that is identifiable apart from the persons. However, if one rejects the *filioque* and claims that the Holy Spirit proceeds only from the Father, how can we distinguish between the Son and the Holy Spirit, who might appear to have the same relation of origin and thus be indistinguishable? These are the traditional horns of the *filioque* dilemma, and, humbly, we offer no resolution or answer to this dilemma.

Historically, the fear that motivated the addition of the *filioque* clause is not only a collapse between the Son and the Spirit but also the subordination of the Son in the form of Arianism. In this way, the unecumenical introduction of the *filioque* into the creed was to firm up the *homoouison* between the Father and the Son.[17] Put most simply, the *filioque* was never really about the Holy Spirit but about the divinity of the Son. Moreover, historians have noted that one cannot understand this change to the Latin creed apart from the ecclesiastical politics of the time, and still today the primary goal for many working on the *filioque* debate is ecumenical humility and reconciliation rather than dogmatic accuracy.[18] More recently, Moltmann (rather polemically) argued that the *filioque* persists out of a jealous "clericalism" because "if God is represented by Christ, Christ by the Pope, and the Pope by the bishops and priests, then—by way of the Filioque in the primordial relationships—the Holy Spirit, with all his charismata and energies in salvation history, is tied down to the operative acts of the priesthood."[19] Whilst Moltmann may overreach here, what is important to note is that these are debates in ecclesiology, both ecumenical and structural. None of the above is concerned with or attentive to the distinctive personhood or revelation of the Holy Spirit.

---

16. Although he strongly denied the implication highlighted here, this was Karl Barth's tactic for finding a middle path in this millennium-old controversy. Karl Barth, *Church Dogmatics*, vol. 1, *The Doctrine of the Word of God*, part.1, trans. G. W. Bromiley, ed. G. W. Bromiley and T. F. Torrance (Edinburgh: T&T Clark, 1975), 486–87. Cf. Wolfhart Pannenberg, *Systematic Theology*, trans. Geoffrey W. Bromiley (Grand Rapids: Eerdmans, 1996), 1:342ff.

17. Avery Dulles sources this concern back to Basil of Caesarea's unfortunate use of the word *cause* in reference to the Son's procession of the Father. Dulles, "The *Filioque:* What is At Stake?," *Concordia Theological Quarterly* 59 (January–April 1995): 32.

18. For example, Yves Congar proposed that the Western church should suppress the *filioque* cause because this "would be a gesture of humility and brotherhood on the part of the Roman Catholic Church which might have wide-reaching ecumenical implications." Congar, *I Believe in the Holy Spirit*, 3 vols., trans. D. Smith (New York: Seabury Press, 1980), 204, 206.

19. Moltmann, *The Spirit of Life*, 294.

SPIRIT CHRISTOLOGY

One form of reaction to the felt subordination of the Holy Spirit to Christ in the divine economy, as mentioned above, is the adoption of a Spirit Christology. There are many variations of Spirit Christology ranging from what could be identified as forms of adoptionism to forms of panthenthe-sism, though this is not a necessary entailment of the position. What we consider to be a minimalist Spirit Christology stems from a robust, possibly overrealised, pneumatology. On this minimalist account, it is "the Spirit who is the point of contact between the divine hypostasis and the humanity of Jesus."[20] Since the person of the Son must act in accord with his human nature without a change in his divine nature, the Spirit is introduced to mediate between the human and divine natures in Jesus Christ. As such, any act of divinity witnessed in Jesus Christ should, in some sense, be attributed to the Holy Spirit's acting through Christ's humanity and not solely to the action of the Son. This mediation of the Spirit acts as a sort of safeguard not only in upholding the divinity of the Son but also, more importantly for most advocating this view, maintaining Jesus's humanity. On this account, the Son is only indirectly related to his humanity, and the man Jesus is only indirectly related to the Godhead.[21] The Spirit plays a significant role in mediating and sustaining the humanity (nature, mind, etc.) of Christ in its relation to the divine person of the Son. It is a bit unclear why one should think that the Spirit does play or would need to play this sort of double mediatory role between (1) the humanity and divinity in the person of Jesus and (2) the person of the incarnate Son and the person of the Father. How does adding another divine person into the mix provide mediation between natures (within Christ) or persons (within the Godhead)?

Ultimately, we are not concerned with whether Spirit Christology is the best way to work out what is going on in the incarnation of the Son. What we are concerned with is how this understanding of Christology facilitates a collapse of pneumatology into Christology (and, oddly enough, might further facilitate a tangential collapse of pneumatology and Christology into anthropology). The beginnings of a collapse that this view implies is concerning in at least three ways:[22] (1) there is a lack of clarity regarding

---

20. Myk Habets, "Spirit Christology: The Future of Christology," in *Third Article Theology: A Pneumatological Dogmatics*, ed. Myk Habets (Minneapolis: Fortress, 2016), 229.

21. Habets, "Spirit Christology," 223.

22. There is a fourth way: because of the close association between the Spirit and Christ in incarnation, the Spirit (most explicitly) post-ascension functions theologically as a *form of Christ*

how to understand the *union* of humanity and divinity in Jesus Christ as the single person of the Son, (2) the complexities of pneumatological doctrine are constrained in that the primary mode of revelation of the Spirit relates to *merely* the humanity of Christ and not Godself, and (3) Spirit Christology seems to presuppose a competitiveness between the divine and human natures such that mediation is required even in the person of Christ.[23] Curiously, this has the effect of making Christ less than fully God while simultaneously making Christ something other than fully human.[24] So how does all this relate to pneumatology proper? On this model, it is the Holy Spirit who facilitates the communication/union of natures and persons within the single person of Christ, within the immanent Trinity (as discussed above), and in God's relation to human persons.

The question "Where is the Spirit?" is answered by advocates of this Spirit Christology view as fundamentally grounded and located "in the humanity of Christ." The way the Spirit acts in Christ's humanity (mediating humanity to Christ and mediating the divinity of the Father to Christ) becomes a model for how the Spirit indwells the human person, except now it is the human Jesus that is mediated to the Christian believer and not the Godhead.[25] We wonder if the Spirit's mediation can be thought to make the relation between something divine and something human really indirect. The Spirit himself *is* divine! Why then, or *how* then, does it work that the Spirit is able to be the mediating one? The only reason we can conceive for why it is that the Spirit is able to do this work (and on a Spirit Christology *must* do this work) is that spirit (inexplicitly) is conceptualised as some semicreated or uncreated stuff.[26] We have, it seems, returned back to the what question, this time via the where question. The Spirit has become either a quasi-divine stuff located in the humanity of Christ or

lacking his own personhood. As John W. Nevin writes, "The Spirit then constitutes the form of Christ's presence and activity in the Church, and the medium by which he communicates himself to his people." Nevin, *Mystical Presence: A Vindication of the Reformed or Calvinistic Doctrine of the Holy Eucharist* (London: FB&C, 2015), 226. See also David Coffey, "The Method of Third Article Theology," in *Third Article Theology: A Pneumatological Dogmatics*, ed. Myk Habets (Minneapolis: Fortress, 2016), 21–38.

23. Thank you to Jared Michelson for helping us to articulate the problematic presupposition in this way.

24. For a more extensive articulation of this argument, see Kimberley Kroll, "Indwelling without the Indwelling Holy Spirit: A Critique of Ray Yeo's Modified Account," *Journal of Analytic Theology* 7 (2019): 124–41.

25. Ray S. Yeo, "Towards a Model of the Indwelling: A Conversation with Jonathan Edwards and William Alston," *Journal of Analytic Theology* 2 (2014): 210–37.

26. Interestingly, this not-so-live option, if it were an option, imitates the three answers to the 'what' question, i.e. material (created), immaterial (divine), and supra-material (created-divine composite).

a relation that holds between divine and created stuff, belonging fully to neither category. In a sense, the "black box" of the Holy Spirit is moved and located in Christ's humanity minimizing both the divine and personal qualities of the Holy Spirit.

SPIRIT AS AGGREGATE OF THE HUMAN PERSON

At first glance, equating the Holy Spirit with a human spirit might appear to answer the what question of spirit (i.e., spirit *just is* human spirit, whatever human spirit is).[27] Yet this move locates the spirit *within* a human and so is also an attempt to answer the question "Where is spirit?" That is, saying that spirit is human spirit does not actually address the question "What is spirit?" Instead, it avoids the what question by locating spirit in something else with concrete spaciotemporal location, that is, human beings. This move ultimately equates a part of a human being with God, the human spirit with divine spirit. Let's call this concept "Spirit anthropology."

The main problem with understanding spirit as merely referring to the human spirit or life-breath of human beings is that it makes either (1) the Holy Spirit something other than divine (denying Trinitarian conceptions of God) or (2) humans in some sense naturally divine (divinizing humans), because (3) the distinction between the human and divine natures is collapsed. Most will not (explicitly) affirm (1), though there might be biblical fodder for this (especially in the Hebrew Bible and Second Temple literature).[28] We do not think proponents of the Holy Spirit as "life-breath" want to confer that Holy Spirit *just is* human spirit because this seems to lead to the immediate collapse of the Creator-creature distinction. Instead, proponents of this view would have to say something like: "Humans have human spirits, and humans are also in a special 'life-breath' relation[29] to the

27. This identification of the human spirit with the Holy Spirit often results from the apparent textual ambiguity on this point in some biblical passages, particularly in wisdom literature. The additional presence of the Holy Spirit indwelling the Christian believer, or as the breath of life "on loan to man during his earthly life" (Wis. 15:16), does not help. However, textual ambiguity is not excuse for metaphysical confusion or collapse. George Montague, *The Holy Spirit: The Growth of a Biblical Tradition* (Eugene, OR: Wipf & Stock, 1976), 102.

28. For an introduction into the biblical conversation regarding human spirit as holy spirit, see John R. Levison, *Filled with the Spirit* (Grand Rapids: Eerdmans, 2009). Levison understands life-breath *as* divine spirit and "filling" ("to the nth degree") as a special endowment upon conversion. For Levison, there is no distinction between the רוּחַ that animates human persons and the πνεῦμα that is experienced in fullness by the faithful. Whatever pneuma is understood to be, it is already present in, and at least partially constitutive of, the human person upon creation.

29. Because humanity is the only creation that receives this "life-breath," spirit is kept back from collapse into all of creation, allowing humanity to maintain a heightened status over the creation.

Holy Spirit such that the Holy Spirit can be said to have been breathed into and added to *all* humans such that *all* human beings have spirit that is also divine Spirit."[30] Oddly, what we have, then, are humans who always have access to the mind of God due to the already present Spirit of God within them; a kind of Schleiermachian "God-consciousness." If this is the case, then the fall from grace has not really had much effect. There is no difference between those in Christ and in the church and those outside of Christ and his church because all have immediate access to God via this divine Spirit—the Holy Spirit is thereby somehow *constitutive of all humanity at creation*.[31]

Similar to Spirit Christology, Spirit anthropology is a form of overrealised pneumatology that both diminishes the divine and turns the human into something other than human. This tendency toward a so-called Spirit anthropology can be seen most often in those that (1) lean toward (or commit to) universalism and (2) understand conversion to be merely epistemic. Regarding (1), Spirit anthropology acts to "fill the gap" between those who come to faith and those who do not. If all humans will enter the loving presence of God and are being moved to eschatological bliss, and if all humans have had the salvation of Christ applied to them, then all humans have immediate access to the divine via the presence of the divine Spirit. Regarding (2), salvation is a coming to know what is already the case rather than a metaphysical change of the person in relation to God. And in the same vein, it is a coming to know through looking within for the God who is already present within (i.e., God is not only closer than one can imagine but seems familiar and unremarkable rather than being a radically transcendent God who "disrupts" through in-breaking). Both of these renderings, to their credit, avoid major theological puzzles (e.g., How is it that the work of Christ is only made manifest in some humans? How is it that we do not have an ontological change of status on conversion through the giving of the Spirit?). But at what cost?

---

30. One of us has previously suggested that the *imago Dei* might be understood as the indwelling of the Holy Spirit, which implies that all human beings are indwelt by the Spirit as part of their creation. I now think that if one argues for a pneumatological basis for the *imago Dei*, which has significant advantages over other standard models, then it should be on the unique *potential* for human beings to be indwelt by the Spirit rather than on the full realisation of this indwelling in all people. See Joanna Leidenhag, "Uniqueness and the Presence of the Image: Towards a Pneumatological Foundation for Human Uniqueness and the Image of God," in *Issues in Science and Theology: Are We Special? Human Uniqueness in Science and Theology*, ed. Michael Fuller, Dirk Ever, Anna Runehov, and Knut-Willy Sæther (Cham, Switzerland: Springer, 2017), 255–70.

31. God obviously acts toward and throughout creation given his omnipresence. However, we see no good reason to consider omnipresence, indwelling, and specialized "local" presence as synonyms or identical notions of God's presence in the world. Indeed, such collapse between different ways God is present to creatures and in creation only leads to deep theological confusion.

Spirit as Aggregate of Creation

Once the Holy Spirit becomes constitutive of a human person, one is only a stone-throw away from understanding Spirit as constitutive of creation. In this way the Holy Spirit is not only collapsed into the human soul or life-force but becomes a "world-soul" or cosmic life force. This trajectory can be seen in the work of Jürgen Moltmann and Wolfhart Pannenberg. As leading proponents of the rediscovery of Trinitarianism in twentieth-century theology, Moltmann and Pannenberg have both given substantial attention to the place of pneumatology in systematic theology. Both theologians also reject what they see as the Hellenising influence on pneumatology that associated *pneuma* with *nous*, a rational mind and subsequent Spirit anthropology, more than with *ruach*, a cosmic and transcendent force. Their goal was to use pneumatology to bridge unacceptable divides between creation and redemption, as well as between natural science and Christian thought, by emphasising the Spirit's role as the power and integrating "connector" throughout the cosmos. For all the many differences between them, both Moltmann and Pannenberg sought to articulate a theology of the person and work of the Holy Spirit through engagement with modern science and so came to define the Spirit as a "vitalizing field of energy."[32] It is ironic that, whilst both Moltmann and Pannenberg decried the influence of Hellenistic philosophy upon Christian pneumatology, the development of spirit as a rational but only quasi-personal force pervading the cosmos remains very close to Philo's Christianized interpretation of the spirit as the Stoic or Platonic "world-soul."[33]

Moltmann's pneumatology starts with the "elemental" experience of spirit as the "divine element"[34] (comparable to water, fire, or air/breath) and consists largely in a description of the Spirit's effects; the outputs of the black box. For Moltmann, the where and who questions of pneumatology are determined by human experience: the experience of being alive, the experience of an empowered or liberated life, the experience of inner peace, and perhaps most importantly, "the space we live in" and "that broad place where there is no more cramping."[35] From this, Moltmann deduces that

32. Jürgen Moltmann, *The Spirit of Life: A Universal Affirmation*, trans. Margaret Kohl (London: SCM, 2009), 55.

33. John R. Levison, *The Spirit in First-Century Judaism* (Leiden: Brill, 1997), 148ff.

34. Jürgen Moltmann, *The Source of Life: The Holy Spirit and the Theology of Life*, trans. Margaret Kohl (London: SCM, 2009), 12.

35. Moltmann, *The Source of Life*, 11, 31, 68. See also Moltmann's critique of the split between experience and revelation in the dialectics of Barth, Brunner, Bultmann, and Gogarten, and his preference to experience as revelation (Moltmann, *The Spirit of Life*, 5–6).

Mother is an appropriate name for the Holy Spirit as the space and lifeforce in which a child in whom the individual human and the entire cosmos lives and grows.[36] The subsumption of pneumatology into the doctrine of creation occurs as much because creation is Moltmann's answer to the question "What is spirit?" as it is his answer to the question "Where is the Holy Spirit?"; the Spirit is found throughout creation as a divine force field of creation. The Spirit, for Moltmann, is "by no means merely a matter of revelation. It [The Holy Spirit] has to do with life and its source and so is in everything and known through every experience."[37]

By contrast, Pannenberg denied the direct experience of God in finite existence and believed that God could only be experienced indirectly through the totality of universal history. Pannenberg tries to articulate this through the language of electromagnetic field theory, whereby the Spirit becomes a universal field of forces manifested in particular corpuscular constellations. This metaphor with field theory is also a modern answer to the what question. It is telling, and often missed, that the primary focus for Pannenberg's discussion of fields of force is the "spirit" as the substance of the Godhead, not the name for the third person of the Trinity. Pannenberg's field of force is the life of the triune God manifest as the pervasive, indirect revelation of the totality of history.[38] Pannenberg's answer to the what question dictates his answer to the where question; the divine force field (spirit) is everywhere, in all history, and so the Holy Spirit is also nowhere in particular. There is no way on such a schema to even start pneumatology, to inquire further into the Holy Spirit as a person, or to probe the distinctive revelation of the Holy Spirit.

For both Moltmann and Pannenberg, the diffusion of pneumatology into all experience and the totality of cosmic history means that pneumatology can have no boundaries, edges, or clear definition. *Spirit* is defined as supramaterial bodily experiences had by all humanity, indeed all flesh and the entire cosmos. The question of how this spirit of creation can also be *Holy*, an uncreated person of the Trinity, remains unanswered. In the attempt to free pneumatology from the anthropological spirits of modern liberal Protestantism, Moltmann, Pannenberg, and numerous other scholars

---

36. This is a move from what the Spirit is (the experience of space and life) to who the Holy Spirit is (Mother). Moltmann, *The Spirit of Life*, 270–74; Moltmann, *The Source of Life*, 27, 35–37.

37. Moltmann, *The Spirit of Life*, 7.

38. Christoph Schwöbel, "Wolfhart Pannenberg," in *The Modern Theologians: An Introduction to Christian Theology in the Twentieth Century*, ed. David Ford (Oxford: Basil Blackwell, 1987), 278; Wolfhart Pannenberg, *Systematic Theology*, trans. Geoffrey W. Bromiley, vol. 1 (Grand Rapids: Eerdmans, 1996), 401ff; 414ff.

in the recent fields of science-and-religion and ecotheology have collapsed pneumatology into the doctrine of creation.[39]

HOW DOES THE HOLY SPIRIT REVEAL?

The above analysis has been something of a ground-clearing exercise. It provides a critical cartography of the field of pneumatology, arguing that, for the most part, theologians have been preoccupied with not necessarily the *wrong* questions but *unhelpful* questions regarding the third person of the Trinity. Preoccupation with the questions "What is Spirit?" and "Where is the Holy Spirit?" has led to either (1) stumbling over thirdness into a pit of abstraction or (2) inserting the black box of spirit into another doctrine that in turn defines the Spirit; both of these diminish or forgo his divine personhood. If this is a fair assessment of the pneumatological landscape, one might wonder how *any* claims can be made about the Holy Spirit. If we can't answer the questions of what (without abstraction) or where (without collapse), then what is a theologian interested in pneumatology to do? This is exactly what makes it so dang hard to work out particularities of pneumatology *simpliciter*! That is, the Holy Spirit is never found alone or in isolation in a way that allows for neat and clear demarcation regarding what or where he is (but, honestly, this is a truth of the whole Trinity). Thus, we propose that one must look first to the primary mode in which the Holy Spirit acts in revelation.

How is it that we should understand the mode of the Spirit's revelation? The Holy Spirit is always pointing to and revealing Christ. For this

39. John Polkinghorne talks of the work of the Spirit in terms of "the input of pure information" into creation. John Polkinghorne, "The Hidden Spirit and the Cosmos,' in *The Work of the Spirit: Pneumatology and Pentecostalism,* ed. Michael Welker (Grand Rapids: Eerdmans, 2006), 169–82. A more recently popular model has been to associate the Holy Spirit with emergence theory as the "emergence of spirit" and the "spirit of emergence." See Philip Clayton, "The Emergence of Spirit," *CTNS Bulletin* 20, no. 4 (2000): 3–20; Denis Edwards, *Breath of Life: A Theology of the Creator Spirit* (Maryknoll, NY: Orbis, 2000); Amos Yong, "*Ruach*, the Primordial Chaos, and the Breath of Life: Emergence Theory and the Creation Narratives in Pneumatological Perspective," in *The Work of the Spirit: Pneumatology and Pentecostalism*, ed. Michael Welker (Grand Rapids: Eerdmans, 2006), 183–204. For a critique of this movement in the science-religion dialogue, see Joanna Leidenhag, "A Critique of Emergent Theologies," *Zygon: Journal for Science and Religion* 51, no. 4 (2016): 867–82; Joanna Leidenhag and Mikael Leidenhag, "Spirit and Science: A Critical Examination of Amos Yong's Pneumatological Theology of Emergence," *Open Theology* 1, no. 1 (2015): 425–35; Joanna Leidenhag and Mikael Leidenhag, "The Unsuitability of Emergence Theory for Pentecostal Theology: A Response to Bradnick and McCall," *Zygon: International Journal in Science and Religion* 53, no. 1 (2018): 258–73. Donald Bloesch raises this objection against the pneumatology of Clark Pinnock, which "tends to begin with the Spirit's work in creation," resulting in a "natural theology of the Spirit" that struggles to say anything distinctively Christian about the Holy Spirit and instead offers a global religion of the Spirit. Donald Bloesch, *The Holy Spirit: Works & Gifts* (Downers Grove, IL: InterVarsity Press, 2000), 25–26.

reason, theologians have come to speak of a "self-effacing," "elusive," or "shy" personality of the Spirit. Curiously, we do not likewise refer to Christ as self-effacing in his pointing and revealing the Father and the promised Spirit. Further, in so far as the Holy Spirit is the *Paraclete* who has come to be present in believers, one might argue that he is currently both *more* present and *more* intimate with his redeemed creatures than either the Father or the Son. The characterisation of the Holy Spirit's nature as "self-effacing," whilst it may contain a grain of truth, seems to function largely as an excuse for the subsumption of pneumatology into more concrete doctrine, as discussed above. Given the difficulties in pneumatology, such a judgement can only be seen as premature. Until we examine the distinct revelation of the Holy Spirit and the manner of this revelation, we cannot know if the Holy Spirit is more timid than the other members of the Trinity—or indeed more assertive!

One cannot imagine or deduce from prior revelation Christology (the revelation of the Son) without *incarnation*—the mode of his revelation. There are certain attributes of the Son that are only revealed or fleshed out through God's unique mode of revelation for the Son (e.g., the humility and condescension of God, that divinity and humanity are not in a competitive relation, etc.). Similarly, one cannot attain to a proper pneumatology (the revelation of the Holy Spirit) by looking (only or primarily) to the revelation of the Son, to theological anthropology, or to the doctrine of creation. To begin one's theological investigation into pneumatology, one must be attentive to God's unique mode of revelation for the Holy Spirit—*indwelling*. Whilst indwelling is not the only mode of the Spirit's revelation in creation, it is a good place to start for theologians working post-Pentecost. It is via this mode of revelation—intimate and internal indwelling relation between two personal *relata* (the Holy Spirit and redeemed human persons)—that the Holy Spirit is revealed to and present in creation as the third person of the Godhead. Note that here the Holy Spirit is *in relation* and is neither a relation nor merely a relator (one who simply facilitates others' relationships).

Indwelling, as a dynamic act in a particular mode of revelation, could inform our understanding of the uniqueness of the Holy Spirit's personhood (avoiding the instrumentalization of the Spirit) and then can also inform our thinking of the Trinitarian God more generally. For it is only now, post-ascension of Christ and post-instantiating the new indwelling relation of the Spirit (i.e., post-Pentecost), that we can even begin to fathom Trinity. More specifically, it is via the Holy Spirit's being in indwelling relation to redeemed human persons that human minds are illumined and receive revelation regarding the Trinitarian nature of the Godhead (and are able to investigate the biblical witness retrospectively in light of Christ and Pentecost). The Holy Spirit is not *merely* a means of revelation, not merely a "black box" connector. And revelation is not merely accomplished *by*, *with*, and *through* the Spirit. He himself *is* being revealed as Holy Spirit, the third person of the Godhead! As such, God the Holy Spirit is also the *object* of revelation along with the Father and the Son and not merely the instrument of revelation. If we examine and seek to understand the uniqueness of this indwelling relation,[40] and we do not act as if the third person of the Trinity is merely a relation, then we might just properly navigate the pneumatological sea toward a robust understanding of the divine person of the Holy Spirit.

40. For a further extensive and constructive account of the indwelling relation of the Holy Spirit, see Kroll, "The Condescension of God."

CHAPTER 4

THE MYSTERY OF THE IMMANENT TRINITY AND THE PROCESSION OF THE SPIRIT

SAMEER YADAV

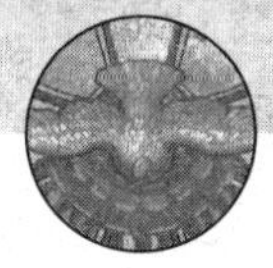

THERE IS IN RECENT THINKING about the Trinity an emerging trend that begins by observing the large and varied proliferation of Trinitarian theologies that have grown out of the twentieth-century revival of Trinitarian theorizing and then proceeds to offer strong cautionary notes about the kind of insights about the inner life of God as Trinity that we can legitimately expect to derive from our theorizing. The cautionary advice often recommends that we dramatically *restrict* our Trinitarian theorizing to recognize significant limits on what the available evidence licenses us to affirm about the inner life of God. This is what I will call a kind of metaphysical *minimalism* about our aims and interests in reflecting on the inner-Trinitarian life of God, a minimalism about how deep or detailed a model of the Trinitarian structure of God's inner life in the so-called "immanent Trinity" we can derive from a traditional interpretation of Scripture. Three recent examples of Trinitarian minimalism have been expressed by Oliver Crisp, Karen Kilby, and Linn Tonstad.[1] Each one offers

1. Oliver D. Crisp, *Analyzing Doctrine* (Waco, TX: Baylor University Press, 2019); Karen Kilby, "Is an Apophatic Trinitarianism Possible?," *International Journal of Systematic Theology* 12, no. 1 (January 2010): 65–77; Linn Marie Tonstad, *God and Difference: The Trinity, Sexuality, and the Transformation of Finitude* (New York: Routledge, 2017).

different reasons to commend different kinds of minimalism as a cautionary note to would-be Trinitarian theologians who wish to maintain a traditional one-substance, three-persons doctrine. Despite their differences, all of them worry about unwarranted speculation in Trinitarian thinking. In what follows I want to object to these restrictive impulses and advocate for a more robust or *maximalist* freedom in Trinitarian theorizing. In this paper, I will focus particularly on the most recent expression of Trinitarian minimalism that we find in Oliver Crisp's *Analyzing Doctrine*.

What does this question of minimalist versus maximalist theorizing about Trinitarian metaphysics have to do with the Holy Spirit in particular? Proposing an intervention on Trinitarian minimalism in the context of this book might seem five years too late, because the theme of *Advancing Trinitarian Theology* was the topic of the 2014 Los Angeles Theology Conference,[2] whereas any treatment of the Nicene tradition for the papers collected in this volume from LATC 2020 are supposed to focus on the third article of the creed and its affirmations about the Spirit. In the history of Trinitarian debates, the primary problem of "third article theology" is the question of the Spirit's procession—whether the Spirit eternally proceeds from the Father only or jointly from the Father and the Son.[3] But the *filioque* controversy has never been more than a stone's throw from wider methodological debates about the proper approach to Trinitarian theorizing per se.[4] So in what follows I will briefly summarize the connection between Crisp's thinking about what Nicene Trinitarianism minimally involves and the *filioque* controversy. Then I'll consider some worries about what Crisp calls the "moderate mysterianism" of his Trinitarian minimalism that would threaten to undercut traditional theorizing about the Spirit's procession. I won't claim that my rejection of Crisp's Trinitarian minimalism gives us

---

2. Oliver D. Crisp and Fred Sanders, eds., *Advancing Trinitarian Theology: Explorations in Constructive Dogmatics* (Grand Rapids: Zondervan, 2014).

3. While Myk Habets describes "third article theology" as a movement in constructive theology that utilizes "a distinctly pneumatological approach to dogmatics," I use it only to signal theology focusing particularly on the theological reflection arising from the third article of the Nicene creed. See the essays gathered in Habets, *Third Article Theology: A Pneumatological Dogmatics* (Minneapolis: Fortress, 2016).

4. As Edward Siecienski notes, in *The Filioque: History of a Doctrinal Controversy* (New York: Oxford University Press, 2010), at issue was not only "the monarchy of the Father, the eternal relationship between Son and Spirit, [and] the transferrable (or nontransferable) nature of the hypostatic qualities" but also "the exact relationship between the economy . . . and theology" (6). Furthermore, "this last issue," Siecienski observes, was "particularly vexing, since the Greeks were more hesitant about blurring the lines between the two, while the Latins insisted that the economy revealed truths about the immanent Trinity, including the sending of the Spirit by/through/from the Son," and it was precisely these "diverse approaches to trinitarian mystery" that raised the question of whether "the two halves of Christendom" had "come to "differing, and ultimately incompatible, teachings about the nature of God" (6).

any particular reason to adopt this or that view of the Spirit's procession *ad intra*. Rather, I only think we ought to lift his proposed restriction.

Oliver Crisp's methodological reflections in his chapter on "Trinity and Mystery" in *Analyzing Doctrine* rely on Bill Wood's explanation of a model as an attempt to schematize a complex set of data in order to gain partial understanding and to serve some particular interests of the inquirer.[5] Like Wood, Crisp emphasizes that models intentionally and often necessarily leave a lot out, and in that respect whatever they seek to model will always remain relatively mysterious while the model will always be representationally inadequate. To cite his favored example, a model airplane is only aimed at resembling the real thing in certain targeted respects and therefore represents reality in a limited and partial way.[6]

Likewise, Crisp thinks that the Nicene orthodoxy about God's triune nature is a limited way of representing how God reveals Godself to be in Scripture. Taking one plausible reading of the complex scriptural evidence as an evidence base, a Nicene model consists in organizing and schematizing that evidence base to arrive at the claim that there is exactly one God and that this God exists in three eternally distinct but coequally divine persons: Father, Son and Holy Spirit. Crisp breaks this down into four component claims: there is exactly and numerically one God, God is coeternally three, the three are individually nonidentical to one another, and the three are equally divine or consubstantial.[7] When considered together, these claims about God constitute a rather minimalistic and "conceptually thin" model of God's triunity, a model that "says very little about the divine nature, and about what divine persons are or how they are related to one another in the divine life."[8] It expresses a plausibly biblically inferred belief *that* God is triune, although it does not model for us *how* God is triune. He does, however, take this minimal model to rule out many alternative possible ways of organizing the biblical material, such as the Arian view that makes the Son a less than divine substance who is not one being with the Father.[9] I would want to add a few further points.

---

5. William Wood, "Modeling Mystery," *Scientia et Fides* 4, no. 1 (2016): 39–59.

6. Crisp, *Analyzing Doctrine*, 87.

7. Crisp delineates these as separate propositions T1–T4: "(T1) there is exactly one God; (T2) there are exactly three coeternal divine persons "in" God: the Father, the Son, and the Holy Spirit; (T3) the Father, the Son, and the Holy Spirit are not identical; (T4) the Father, the Son, and the Holy Spirit are consubstantial." Crisp, *Analyzing Doctrine*, 86.

8. Crisp, *Analyzing Doctrine*, 78.

9. Crisp, *Analyzing Doctrine*, 85.

The first has to do with the scriptural evidence that served as the basis for inferring these parameters that make up a minimally Nicene Trinitarianism. Here it is important to emphasize that the parameters in question were formed primarily by reading the monotheism of Israel's religion alongside the so-called "missions" of that God in the sending of the Son and the Spirit as revealing a pattern within God's own life.[10] Israel's one God is revealed in redemptive relationship to us *ad extra* as a Father begetting a Son and breathing a Spirit, precisely because Israel's one God in fact *is* a Father begetting a Son and breathing a Spirit *ad intra*, independently of God's relation to creatures.[11] It is this reading of God's missions as revelatory of relations of origin within God that sets the parameters for the Nicene picture of God's triunity: if Israel's one God really is in some sense a divine Father begetting a divine Son and breathing a divine Spirit, then we must at a minimum affirm the claims about God's numerical oneness and coeternal, nonidentical, and consubstantial threeness that Crisp identifies with Nicene minimalism.

The second point is that the parameters that make up the minimal claim about God's triunity can be equally well identified negatively by three of the most important possibilities for reading the biblical evidence that it rules out: polytheism, modalism, and subordinationism. So the parameters of God's numerical oneness and the consubstantiality of the three rules out polytheism,[12] the eternality and nonidentity of the three rules out the modalist idea that God's threeness is a merely optional way God chooses to appear rather than how God necessarily is,[13] and the parameter of coequal

10. As Fred Sanders puts it in *The Triune God* (Grand Rapids: Zondervan, 2016): "The Bible tells a unified story of God's way with his people . . . in the visible missions of the Son and the Holy Spirit. Interpreting these missions correctly as divine self-revelation is central to the exegetical establishing of Trinitarian theology. What the missions reveal about the life of God is that his life takes place in eternal relations of origin" (93).

11. See Sanders, "Entangled in the Trinity: Economic and Immanent Trinity in Recent Theology," *Dialog: A Journal of Theology* 40, no. 3 (2001): 175–82. For a helpful synopsis of the various ways that the inference from economy of the Spirit to the immanence of the Spirit in the divine life, see Brian Daley, "Revisiting the 'Filioque': Roots and Branches of an Old Debate. Part One," *Pro Ecclesia* 10, no. 1 (Winter 2001): 31–62.

12. See Gregory of Nyssa, *Ad Ablabium Quod non sint tres dei*, in *Gregorii Nysseni Opera*, vol. 3, part 1, ed. Friedrich Muller (Leiden: Brill, 1958), 35–58, and translated as *On "Not Three Gods": To Ablabium*, in *Nicene and Post-Nicene Fathers*, 2nd series, vol. 5, trans. and ed. H. A. Wilson (New York: Christian Literature Company, 1893), 331–36. See also the discussion of early Christian thinking about the kind of unity a triune God must possess in Giulio Maspero, *Trinity and Man: Gregory of Nyssa's Ad Ablabium* (Leiden: Brill, 2007); and Lewis Ayres, *Nicaea and Its Legacy* (New York: Oxford University Press, 2004), 344–63.

13. Khaled Anatolios, *Retrieving Nicaea* (Grand Rapids: Baker Academic, 2011), defines the modalism of Sabellius and Paul of Samosata as the view that God is a "radically singular being" with "Son and Spirit as merely modes of divine operation" (16). This may not be an entirely accurate way of glossing the view insofar as we can also find it expressed by pro-Nicenes. In *Ad Ablabium*,

divinity among the three rules out the subordinationist idea that any one person is anything less than a distinct way of manifesting the very same divinity that is also distinctly manifested by each of the other two persons.[14]

According to Crisp, this sort of minimal model of Trinitarianism is minimal because it involves only identifying a few necessary biblical parameters for defining what Christians mean when we say *that* God is triune. What it does not even so much as attempt to model is *how* God satisfies all of these parameters and hence *how* God is triune.[15] Offering a model that shows how God satisfies the minimal model would count as a kind of "maximal" model of God's triunity. It would show us more specifically what form God's exemplification of triunity takes and how these parameters cohere, and this would require us to say much more than what we find in minimalism. A maximal account would have to specify the metaphysical structure that God's one-and-three-ness consists in, and hence explain how the parameters constitutive of Nicene Trinitarianism hang together. Crisp identifies the two most historically dominant families of theological theory that have been offered as maximalist models of the Trinity: Latin models that theorize God as a single mind and will who exhibits the real and distinct subsistent relations of origin that mark off each person from the other,[16] and social-Trinitarian models that theorize God as the perfect unity between three individual minds and wills distinguished by relationships of origin.[17] To these he adds a third: the more

Gregory of Nyssa describes Father, Son, and Spirit as "modes" of a singular existence and then goes on to say, "It does not seem to me absolutely necessary, with a view to the present proof of our argument, to contend against those who oppose us with the assertion that we are not to conceive '*Godhead*' as an operation. For we, believing the Divine nature to be unlimited, conceive no comprehension of it." Rather, modalism consists in holding that the three modes of the divine being are operations of the divine being *contingent on the divine will* that *fail to track anything of the divine nature*. It is consistent with rejecting that view, Gregory thinks, to hold that one knows by way of revelation *that* it belongs necessarily to God's nature to be manifest in three distinct modes of divine operation, expressed in a unity of action, while not knowing *how* the divine nature manifests those modes of operation in itself, apart from their manifestation in God's external acts.

14. For an assessment of the Arian controversy and its formative role in shaping the Nicene consensus, Rowan Williams, *Arius: Heresy and Tradition* (Grand Rapids: Eerdmans, 2001), remains unsurpassed.

15. Crisp, *Analyzing Doctrine*, 93–94.

16. Richard Cross argues persuasively that while the differences between so-called "Latin" vs. "Greek" Trinitarianism are not as stark as often imagined, Latin Trinitarianism remains distinctive for holding that the only distinguishing mark individuality one divine person from another is one of mutual relations. See his "Latin Trinitarianism: Some Conceptual and Historical Considerations," in *Philosophical and Theological Essays on the Trinity*, ed. Thomas McCall and Michael Rea (New York: Oxford University Press, 2009), 201–16. For a contemporary expression of Latin Trinitarianism in just this sense, see Brian Leftow, "A Latin Trinity," *Faith and Philosophy* 21, no. 3 (2004): 304–33.

17. Carl Moser characterizes social Trinitarianism as committed to the idea that the divine unity consists in the "mutual indwelling" or periochoresis of Father, Son, and Spirit, each construed as a

recent advent of "constitutional" theories that regard the oneness of divine matter to exist eternally in three distinct forms.[18] I will not dwell on these three types of maximal or conceptually thicker models. The point is just that Crisp claims that they go *beyond* the conceptual thinness of a minimal model in virtue of offering nontrivially different and mutually incompatible ways of specifying how the four parameters of God's triunity are actually exemplified by God.

Against this background Crisp advocates for what he calls a moderate Trinitarian mysterianism. He suggests that the problems that afflict Latin, social, and constitutional Trinitarianism are not merely evidence of the difficulty of specifying how God's threeness-in-oneness works, but it is instead evidence of the impossibility of specifying how it works. All maximal models of the Trinity fail for the same reason, he says, which is that in trying to move beyond the minimal parameters for saying *that* God is triune to specify *how* God is triune, maximal models say too much.[19] More specifically, he thinks they attempt to say more than we are cognitively capable of knowing. His view is therefore mysterian in denying that we have sufficient grounds for theorizing the underlying metaphysics that ground or explain the parameters revealed in Scripture. Any apparent contradiction that arises from trying to understand how those parameters consistently hang together is merely apparent, arising from some kind of equivocation regarding God's oneness or threeness (or both) that we cannot articulate because it is beyond our capacity to comprehend.[20] It follows that maximal theorizing is a fool's errand. To use the analogy he develops, it would be like 2-D creatures living in Flatland trying to comprehend a spherical being; such a being could only show up to Flatlanders as a series of points. The explanation of a 3-D being would not be merely difficult for 2-D beings to understand but impossible. So too God's triunity that shows up for us

---

fully fledged "person" in the modern sense involving distinct agencies or centers of consciousness. See Moser, "Fully Social Trinitarianism," in McCall and Rea, *Philosophical and Theological Essays on the Trinity*, 131–50. Perhaps the most influential modern expression of social Trinitarianism is to be found in Jürgen Moltmann, *The Trinity and the Kingdom: The Doctrine of God* (Minneapolis: Fortress, 1981). For a recent defense of social Trinitarianism, see William Hasker, "Objections to Social Trinitarianism," *Religious Studies* 46 (2010): 421–39.

18. See Jeffrey Brower and Michael Rea, "Material Constitution and the Trinity," *Faith and Philosophy* 22, no. 1 (2005): 57–76. In addition to Latin, Social, and Material Constitution accounts, we might add the recent defense of a "Latin Social Trinity" by Scott Williams in "Unity of Action in a Latin Social Model of the Trinity," *Faith and Philosophy* 34, no. 3 (2017): 321–46.

19. "I think all these existing ways of conceiving the Trinity fail for a similar reason—namely, *they attempt to say too much about the triunity of God*" (Crisp, *Analyzing Doctrine*, 82).

20. According to Crisp, Christian Trinitarianism is mysterious insofar as it involves what James Anderson has called a "MACRUE," an acronym for a "*merely apparent contraction resulting from unarticulated equivocations*" (Crisp, *Analyzing Doctrine*, 93).

as the parameters of the minimal model is a partial revelation grounded in something beyond our ken.[21]

Crisp takes this mysterianism to be "moderate" because in affirming a minimal model it claims that God's triunity is partially intelligible and knowable. He therefore denies "apophaticism," which he takes to imply a radical skepticism about what it means to call God "triune." But he is nevertheless a mysterian in denying that a traditional reading of the biblical evidence licenses us to move beyond a minimal model to the kind of theorizing displayed by maximal models (we can only manage to say *that* not *how*).[22] The relevant implication of this for the topic of this conference is that the *filioque* controversy can only be understood against the background of maximalist theorizing—it proposes single procession from the Father versus joint procession from Father and Son as two alternative metaphysical structures for explaining the individuation of the Spirit within the inner life of God.[23] But arguably this is a matter of *how*, not *that*; it purports to identify what the nonidentity of Spirit from the other persons consists in and also traditionally involves the question of what the consubstantiality of God consists in, whether the monarchy of the Father that ontologically grounds both Son and Spirit on a single procession view or the bond of the Spirit that grounds the union of Father and Son on the joint procession view.[24] But if all determinate metaphysical theorizing about the minimal claims

21. Crisp, *Analyzing Doctrine*, 96–97. For a similar appeal to Abbott's nineteenth-century story of *Flatland* to illustrate divine incomprehensibility, see David Holley, *Meaning and Mystery: What it Means to Believe in God* (Oxford: Wiley-Blackwell, 2010), 110; and Steven Boyer and Christopher Hall, *The Mystery of God: Theology for Knowing the Unknowable* (Grand Rapids: Baker Academic, 2012), 3–18.

22. "Although I am sympathetic to the intuition that motivates some apophatically minded systematic theologians to be leery of any but the thinnest conceptual content to the doctrine of the Trinity, I am also skeptical of the claim that we can know nothing, or next to nothing, about the divine nature. . . . But nor am I as optimistic as some analytics and social Trinitarians seem to be about what we can say regarding the divine nature. What I am after is something between these two sorts of views" (Crisp, *Analyzing Doctrine*, 84).

23. As Stephen Holmes puts it: "Within the bounds of classical Trinitarianism, the *filioque* debate was, in retrospect, inevitable: two relations of origin are proposed, the generation of the Son and the spiration of the Spirit. There are thus four relational terms: generating; being generated; spirating; and being spirated. These four terms then need to be divided between three *hypostases*. Two options appear natural and obvious: to identify the One who generates with the One who spirates, thus teaching the Father as the sole cause and denying the *filioque*; or, following Thomas Aquinas, to affirm the *filioque* by making spiration a joint action of Father and Son, and so a non-hypostatic causal principle. (Other solutions are logically possible . . . but all seem sufficiently obviously foreign to the economic order revealed in Scripture to be immediately excluded)." Holmes, *The Quest for the Trinity: The Doctrine of God in Scripture, History, and Modernity* (Downers Grove, IL: IVP Academic, 2012), 164.

24. For a detailed analysis of the purported theological consequences of a single versus dual procession account of the Spirit, see A. Edward Siecienski, *The Filioque: History of a Doctrinal Controversy* (New York: Oxford University Press, 2010).

regarding the intrinsic structure of the immanent Trinity necessarily say too much, then this, the most longstanding theological dispute in Christian history, turns out to be a kind of hubristic mistake. The minimal parameters give us no basis for getting a disagreement off the ground in the first place.

Given the divisive character of the *filioque* controversy across various quarters of the church, perhaps setting it aside as an illegitimate dispute counts as a benefit rather than a deficit of this view. But while Crisp's moderate mysterianism would permit us to dissolve rather than attempt to solve the *filioque* controversy, I think there is a deep tension in his view that borders on incoherence. It seems to me that what he identifies as a moderate view is rather made up of two distinct components that are presented as compatible but in fact run contrary to one another. One component is what we can call "accommodationist"—it is the view that the minimal parameters for Trinitarianism derived from a traditional reading of Scripture are divine accommodations to our understanding that give us a genuine, albeit partial, picture of what the divine nature is like. A model airplane may not adequately resemble the avionic engineering of its archetype, but it can still adequately resemble other features, like its shape and relative proportions. Similarly, the volumetric figure of a sphere may be incomprehensible to a 2-D Flatlander, but the points manifest by that sphere on the 2-D plane are perfectly well comprehensible in just the terms used and understood by the Flatlander because they are accommodated to the Flatlander's 2-D capacities.

But suppose this is how we understand the minimal parameters of Trinitarianism derived from a traditional reading of Scripture. Our talk of God's inner life is like talk of the 2-D points that show up in virtue of the sphere that intersects our plane of existence. It is characterized by concepts perfectly well intelligible to us: relations of origin—begottenness, unbegottenness, procession, and so on—that mark off each of the three persons from one another, while each of those three is a real and fully divine manifestation of the same singular being of God. If the oneness and threeness implied by scriptural talk about God's singular being exhibiting triadic interrelations is an accommodation, then we ought to be able to understand the truth conditions of the minimal parameters and the satisfaction conditions of their key terms in the same way that Flatlanders can know both the truth conditions for something's showing up as the patterns of points accessible to them and the satisfaction conditions of the geometric terms describing those patterns.

The task of specifying the truth conditions of a minimal Trinitarianism by way of identifying the satisfaction conditions of its key terms is exactly what the maximal models are trying to do. Latin, social, and constitutional Trinitarian theorists are not like Flatlanders trying to describe the sphere and explaining how and why it must essentially appear in the 2-D ways it does to them. Instead, they are like Flatlanders trying to find a coherent scheme that describes what a sphere *means for them* by incorporating all the appearances of its 2-D manifestations available to them as manifestations that purport to describe a single being.[25] Likewise Trinitarian theorists are trying to offer a minimally coherent interpretation of what "triunity" *means in light of what has been revealed*.[26] This is why the main reasons that Latin and social Trinitarian have offered to accept their theory and reject its alternatives are no different than the kinds of reasons that motivate Trinitarianism in the first place. Crisp observes that the formation of a minimal understanding of God's triunity implied the rejection of Arian subordinationism, and to this I have also observed that it was also understood to imply the rejection of tritheism and modalism as well. But as Crisp himself observes, the primary arguments of Latin Trinitarians against social Trinitarians has become precisely that they violate a minimal parameter of avoiding tritheism, while the objection to the Latins is that they violate the antimodalist parameter.[27] There is no way of articulating a minimalistic Trinitarianism that is not already somehow metaphysically loaded to specify what kind of oneness and threeness is minimally required to keep us from these heresies. So what I am suggesting is that if we can truly understand the minimal parameters of a traditional Trinitarianism as accommodations to our cognitive limits, then we are automatically propelled exactly toward the kind of maximalist theorizing that Crisp seems to want to rule out as overdetermined.

The question of single versus joint procession arises from a key interpretive assumption in the formation of a minimal Trinitarianism. It is the

---

25. In the case of scriptural revelation, however, the "appearances" that we are trying to coordinate into a single scheme are not only phenomenological, but also propositional, and perhaps testimonial.

26. For the distinction between various types of revelation, see Mats Wahlberg, *Revelation as Testimony: A Philosophical-Theological Study* (Grand Rapids: Eerdmans, 2014); and Yadav, "Biblical Inspiration and Biblical Revelation," in *The Oxford Handbook of Divine Revelation*, ed. Balázs M. Mezei, Francesca Murphy, and Kenneth Oakes (New York: Oxford University Press, forthcoming).

27. See Joost van Rossum, "The Experience of the Holy Spirit in Greek Patristic and Byzantine Theology," *Communio viatorum* 53, no. (2011): 25–39: "Patriarch Photius, 9th century, who wrote the first systematic treatise against this doctrine, considered the *Filioque* to be another form of Sabellianism, since in this theology the Father and the Son are merged together into one Person" (35). See also Sciecienski, *The Filioque*, 133–34.

assumption that the divine missions reflect the divine nature. Since in biblical passages describing the divine mission of sending us the Spirit we can find talk of receiving the Spirit from the Father, jointly from the Father and the Son, and also as from the Father through the Son, the question is how to translate these forms of divine agency into a characterization of the relation of origin that individuates and defines the personhood of the Spirit.[28] In the historical theorizing over this question, the primary stakes have been to understand what it is about the divine life we mean when talk about "the Spirit" as a divine person nonidentical while also consubstantial and coequal with Father and Son. Accordingly, the metaphysical arguments for one model and against another appeal to the same kinds of reasons that motivate the minimal model: each argues that the other entails some form of subordinationism or fails to preserve a form of nonidentity between the Spirit and the other persons that also preserves the Spirit's consubstantiality and so on. Of course some have suggested that both models do equally well.[29] If so, then the *filioque* controversy may indeed be underdetermined by a minimal Trinitarianism not because the minimal view is semantically incomplete but because its determinate meaning is compatible with both single and joint procession. But it remains the case that a conclusion like that would need to be shown by appealing to the metaphysical implications of single versus joint procession interpretations of the minimal model, not by ruling out the legitimacy of interpreting the metaphysics required to understand that model in the first place. On Crisp's accommodationist line, therefore, minimalism does not rule out maximalist theorizing but motivates it.

On the other hand, Crisp seems to recognize that a maximal modeling might be a way of interpreting the meaning of a minimally defined Trinitarianism rather than trying to explain it or go beyond it, and he therefore goes on to articulate a second component to his mysterianism. It is the claim that we ought to regard the minimal model itself as semantically underdetermined. In other words, he suggests that the kind of threeness and oneness claimed by the minimal model—the meaning

28. See, for instance, the helpful summary of the subtle inferential reasoning from economy to immanence that we find in Staniloae in Viorel Coman, "Dimitru Staniloae on the *Filioque*: Trinitarian Relationship between the Son and the Spirit and Its Relevance for the Ecclesiological Synthesis between Christology and Pneumatology," *Journal of Ecumenical Studies* 49, no. 4 (Fall 2014): 553–75.

29. Holmes, for example, claims, "It is clear that neither position on the filioque does violence to the received orthodox and catholic tradition. Historically, there was full communion between [those holding single and dual procession]. . . . This does not of course mean that the issue is trivial, or in principle insoluble." Holmes, *The Quest for the Trinity*, 164.

of terms like *numerical oneness*, *consubstantial*, and *nonidentical threeness* are merely "placeholders" and that "we do not have a clear conceptual grip on their semantic content."[30] But if that is so, then it is not the question of *how* God is triune but the very claim *that* God is triune that is necessarily underdetermined on Crisp's mysterianism, like variables with inscrutable values. In the absence of any kind of truth-conditional interpretation of the minimal model, we would have to regard it as literally unintelligible. If it is semantically incomplete then we literally do not and cannot know what we mean when we say that God is three and God is one.[31] If we cannot have a grip on the semantic content of the oneness and threeness talk internal to the minimal model, then—just as Crisp claims—many different more robust Trinitarian models would be radically underdetermined, including both those metaphysical models that posit a single procession of the Spirit from the Father and those that posit a dual procession from the Father and the Son. But a semantically incomplete Trinitarianism would also equally well underdetermine an orthodox rejection of tritheism, subordinationism, and modalism, since denying those views would likewise require us to know enough about what our oneness and threeness talk means to rule them out. If God is just *somehow* one, then we could not say that God is precisely one in such a way as to not multiply beings or entities; if God is just *somehow* three, then we could not say that God is precisely three in such a way as to admit of intrinsically distinct principles of individuation.

It therefore looks like Crisp's moderate mysterianism is either not mysterian in any way that ought to restrict our Trinitarian metaphysical theorizing, or else it is indeed mysterian but of a rather radical sort that entails the unintelligibility of even the most minimal model of God's triunity by imposing semantic indeterminacy on its key terms. We might try to alleviate this tension by noting, as Crisp does, that his mysterianism is compatible with a Thomistic style doctrine of analogy in our theological semantics.[32] But I don't think that helps. If the point is simply that our attempts to find an intelligible oneness-threeness claim minimally projected by Scripture needs to be qualified as merely analogical of whatever it is about, then we have moved out of the mysterian territory that restricts

30. Crisp, *Analyzing Doctrine*, 100.

31. Perhaps it is false that knowing the meaning of a proposition *just is* knowing the truth conditions of that proposition. Still, it seems that knowing what a proposition means necessarily *involves* grasping at least some of its truth-conditions.

32. The rhetorical structure of Crisp's talk about the Trinity is similar to that of the Thomistic line of rejecting univocity without embracing a kind of equivocity that undermines literal meaning—hence settling on analogy to escape between the horns.

our theorizing and back into accommodationist territory that allows it: an analogical semantics can't provide any reasons to limit the traditional wrangling over better and worse metaphysical interpretations of a minimally Trinitarian model (as evidenced in part by the fact that a great many "maximalists" endorsed it).[33] A doctrine of analogy just implies that whatever metaphysically specified theory we have reason to prefer as the best interpretation of our minimal parameters, we must claim that it is at best *analogically* true of God's triunity rather than univocally true of it. But clearly that is no constraint on Trinitarian theorizing, only a constraint on the status of our theories.[34]

So to summarize the argument I've been developing: Crisp's allegedly moderate Trinitarian mysterianism presents us with two incompatible ways of theorizing about the Trinity. The first way is quite permissive: the full gamut of traditional theorizing in the Nicene tradition is just an attempt to articulate a minimally coherent understanding of God's revealed accommodations to us as a single being who eternally exists as a Father begetting a Son and breathing the Spirit without mutual subordination or collapse of individual identity between the three. Analyzing what the key terms in this understanding ought or ought not ontologically commit us to is inevitably controversial. As such, it predicts genuine metaphysical dispute. The resultant theorizing cannot therefore rightly be regarded as unnecessary, overly speculative, or overweening. Alternatively, we can opt for the radically skeptical way of regarding the oneness and threeness of God projected by a traditional reading of Scripture as involving a fundamental semantic indeterminacy that prevents any analysis of those constituent concepts. As such, every particular theoretical interpretation of God's triunity would be underdetermined. But this comes at the cost of the very idea of God's triunity being literally unintelligible to us, an *unaccommodated* rather than *revealed* mystery, one that fails to tell us about God in terms we can possibly understand. From an indeterminate oneness and threeness, neither the affirmations nor the denials of the Nicene orthodoxy could follow.

33. See Holmes, *The Quest for the Trinity,* 154–59. For an antimetaphysical reading of Thomas, see Karen Kilby, "Aquinas, the Trinity and the Limits of Understanding," *International Journal of Systematic Theology* 7, no. 4 (2005): 414–27. Gilles Emery, however, seems to offer a reading more historically and contextually faithful to Thomas in regarding his skepticism as aimed at necessary reasons for Trinitarian properties and relations, rather than being aimed at positive knowledge of those properties and relations per se. See Emery, *The Trinitarian Theology of St. Thomas Aquinas* (New York: Oxford University Press, 2010), 18–35.

34. See William P. Alston, "Aquinas on Theological Predication: A Look Backward and a Look Forward," in *Reasoned Faith*, ed. Eleonore Stump (Ithaca: Cornell University Press, 1993), 145–78.

Given these options when reflecting on the procession of the Spirit within the divine life, therefore, it seems best to take the more permissive route of allowing the wind to blow where it wishes in our theorizing rather than quenching the spirit of inquiry for fear of saying too much.

This argument leaves an important question unanswered: namely, whether the rejection of the mysterian skepticism implied by Crisp's view entails a rejection of a Trinitarian apophaticism per se. It seems to me that it does not. One way to construe the apophatic gesture is to regard it not as a matter of denying us any (significant) knowledge of God's nature per se—but rather as a matter of denying us knowledge of God's nature *in* se. This would be to regard God's triunity as a revealed accommodation that manages to truly track the way things stand with God, while doing so in a necessarily *relational* way according to our cognitive limits rather than according to the way God is in and for Godself. Whether an apophaticism of *that* sort is defensible, however, is a matter best left for another time.[35]

35. For some hints of how an apophaticism of this sort might go, see Sameer Yadav, *The Problem of Perception and the Experience of God* (Minneapolis: Fortress, 2015); and Yadav, "Mystical Experience and the Apophatic Attitude," *Journal of Analytic Theology* 4 (2016): 17–43.

CHAPTER 5

"SPIRITUAL ENLIGHTENMENT"

Contributions of a Pneumatological Epistemology

DANIEL CASTELO

OVER THE YEARS, I have begun asking my students to wrestle with a key question: What kind of knowledge is God-knowledge?[1] I have stressed this question for a number of reasons, but the prompt for it is partially a result of the context in which I raise the question.

I teach at a Christian liberal arts university, and I have several non-theology majors in some of my classes, especially in the required, general education ones. In these classes, having a majority of science majors is very different from having a significant swath of art majors: the conversations are different, the questions significantly vary, the intellectual sensibilities are wide-ranging, and so on. This observation is not meant to denigrate one kind of thinking over another, but it is to suggest precisely the point: there are different ways of thinking and so different kinds of knowledge available out of which people process and reason. A university context

1. Naturally, the question itself assumes that God-knowledge is a legitimate and reliable kind of knowledge, a point significantly disputed in certain contexts. In many cases, the verdict is already in: rather than a branch of knowledge, God-knowledge is based on belief, a gesture no doubt aimed at a kind of intellectual marginalization. For a helpful consideration of some of the issues, see "Theology as Knowledge: A Symposium," *First Things*, May 2006, https://www.firstthings.com/article/2006/05/theology-as-knowledge.

highlights this point exceedingly because the options are so many and their formative work so profound within a concentrated location and experience. The options truly are *disciplines* because they represent a kind of intellectual formation—a process of disciplining the mind and the self so as to shape *not only what* a person thinks but also *how* a person thinks and processes.

In light of these disciplinary dynamics, are we clear where God-knowledge fits among other kinds of knowledge? Theologians are inclined to think that God-knowledge is its own kind of knowledge, and I agree with that point. After all, its subject matter, namely the God of Christian confession, is unique. When engaging in interdisciplinary discussions, theologians may charge themselves or be charged with the role of helping the other disciplines think about a broader picture, one in which questions of purpose and meaning come to the fore in the midst of specialized training. We encounter this situation quite repeatedly at Seattle Pacific University. When we hire scholars in nontheological areas who confess Christian identity, we tend to think that they will naturally make the connections between their discipline and their faith. If these candidates cannot make these connections (perhaps because their educational training has been in nonconfessional settings such as state schools), the School of Theology is typically called upon to lend an awkwardly helping hand. The scenario is awkward in that those of us in the School of Theology typically do not know the other disciplines well enough to engage in a meaningful back-and-forth on their disciplinary grounds. In such exchanges, we in the School of Theology typically listen, learn, and maybe offer a theme or trope to aid these colleagues as they work toward tenure, and that is about the extent of what we can do. At play in this framework are a number of undergirding assumptions, including that theology should have something significant to say to the disciplines of biology, chemistry, history, and English. After all, "all truth is God's truth."[2]

For the purposes of this exercise, I am not interested in speaking to the matter of how theology can contribute to other disciplines; I am more interested in thinking broadly about how other disciplines may contribute to theology. That is not to say that I am relativizing the subject matter of theology in light of other disciplines. I am not saying that God and Chaucer (for instance) are equally important subjects to be explored in the grand scheme of things. Chaucer, after all, is not God (which may be news to

2. This is a common enough phrase, but the larger point was registered for me in reading John Henry Newman, *The Idea of a University*.

only a few people). But, pressingly for the rhythms of institutional life, a Chaucer specialist teaching at a Christian university will need to know more about theology than a theologian will need to know about Chaucer when questions of mission-fit are debated in tenure-decisions. This is just part of the reality of teaching at a Christian university.[3]

What I am interested in is exposing how theology engages its craft and how it casts a vision regarding the pursuit of its subject matter. The subject matter of theology may be unique, but there is not a singularly unique way of pursuing theology. Simply peruse a number of theology textbooks and theological faculties, and see how they define and do theology differently. Questions of method in addition to matters of epistemology vary widely across the discipline of Christian theology. Perhaps that is to be expected, as there are different schools of thought within the other disciplines as well. But on the ground this reality may be difficult for theological practitioners to admit, in part because of the distinction theology is given as a result of its subject matter.

And this last point raises a significant issue. Theology's subject matter may be unique, but theology's practitioners are not. Theologians are humans, as are chemists, physicists, and Chaucer specialists. As humans, theologians are shaped intellectually by their contextualizing influences, including their teachers, environments, experiences, and values. Again, we may want to believe that theology's subject matter would put everybody on the same methodological and epistemological page, but experience says otherwise. Yes, the subject matter of theology is the God of Christian confession, but the "specialists" of this field vary considerably in their intellectual orientations. These differences in intellectual orientations and thus formations are part of the reason why theologians define theology differently, why they pursue different theological aims, and why they produce different scholarly products.

I begin my essay in this way because I am committed to the notion that much of how theology is undertaken in the scholarly theological traditions

---

3. I limit myself to the Christian university in that the claims I am making about interdisciplinary interaction assume an intrasystemic confessional basis. Disciplines cast in a secular way could make any number of contributions to the theological task, but that conversation is a broad one I do not wish to explore here. Stanley Hauerwas generalizes that the Christian university may be no different than a secular university in terms of how work is done in the academic disciplines, a point that I believe would have to be pressed on a case-by-case basis, but the generalization is understandable given the power of the secular academy for determining what are legitimate kinds of knowledge and how to pursue and frame them. See Hauerwas, *The State of the University* (Malden, MA: Blackwell, 2007).

that I am aware of is pneumatologically anemic. Pneumatology is often not considered basic to questions related to theological method and theological epistemology.[4] If this assessment is correct, then one wonders why this is the case. What things are involved that often make pneumatology incidental or highly tangential to questions of theological method and epistemology? The culprit certainly would not be the subject matter, in that the Holy Spirit is an eternal person of the triune God. Chaucer is not God, but the Holy Spirit is God. The point should matter for all aspects of theological inquiry, including method and epistemology. A major factor in all of this would have to be theology's practitioners, many of whom would not think—given their intellectual formations and orientations—that one's pneumatology would have a bearing on questions of method and epistemology. But if this is so, one wonders: And why would *that* be the case?

My hunch is that within accounts of God-knowledge there are competing accounts of knowledge, and these manifest themselves especially at the level of method and epistemology. To extend the example mentioned earlier, certain theologians approach their craft as scientists; others approach it as artists. Furthermore, certain accounts of knowledge are more Spirit-friendly than others, or at least, certain approaches within certain domains of knowledge are more Spirit-friendly than others ("Spirit-friendly" meaning the welcoming of aspects that Christians typically associate with the Holy Spirit.) Put another way, there are competing accounts of knowledge within the field of God-knowledge itself, as it is understood and pursued by its practitioners. As a result, in these epistemic contestations, some things are allowed; other things not so much. Openings and closures fill this disciplinary landscape, and one potential loss in such contestations is pneumatology. Why would pneumatology be especially vulnerable in such contestations?

A significant reason why pneumatology would be vulnerable is that we who are products of north transatlantic culture do not know how to accommodate pneumatology in our intellectual social imaginaries. At some

4. That is not to say one cannot find these proposals. I am heartened by what traffics as "third article theology," a movement spurred by the likes of Lyle Dabney and Myk Habets. These proposals stress that the very conceptual formulation of faith and confession requires an admittedly explicit pneumatological orientation. In this vein, see the following: Myk Habets, ed., *Third Article Theology: A Pneumatological Dogmatics* (Minneapolis: Fortress, 2016); D. Lyle Dabney, "Otherwise Engaged in the Spirit: A First Theology for a Twenty-first Century," in *The Future of Theology*, ed. Miroslav Volf, Carmen Krieg, and Thomas Kucharz (Grand Rapids: Eerdmans, 1996), 154–63; and Kenneth J. Archer and L. William Oliverio Jr., eds., *Constructive Pneumatological Hermeneutics in Pentecostal Christianity* (New York: Palgrave Macmillan, 2016).

level, pneumatology and all its features just do not make sense for how we understand, structure, and engage our world. We may have an easier time accommodating other themes associated with Christian theology generally and with the doctrine of God particularly, but pneumatology has tended to be a stumbling block to those of us who trace our intellectual lineage to various upheavals of thought where the "order of things" became increasingly demythologized, disenchanted, secularized, naturalized—in short, despiritualized.

It is no wonder, then, that the conference call for Los Angeles Theology Conference 2020 demonstrates some concern surrounding pneumatology when it stresses that pneumatology may seem "scattered or diffused across the surface of contemporary thought." This appearance may be due to the wide applicability of pneumatology, as the call mentions earlier; but it may also be due to this latent unease with how to navigate pneumatology in the first place—an unease directly related to the intellectual and cultural resources we have at our disposal at this given moment and location. What are we to do in the midst of these circumstances? How can pneumatology be more central to the task of theology at the methodological and epistemological level?

Let me offer two general proposals along these lines. The first would be to seek the aid of the other disciplines, that is, the other kinds of knowledge available. How would this work? In short, these other kinds of knowledge can help those who pursue God-knowledge to see how they may singularly and myopically pursue their work by exposing the limits and reductions of the very methods they use and the forms of knowing and reasoning they appeal to. To harken back to my example, the goal is not to have all science or art majors in a class pursuing theology. The vitality of exchange comes through when the class contains a mix of science, art, and other majors. By this very exchange and even contestation of different ways and means of knowing, those who pursue God-knowledge can see how they may overrely on certain methods and rationalities and possibly ignore or diminish other methods and rationalities. This commitment stems from the notion that God-knowledge is not owned by theologians and that there is not a singular way of pursuing theology—the subject matter just does not lend itself to such strictures. Christian scientists and artists can and do have things to say about God-knowledge, things that theologians need to hear. Furthermore, theologians are in need of fostering intellectual modesty precisely because of the uniqueness of their subject matter. One way of actively cultivating that modesty is by being told by a Chaucer specialist that interpreting God's revelation and interpreting Chaucer are different kinds of activities, which the theologian may recognize explicitly but maybe not methodologically in all the pertinent aspects. A person who specializes in the reading of ancient texts may have thought through many of the applicable hermeneutical dimensions of doing such work, including the possibilities and limits of that work. Only certain theologians have specialization in hermeneutics; therefore, chances are that hermeneutical tendencies could be underdeveloped in certain theological proposals. If this is the case, the default would be to appeal to customary and well-known approaches simply because they are customary and well-known. Summarily put, theologians need input from experts in other fields of knowledge in order to do theology well, but this input is of a kind of not simply filling informational gaps but also of exposing methodological and epistemological inclinations and biases. Pneumatologically framed, theologians may need the help of other disciplines to understand why their proposals tend to be pneumatologically anemic. The issues at play are not simply theological; they may very well be intellectual in a broad yet determinative way. Competing "enlightenments," then, may need to be brought to light.

The other proposal I wish to offer as to how pneumatology can be more central to the task of theology at the methodological and epistemological level is to see how other traditions and contexts beyond our intellectual-cultural milieu have and continue to pursue the theological task. Now, rather than engaging different kinds of knowledge, theologians can appeal to past and present voices across the Christian tradition so as to locate their preferred methodological and epistemological tendencies within the intellectual narratives that brought them to be, all the while highlighting that alternatives to those preferences exist within the tradition itself. One thinks, for instance, of a number of patristic voices that stress not simply intellectual virtuosity but spiritual sanctity as necessary for those who wish to pursue theology well.[5] The private-public dichotomy—one that we in the American context know all too well—and its relegation of Christian commitments to the private realm would not hold here. Pressing our concerns and conundrums on such ancient accounts would tend toward anachronism; to understand these voices as best we could, we would have to attempt to enter different theological worlds. A working displacement

5. For a beautiful elaboration of this point, see Hans Urs von Balthasar's chapter "Theology and Sanctity," in *Word and Redemption: Essays in Theology 2* (New York: Herder and Herder, 1965), 49–86.

and reorienting process would be required at some level, which in turn could have a pneumatological payoff. Furthermore, the witness of Christians throughout the world would be important to hear in that many of these contexts happen to be relatively underdetermined intellectually by some of the upheavals of thought associated with north transatlantic culture, yet interestingly, many of these contexts also happen to be charismatically oriented. I am inclined to think that these two characteristics of Christianity in the so-called Global South are not coincidental to one another; there is a link to expose here.

These have been some thoughts regarding why accounts of God-knowledge in our setting may be pneumatologically anemic, and I have offered some general ways to ameliorate this situation. In what follows, I wish to offer brief sketches on what kind of knowledge God-knowledge is and to do so within a pneumatological framework. I will offer different Pauline tropes to expand on what I am labeling different "registers" of theological engagement and reflection. My goal in offering these sketches is to offer a vision of what "spiritual enlightenment" could look like,[6] a kind of enlightenment that puts pneumatology at the center of an account of God-knowledge, as awkward and unclear as such a move would be for us in the contemporary setting. One feature of this vision that I should highlight from the start is that these registers run "deep," if I may riff on a book-title of one of the sponsors of this event.[7] What do I mean by *deep* in this case? I mean that God-knowledge touches us at registers that are both difficult to penetrate, yet these are the registers that make us largely who we are. *God-knowledge is a kind of knowledge that cuts to the core of who we are and how things are*, and that framing of going deep is work that the Spirit uniquely and properly does. Notice that I am not making a strictly anthropological argument; I am not suggesting that *we* go deeper *into ourselves* so as to find *who we are* in a perpetual quest of self-discovery. What I am saying is that the Spirit of God is the One who can go deep into ourselves, deeper than we can at any given moment, and in turn the Spirit does work in those deep spaces that we cannot do. And why does the Spirit do this kind of

6. I draw this phrase of "spiritual enlightenment" from the work of the Cappadocians; although debated that it in fact could have been written by Gregory of Nyssa, "Letter 38," attributed for quite some time to Basil of Caesarea, has the following important, epistemological claim: "For it is not possible for any one to conceive of the Son if he be not previously enlightened by the Spirit." In *Nicene and Post-Nicene Fathers*, 2nd series, ed. Philip Schaff and Henry Wace (New York: Christian Literature Company, 1895), 8:138.

7. Fred Sanders, *The Deep Things of God: How the Trinity Changes Everything*, 2nd ed. (Wheaton, IL: Crossway, 2017).

work? To accomplish the purposes of God in the world and to provide a distinct but necessary kind of "enlightenment" as to who we are, who God is, and how things are.

"SIGHS TOO DEEP FOR WORDS"

Let us move, then, to the first major register I wish to highlight, what can be labeled "sighs too deep for words." When the apostle Paul highlights that the Spirit helps us with "sighs too deep for words" (*stenagmois alalētois*) in Romans 8:26,[8] key points are implied. First, the Spirit is in the business of helping us; aiding us is part of the Spirit's "job description" and character, a point that substantiates further the paracletic profile of the Spirit stressed in the gospel of John. We may be at a loss for words at moments of distress; we may not know how to pray. But a lack of words need not lead to despair; the Spirit helps us when we are speechless.

Second, the kind of help highlighted by Paul has to do with penetrating registers that run deeper than words. This is a vital point. One sometimes hears the phrase (and I have used it myself repeatedly, I must admit) that "all we have are words" when we talk about communicating and relating. When more rigorously pressed, the phrase is simply not true. Body-language experts, for example, would have something to say on this point. We do have more than words. As to the verse, it is not clear what "sighs" or "groans" are per se,[9] but what is clear is that they press deeply into *properly theological* realms, ones that go beyond words. To stress the point pneumatologically, words are not all that God's Spirit has either. When making intercession on our behalf, the Spirit's choice here is to go beyond words. There are such things as sighs or groans that are significant to God when the Spirit intercedes for us since the Spirit's very self uses them.

Third, that the Spirit groans on our behalf is an act of solidarity, given that the whole of creation groans under the pressure of the present age, as highlighted earlier in Romans 8 (vv. 22–23). The suggestion is that the

8. Unless otherwise indicated, Scripture quotations in this chapter come from the NRSV.

9. Interestingly, Gordon Fee is of the opinion that what Paul has in mind here is akin to what he describes in 1 Corinthians 14, namely speaking and praying in tongues; see Fee, *God's Empowering Presence* (Peabody, MA: Hendrickson, 1994), 584. This reading certainly is possible, but my aim is not to identify these as such as it is to suggest their role not only for this passage but for understanding a wide range of conduits for expressing theological meaning on the whole. Certainly, tongues can do that kind of theological work, one may even say theological-philosophical work, as highlighted by James K. A. Smith's compelling title *Thinking in Tongues* (Grand Rapids: Eerdmans, 2010).

natural order and humans, who are part of it, groan in their duress, and as a matter of tending to this situation, the Spirit groans in solidarity with the creation as the Spirit makes intercession on our behalf. Therefore, groans and sighs (i.e., inarticulate, unutterable, wordless expressions) mark a key register of interconnectivity and solidarity between creation, humans, and God.

The reason for emphasizing this phrase and many of its dimensions here is to show that *God-knowledge runs deeper than words*. Based on this passage, how the created realm expresses itself, how humans express themselves, and how the Spirit expresses the Spirit's self can be collectively understood in terms that run deeper than words. As important as words are generally for humans and specifically for theologians and their work, words are not all that we have for connecting to God and understanding God.[10] God-knowledge runs deeper than words, and this point should be understood as "helpful" to those who have the first fruits of the Spirit. There are times when words fail us, when our limits and the limits of words collide, thereby making us speechless and perhaps leaving us feeling as if we have no recourse. This passage suggests hope in such circumstances because we have available other things besides words to connect with and understand God. God's Spirit in fact uses other things besides words at critical junctures of the Spirit's helping us within the economy.

One way to collectively hold these points is to highlight the apophatic dimensions of the theological task. Apophaticism, of course, can be understood in different ways.[11] It can simply point to the mode of denial, of saying what God is not in contradistinction to saying what God is, that is, the mode of cataphaticism. Apophatic dimensions of God-talk are important to point out in that oftentimes they are assumed and thus implicit. For instance, saying that "God is love" cataphatically bears with it (or at least it should bear with it) an apophatic dimension: "God is love *but* not in the way we humans typically understand love." The same can be said

10. I realize that this point is a difficult—if awkward—one to stress at an academic conference. During the conference itself, I heard some light-hearted joking surrounding the notion of groans. Then again, an academic conference is not a place where we tend to be forthcoming and vulnerable before God and one another. The setting matters for both the intelligibility and meaningfulness of something within this domain. My aim in registering the notion within an academic conference is to remind us that a conference is not the only venue, and maybe even at some level it is an inadequate venue, for transmitting and sharing certain aspects of God-knowledge.

11. I do not wish to offer an elaborate taxonomy at this point beyond what I do in the text above, but perhaps a general orientation would prove helpful; for this, see Denys Turner, "Apophaticism, Idolatry, and the Claims of Reason," in *Silence and the Word*, ed. Oliver Davies and Denys Turner (Cambridge: Cambridge University Press, 2002), 11–34.

with other divine attributes and characterizations. The way of denial is an apophatic strategy, but it can be understood not simply as a counterpoint to affirmation; cataphatic and apophatic strategies use words, but the apophatic strategy of denial is not simply a parallel process to cataphaticism. Distinctively, apophaticism can also point to the work of exposing limits. The exercise of denial can be understood not simply as a stopping point (by saying something like, "God is not") but as a marker along a specific path—a path of recognizing the limits of words (and by implication, our own limits). In connection to what we said earlier, if we are exposing the limits of words, we could be on the path of recognizing the theological significance of groans. Apophaticism may be understood, then, as a theological methodological approach to enlighten us as to the importance of the biblical claim that the Spirit renders help when interceding with "sighs too deep for words." Put another way, apophaticism may be a way of getting at the theological significance of expressions and modalities that are unutterable and so beyond words. Why is that important work?

The reason why this is important work is because one wonders the degree to which we may be inclined or disinclined to think of something like "groans" or "sighs" as theologically significant. If groans and sighs are important to God and God's Spirit, we must ask: Have we made idols of our words? Do we have a theologically problematic relationship with our capacity to speak? Would certain majors or intellectual orientations help us see those possibilities better than others? How are we aided or hindered in recognizing the theological significance of the Spirit's nonverbal forms of intercession on our behalf? The depth imagined here is work that the Spirit can do in expanding our imaginations as to the possibilities of what is theologically significant. Words are not all we have in discussing that which can be expressions of theological meaning.

It should be noted that within the context of Roman 8:26 we are talking about the modality of prayer. *God-knowledge is a deep kind of knowledge because it is learned on one's knees.*[12] That sounds awfully pious, doesn't it? But why? Because for some reason, we tend to be comfortable with theology being something other than spirituality and contemplation.[13] What precisely is

12. For reflections on prayer as an "epistemological presupposition" for the act of theologizing itself, see Gavin D'Costa, *Theology in the Public Square* (Malden, MA: Blackwell, 2005), beginning on p. 112.

13. I find Sarah Coakley's adumbration of these points compelling: "[Theology] is the actual *practice* of contemplation that is the condition of a new 'knowing in unknowing.' It must involve the stuff of learned bodily enactment, sweated out painfully over months and years, in duress, in discomfort, in bewilderment, as well as in joy and dawning recognition. . . . For contemplation

at work here? One assumes that there are many reasons—the separation of the church and academy, the professionalization of the theological guild, the regnant intellectual and cultural forces we are shaped by, and so on—but one certainty is that the character of God-knowledge has already been decided in a certain sense if the theological significance of Romans 8:26 is undetectable or, more worrisomely, inadmissible. It could be that we are more comfortable with certain kinds of knowledges than others. And if this is in fact the case, God-knowledge cannot help but be impoverished or maybe even misconstrued as certainly one kind of knowledge but definitely not another. A pneumatic sensibility here is that certain things of God are only learned and known in the modality of prayer and worship. As we will develop further at a later point, when we approach God as one to be worshiped, things come to light that are not available when God is approached simply as a topic of study. Both approaches involve learning, but their significance involves a differentiation of modalities of learning, which in turn rely on different registers and produce different outcomes. We may not have the words or concepts to account for whatever comes to light, but that does not take away from its theological significance. The welcoming of a pneumatologically framed apophatic mode of participating in God-knowledge opens up these possibilities.

I should add here that I do not hear of apophaticism as a theological methodological strategy in many academic theological circles. Yes, there is something like an "apophatic turn" in certain currents of theology that rely on what traffics as postmodern sensibilities, but the impact of this work comes across at times as limited to only certain theological orientations. I certainly do not hear much about apophaticism within many evangelical theological circles, which, at day's end, is quite ironic, is it not? Why would traditions that stress conversion, mission, biblical authority, the prevalence of sin, and the like *not* find appealing an apophatic mode of stressing God-knowledge? Apophaticism exposes human limits, maybe even human idolatries, all the while creating conceptual space for the majesty and glory of God; these and other themes appear to be ones that evangelicals could strongly support. But then again, the kind of apophaticism I am stressing through the language of Romans 8 involves dependence and

is the unique, and wholly *sui generis*, task of seeking to know, and speak of God, unknowingly; as Christian contemplation, it is also the necessarily bodily practice of dispossession, humility, and effacement which, in the Spirit, causes us to learn incarnationally, and only so, the royal way of the Son to the Father." Coakley, *God, Sexuality, and the Self* (Cambridge: Cambridge University Press, 2013), 45–46.

a certain account of losing control. This is all hinted in Romans 8 within an elaboration of human weakness, which in turn occasions the Spirit's work of helping and intercession. Yes, pneumatology may be "diffused" and "scattered" and in need of being more dogmatically disciplined within the doctrine of God; it may also be the case that our doctrine of God and our account of God-knowledge may need to be open to the significance of "sighs too deep for words."

"GOD'S LOVE BEING POURED OUT INTO OUR HEARTS"

Let us move now to a second register. The first had to do with "sighs too deep for words." The second register has to do with "God's love." It is painfully obvious that a basic claim of Christianity is that the sum of the law is to love God with all that one is and one's neighbor as oneself. Given the culminating nature of this claim, it is hard not to make reference to it somehow when elaborating the kind of knowledge God-knowledge is, especially when approached pneumatologically. The more pressing question to raise for our present purposes is how these love commandments actually affect, order, and substantiate the work of theologizing. For instance, one rarely hears a theologian in writing claim explicitly and repeatedly one's love for God. When I once was asked by a student why I do the work I do as a theologian, I surprised myself by stating quite spontaneously that I do this work because I love God. I must admit that as spontaneous as the response was, it nevertheless felt somewhat strange once I said it. Yet it is a vital and pressing question on Christian grounds if one could properly, fittingly, and faithfully pursue theology apart from the love of God. The same could be said about the second love commandment: How could something like Christian theology be properly pursued apart from some sense of love of neighbor?

Because there is much to unpack with these love commandments, let us split them as two additional features of the Spirit's work of enlightening us as to the kind of knowledge that God-knowledge is. We will focus on the first in what follows and on the second in the next major section.

As Christians we are not called to define or to conceptualize God with all our heart, soul, mind, and strength, but for those of us who theologize, we certainly spend quite a bit of time and effort doing just that. Our love for God may be implied and on display, but as we have just stated, for some reason, it is something rarely explicitly claimed in theological scholarship.

Part of the issue may be the awkwardness of revealing something so personal within the venue of scholarship. After all, love runs deep. Loving is a deep kind of relating, and so it is a deep kind of knowledge that is difficult to share publicly, especially in certain spaces. And of course, we live in a highly sentimentalized culture in which the language of love is often given an uncritical pass so as to allow it to be both obvious and self-authenticating. Therefore, the challenges of integrating love within the domain of theological methodology and epistemology are formidable.

Appealing to Paul once again, we see that love can do some heavy pneumatological lifting, and this also related, as in Romans 8, to matters of both suffering and hope. Paul notes in Romans 5, "And not only that, but we also boast in our sufferings, knowing that suffering produces endurance, and endurance produces character, and character produces hope, and hope does not disappoint us, because God's love has been poured into our hearts through the Holy Spirit that has been given to us" (vv. 3–5 NRSV). As with Romans 8, Romans 5 has several parts to explore for our present purposes.

First, as initially noted, this remark is in the context of highlighting human weakness and need, now in relation to the work of Christ that establishes peace between us and God. As Paul notes, "We boast in our hope of sharing the glory of God" (v. 2). At play here is a kind of "proper confidence,"[14] a kind of epistemic certainty hinted in the language of "boasting," that is, we can know and proclaim boldly that the work of Christ of reconciling us to God is real and efficacious. This kind of confidence and certainty is not only possible in seasons of flourishing; the apostle Paul remarks that it is also possible in times of suffering. Naturally, through various critical methods we may fittingly speculate what kinds of suffering Paul's original hearers may have been facing. To broaden this theme to our current context, though, it is certainly the case that Christian theologians may have their own kinds of suffering proper to their specific kind of work. If God-knowledge is ultimately a revelatory, receptive kind of knowledge, there is built into it a form of dependency that may seem on the surface to be irreconcilable with boasting, confidence, and certainty. Our agency in this form of endeavoring is somewhat problematized. We may find it easier to boast or have confidence and certainty in those things that we can control. But again, Paul is pressing for the possibility of boasting precisely in times of suffering, at those moments when our limits and weakness are especially prominent.

---

14. The echo here is to Lesslie Newbigin, *Proper Confidence* (Grand Rapids: Eerdmans, 1995).

How is boasting possible in times of suffering? In a second point from the passage worth noting, Paul stresses the primordiality of God's love being poured into our hearts through the Holy Spirit who has been given to us (v. 5). The ground of Christian confidence, certainty, and boasting is a pneumatological condition and reality. What kind of knowledge is God-knowledge? *It is a kind of knowledge made possible by the Spirit pouring out God's love upon our hearts, that very center and core of who we are.* In other words, this language runs deep. This knowledge is not so much seized but received, not so much generated but participated in. By being such, it can occasion boasting in times of suffering because it forces us to look beyond ourselves and our circumstances to something greater. As such, the one who is transcendent has broken into the immanent rather than a creature perpetually grasping to achieve transcendence.

A third point worth stressing about this passage is that this pouring out of God's love upon our hearts by the Spirit is primordial when cast within a context of time and formation. Notice that Paul highlights a sequence of "production": suffering produces endurance, endurance produces character, and character produces hope (vv. 3–4). God's love is hopeful when it reflects a time-driven habituation of those who live out of this love within the features of everyday life.[15] Boasting, confidence, and, yes, hope are all reflective of a seasoned form of intentional embodiment in which endurance and character are critical pieces. The expansion of God's love that is poured out is continual and ongoing, its effects made manifest over time. Some may wish to stress an instantaneity dynamic to all of this, but Paul has in mind the long view in these particular claims. Humans change and are shaped by time-driven processes. Becoming God-like—participating and being shaped by God's love so as to be able to boast of this hope—requires time, intentionality, and embodiment amid fluctuating circumstances.

These aspects surrounding the Spirit pouring out God's love on our hearts is crucial for a number of epistemic concerns, but let us press into the issue of discernment. One line of perennial questions surrounding God-knowledge have to do with detecting it, identifying it, and so on. *Discernment* has become a catch-all category to denote all of this. How do

15. It is worthwhile considering how often the Spirit is tied to virtue; certainly this is the case with Thomas Aquinas, but the tradition runs deeper still: Didymus's *On the Holy Spirit*, one of the earliest Christian pneumatological texts, notes, "Now the Holy Spirit is only introduced to those who have forsaken their vices, who follow the choir of the virtues, and who live by faith in Christ in accordance with and through virtue." See "On the Holy Spirit," in Athanasius the Great and Didymus the Blind, *Works on the Spirit*, trans. Mark DelCogliano, Andrew Radde-Gallwitz, and Lewis Ayres (Yonkers, NY: St. Vladimir's Seminary Press, 2011), 211 (V, 222).

we discern God's presence, God's purposes, God's will? Often, the question of discernment is pneumatologically cast, but this is one place where the "diffusion" or "scattering" that this conference has set as concerns may play a role. Is it not the case that people sometimes seek a pneumatological stamp of approval by claiming, "the Spirit is saying this," or "the Spirit did this"? Such efforts debilitate and discredit pneumatology because they reek of projection. And let us be clear: projection is no small matter theologically, but it is especially egregious pneumatologically when various passages of Scripture point to the delicacy and subtlety of the Spirit's operations in our midst. The biblical themes of blaspheming (Matt 12:31–32), lying to, (Acts 5:3), testing (Acts 5:9), opposing (Acts 7:51), grieving (Eph 4:30), quenching (1 Thess 5:19–21), and outraging (Heb 10:26–29) the Spirit point to a synergistic dynamic in which the love of God may be poured on our hearts by the Spirit, but we in turn have a role to play in how that love is stewarded and held. Sadly, that role can easily be distorting, if not malignant, not only in relation to the Spirit's presence and work but in our formation and character. To take one example, quenching the Spirit not only has a deleterious effect on the work of the Spirit in our midst, but it has a deleterious effect on the one who is doing the quenching in terms of both formation and the ability to recognize and participate in the work of the Spirit in the future.[16] Therefore, to recall another passage, part of the Spirit's job description is to remind us of the words and teachings of Jesus (John 14:26), but what is done with those memories is itself a formational concern. As Jesus said in this very same portion of Scripture, "They who have my commandments and keep them are those who love me" (John 14:21); he adds, "Those who love me will keep my word, and my Father will love them, and we will come to them and make our home with them" (John 14:23). In my view, these matters have significant implications for discernment. How so?

Simply put and working off of John 14, discernment is not possible apart from the triune God making a home in the one seeking to discern. To cite another Johannine verse, "Anyone who resolves to do the will of God will know whether the teaching is from God" (John 7:17). Welcoming God, desiring God, and obeying God—these form some of the preconditions for discerning God-knowledge. With discernment, the issue is not calculation but renunciation and growing conformity. The goal is not projecting onto

---

16. Interestingly, in Stephen's speech where he speaks of "opposing" the Spirit (Acts 7:51–53), he makes reference to the intergenerational feature of this "sin against the Spirit." In other words, Stephen is pointing to systemic, tradition-related dynamics and not simply to isolated ones when he references opposition to the Spirit.

God, but reflecting and beholding God. The mode of reasoning at work is not a hard rationality but a Spirit-driven logicality in which deep things of the self and the deep things of God are on the table and so purposefully and transformatively interactive.

What kind of knowledge is God-knowledge then? *It is the kind of knowledge that the Spirit pours out in the form of love and that we in turn must care for and steward so that it may thrive in our lives.* Only then can we be enlightened by it, grow in it, and so recognize it. Recognition and discernment of God-knowledge are not features of an unconditioned, preliminary process; rather, they are culminations of Spirit-led lives.

"WALKING AND LIVING ACCORDING TO THE SPIRIT"

I mentioned earlier that we would get around to mentioning the second love commandment, loving one's neighbor as oneself. Again, these commandments are brutally basic to Christian self-understanding. Interestingly, however, in Matthew's account of the passage, he has the following words appended between the commandments that are not found in the Lukan (10:27) and Markan (12:30) accounts: "And a second [commandment] is like it" (Matt 22:39). It may be the case in renditions of these commandments to think of them as sequentially ordered in terms of importance, that the first is more important than the second. In Matthew's case, the second is not simply after the first but is said to be similar to the first. In what ways could the similarity be understood?

One of the stubborn challenges in pneumatology, at least how we in English-speaking cultures see it, is that it tends to privatization, individuation, and so to aspects that are nondiscursive and publicly unavailable. One may even tend to think that this is a critique that could be leveled at the previous registers we have considered. My response to this charge is that it all depends on the circumstances. Again, given that the references we have thus far made to both Romans 8 and 5 are to circumstances of suffering and weakness, these could be privately held and negotiated, but they could also be quite public and available to an onlooking world. A person may encounter "sighs too deep for words" in one's prayer closet, but one may also encounter them at funerals of those senselessly killed by rampant gun violence. One may steward the Spirit-poured love of God in one's heart in a steadfast, private way, but one may also demonstrate endurance and character in exceedingly public ways as well. In fact, the public, collective, and communal dimensions of these are indispensable. God-knowledge and growth in God-knowledge are not simply private matters; quite the contrary, involved are important public dimensions as well. How is the second love commandment similar to the first then? One way to think of this is to say that loving one's neighbor is not dissimilar to loving God; in fact, one could argue that certain aspects of God-knowledge can only be gained by loving one's neighbor. So, to raise once again the refrain of our session: What kind of knowledge is God-knowledge? *It is the kind of knowledge that is gained in some sense by being lovingly engaged in and with the world.* That this statement can hold with any significance is a result of a deep, pneumatological sensibility.

One of the challenges of biblical pneumatology is its wide-ranging features. On the one hand, one sees a particularizing, specifying, personhood-related dynamic. We could call this *Trinitarian pneumatology*. For Christians, this feature is most on display in the ways that the Spirit is talked about as an agent in the New Testament. The phrase "another Paraclete" from John 14:16 lifts up the point starkly—that this one will be similar to Jesus, the first Paraclete. But other New Testament passages reinforce the point as well, including the preparatory work of the Spirit for the Messiah's coming in the early chapters of Luke and the manifest work of the Spirit throughout various portions of Acts. One could say that this dynamic is even at times on display in the Old Testament, when the Spirit of YHWH comes upon and stirs people at key moments. Given the evolving Trinitarian commitments of the Christian tradition, this pneumatological dynamic is fundamental to Christian theological reflection.

And yet, on the other hand, biblical pneumatology is far-ranging and expansive as well. The terms *ruach* and *pneuma* function at times as loose, somewhat metaphysical categories that can apply widely. We can say not only "God's Spirit" but also "God is spirit" (John 4:24), and anthropological references, malignant forces, and others could also be referenced in terms of broad uses of these words. For the sake of convenience, let's call this usage *metaphysical pneumatology*. That such language can be used so widely may be difficult for us in our setting to accommodate. After all, in a demythologized environment such as this one, we do not tend to think of the world as being governed by "spirits," with "God's Spirit" being the most powerful, as other Christian cultures and worldviews may hold. As cumbersome as all these factors are, my point in raising them here is to stress that this second, wide-ranging feature of biblical pneumatology may be harder for us Westerners to accommodate than the first.

One way to bridge this conceptual gulf is to link the doctrine of creation to what we are calling Trinitarian pneumatology in constructive ways. Through such a link, the Spirit would not simply be highlighted in such works as sanctification but also in the very constitution of creation, both as God intended it and as we understand it. The repercussions of this move are important; if we say that the created order proclaims or reflects God and that humanity's uniqueness can be stressed in terms of "the image of God," these claims can be thought of as viable and meaningful along pneumatological lines. The constructive conclusion to draw from this is that the world that the triune God created, by being created by God, is in turn a Spirit-drenched world. Obviously, the world is fallen and broken to be sure, but it is also not bereft of God's presence, design, and purposes.

I realize that I am introducing a number of variables and themes that cannot be adequately treated in what follows. But my reason in doing so is to press a larger point: God-knowledge is not cultivated apart from worldly engagement, engagement with one's neighbor, engagement with all that sustains and makes the world beautiful, good, and true, and engagement that resists injustice, violence, and abuse and in turn stands for the oppressed, the hurting, and the marginalized. That we as Christians have a sense of what is good, true, and beautiful harkens back to the possibilities at work with the second register we have stressed: we must have God's love poured into our hearts so that we may know what true love is and, in turn, how to love truly. But in the act of loving, there are aspects of God-knowledge to be learned. God-knowledge is not something simply learned in the abstract or through a lecture or book; it is something that is learned via intentional action and living.

If we can press into service one more Pauline phrase, one that seems apropos to the notion of active living, it would be that of "walking and living according to the Spirit," a theme also mentioned in Romans 8. In this portion of Romans 8, Paul is developing a contrast with the flesh; he states in verse 5, "For those who live according to the flesh set their minds on the things of the flesh, but those who live according to the Spirit set their minds on the things of the Spirit." The contrast, as obvious as it is, is ambiguous in terms of particulars. What in fact is meant by living according to the flesh and living according to the Spirit? With such ambiguity, we may fill in the gaps and make a number of assumptions so as to substantiate the claims. One assumption that often presents itself with regard to this passage is that this all has to do with individual striving and living. Again, the tendency here may be to think of individual struggles with sin, individual victories over sin, individual resolutions to follow the things of the Spirit, and so on. But living and walking are very much public affairs. Fleshly tendencies are active not only within individuals but also within systemic and communal arrangements in the world; the Spirit is also active not only within individuals but within collectives, groups, and systems to defy the principalities and powers that govern this world.

This speaks to a larger point about how humans learn and grow. Certain things can only be appreciated through actually experiencing and performing them, a point stressed by certain philosophical, psychological, and other disciplinary orientations. Any number of examples could prove the point. Why would God-knowledge be any different? Theology in a sense is a practical discipline: it can only be lively and significant as it is enacted and embodied.[17] Doctrines must have some role to play in shaping and substantiating behavior. If the Spirit dwells in us (Rom 8:9), then that reality should matter for how we pursue our politics, what we protest, how we vote, how we spend our time and money, what and how we consume, and so on. These are not incidental or ancillary matters to one's understanding of the doctrine of God. If God desires obedience, if God commands love of neighbor, then something of God's very self is missed if these are not heeded.

Walking and living according to the Spirit, then, is a form of lively and loving engagement with the world that involves looking for God-knowledge wherever it presents itself. It involves a mode of engagement that includes curiosity, humility, revisability, and contrition.

Why have I stressed this last section regarding "spiritual enlightenment" in this manner? What may be the subtext for thinking of God-knowledge as a kind of practical field, one that requires love of neighbor and engagement with the world? I do not think it pneumatologically inconsequential that Christians, especially those of us who are Western Christians in broadly Constantinian arrangements, perpetually struggle with hypocrisy and indifference. These are not simply ethical or moral problems; these are properly theological problems. Somehow it is possible to engage the doctrine of God on the one hand and to be impervious to the world's ills on the other.

---

17. Lurking in the background are theologies of perfection and holiness. Basil of Caesarea elaborates the point well: "All things thirsting for holiness turn to [the Spirit]; everything living in virtue never turns away from Him. He waters them with His life-giving breath and helps them reach their proper fulfillment. He perfects all other things, and Himself lacks nothing. He gives life to all things, and is never depleted. . . . He is the source of sanctification, spiritual light, who gives illumination to everyone using His powers to search for truth—and the illumination He gives is Himself." Basil, *On the Holy Spirit* (Crestwood, NY: St. Vladimir's Seminary Press, 2001), 43 (9.22).

This is a credibility crisis to be sure, but it runs deeper than that. The haunting concluding words of the Sermon on the Mount should, again, drive us to our knees, but in this sense as an act of confession on the way to restoration and transformation: "Not everyone who says to me, 'Lord, Lord,' will enter the kingdom of heaven, but only the one who does the will of my Father in heaven" (Matt 7:21). We are not simply talking of our knowledge of God but of God's knowledge of us—not an enlightenment that makes us more clever but a process of ourselves coming to the light of Christ so as to be exposed in terms of our pride, our shortcomings, our vices, and our prejudices—in short, our sin. What kind of knowledge is God-knowledge in this sense? *It is knowledge that is deeply exposing; it is knowledge that makes us deeply vulnerable to how we fall short of the gospel we claim to value and live by.* This is not exposure for exposure's sake; this is exposure on a path toward healing and conformity to the God of Christian confession, whom we confess to be ultimate truth, beauty, and goodness.

In conclusion, the deep registers we have considered—namely, "sighs too deep for words," "God's love being poured out into our hearts," and "walking and living according to the Spirit"—collectively suggest a specific form of spiritual enlightenment, a kind of pneumatological orientation to God-knowledge that is both challenging and vitalizing. This vision of this uneasily categorized kind of knowledge suggests that it and its practitioners must in turn be disciplined by its own subject matter and wider voices. Some things must be deeply impressed; others must be exposed; and others still must be picked up and enacted. As risky and disquieting as that may sound, such pneumatological contributions undergird and substantiate theologizing as meaningful, worthwhile, and ultimately transformative activity. God-knowledge can and should make a deep difference.

CHAPTER 6

WHO'S ON THIRD?

(Re)Locating the Spirit in the Triune Taxis

JEROME VAN KUIKEN AND JOSHUA M. MCNALL

FAMOUS COMEDY ROUTINES do not normally provide the reverential fodder for constructive treatments of the Trinity. Among the most famous comedic sketches of all time is the 1930s bit entitled "Who's on First?" by Abbott and Costello. The gist of the routine is to illustrate the hilarious confusion that results from a baseball game in which the baserunners have some strange names: "Who" is on first; "What" is on second; "I Don't Know" is on third. (For what it's worth, "I Don't Care!" is the shortstop.)

In turning from comedy to Trinity, the language of first, second, and third also has precedent. Theologians have traditionally assigned the Spirit third place in the triune *taxis* both economically and immanently—though not, of course, in temporal sequence, ontic hierarchy, or authoritative subordination. Some recent scholarship, however, has challenged this placement by virtue of what we will refer to as the *Spirituque:* the idea that the much-debated *filioque* of intra-Trinitarian relations should be complemented by the notion that the Spirit participates with the Father in the Son's eternal generation so that it may be correct to say (at least in some sense) that the Son's eternal generation involves both the Father *and* the Spirit. The result of this *Spirituque* speculation is a question that sounds vaguely similar to those of Abbott and Costello: Who is "on third" (or second or even first!) within the triune *taxis*? And on what basis may we answer that question?

In this chapter, we evaluate three modern *Spirituque* proposals as they come to us from three historic "clubhouses" of the Christian tradition (to continue the baseball metaphor): first, from Anglican Protestant

Sarah Coakley, a Spirit-leading approach; second, from Catholic Thomas Weinandy, a Spirit-mediating perspective; third, from Eastern Orthodox Sergei Bulgakov, a Spirit-completing proposal.

In addition to examining the biblical coherence and theological fruitfulness of these three proposals, we must address the largest objection to any version of the *Spirituque*: the "umpire" of church tradition has almost universally called an "out" on this theological proposal. Without giving away all our conclusions, our favored version of the *Spirituque* must be biblically rather than politically or aesthetically driven; it must avoid the radicalizing of Rahner's Rule; and it must prevent the blurring of distinctions among Trinitarian persons. To accomplish this goal, we will lean not only on our three representatives but also upon Augustine's vision of the Spirit as the *vinculum amoris* between the Father and the Son. Now for our first representative.

"I Don't Know" Is on First: Sarah Coakley's Spirit-Leading Trinitarianism

In the closing paragraphs to the first installment of her systematic theology, Sarah Coakley reaches a "radical ontological conclusion." There can be "no Sonship which is not eternally 'sourced' by 'Father' *in the Spirit* (in such a way, in fact, as to query even the exclusive meanings of Fatherly 'source' . . .)."[1] Herein lies the first example of what we have referred to as the *Spirituque*: the suggestion that the Son is eternally generated by the Father "and the Spirit" so that traditional assignments of "source" and "place" within the triune *taxis* (first Father, then Son, then Spirit) are called into question.

Coakley's interdisciplinary project (a *théologie totale*) is rooted in a heady blend of Pauline, Platonic, pictographic, practical, patristic, and (anti-)patriarchal concerns.[2] Though a treatment of this alliteration cannot detain us,[3]

1. Sarah Coakley, *God, Sexuality, and the Self: An Essay "On the Trinity"* (Cambridge: Cambridge University Press, 2013), 332. Italics hers.

2. In *God, Sexuality, and the Self*, these themes break down as follows: Platonic, through the use of (neo)Platonic insights from Origen to Pseudo-Dionysius (ch. 6); pictographic, in a survey of the Trinity as depicted in Christian iconography (ch. 5); practical, in the attempt to ground theology in "fieldwork" done in local Charismatic churches (ch. 4); patristic, by a retrieval of the "neglected patristic tradition" of "Praying the Trinity" (ch. 3); patriarchal, by the use of feminist resources to critique hierarchal and male-dominated emphases (ch. 2); Pauline, by reference to Romans 8 (ch. 1).

3. See Joshua McNall, "Shrinking Pigeon, Brooding Dove: The Holy Spirit in Recent Works by Sarah Coakley and N. T. Wright," *Scottish Journal of Theology* 69, no. 3 (2016): 295–308; E. Jerome Van Kuiken, "'Ye Worship Ye Know Not What'? The Apophatic Turn and the Trinity," *International Journal of Systematic Theology* 19, no. 4 (2017): 401–20.

the goal is clear: it is to counter a "linear" and hierarchal version of the Trinity that prioritizes the masculine dyad of the Father and the Son while reducing the Spirit to what appears, in iconography at least, like an ever-shrinking "pigeon"—"small, shadowy," and functionally redundant.[4] In contrast, Coakley proposes an "incorporative" model of the Trinity in which the Spirit leads us into an experience of the triune life of God by enflaming and purging our desires, often in deep forms of prayer.[5]

The crucial biblical text for Coakley is Romans 8:9–30, where the Spirit brings our adoption and "bears witness" within us so we cry out, "Abba, Father" (Rom 8:15–16). Coakley's claim is that the Spirit is herein granted a "priority" both "logically and experientially."[6] But this priority is not the only takeaway from Paul's passage. This mystical experience of prayer provides, for Coakley, the "only valid *experientially based* pressure towards hypostatizing the Spirit," allowing us to say "three" with regard to divine persons.[7] Further, since the Spirit's speech is likened to *groaning* (as opposed to ordered words) the experience transcends the logocentric realm of hierarchy and reason in "a strange subversion of all certainties."[8] And since the groaning is compared to "birth pangs," the gendered metaphors for God and believers[9] are blurred by a "ray of darkness."[10] In all of this, the Spirit's priority is made apparent, as are certain connections between God, sexuality, and the self.

Church tradition moved, allegedly, to quash this Spirit-leading Trinitarianism because of the early threat of Montanism and the propensity for a charismatic "loss of control" to be confused with a *sexual* one.[11] "Book and bishop" therefore supplanted "Brooding Dove" as guiding forces in the church, and the "linear" model of the Trinity all but obliterated the "incorporative" approach so that Coakley must forage in the "margins" in order to retrieve it. This retrieval, however, is made all the more impor-

---

4. Coakley, *God, Sexuality, and the Self*, 212. Coakley credits Meg Twycross for the evocative description of a "diminished" Spirit that looks more like a tiny pigeon than a brooding dove.

5. See Coakley, *God, Sexuality, and the Self*, ch. 3.

6. Coakley, *God, Sexuality, and the Self*, 112. Italics hers.

7. Coakley, *God, Sexuality, and the Self*, 113. Italics hers. See also Sarah Coakley, "Why Three? Some Further Reflections on the Origins of the Doctrine of the Trinity," in *The Making and Remaking of Christian Doctrine: Essays in Honour of Maurice Wiles* (Oxford: Clarendon, 1993), 29–56.

8. Coakley, *God, Sexuality, and the Self*, 342.

9. With regard to believers, Coakley cites Paul's flip-flopping between "sonship" and "children of God" (*tekna*) language in Rom 8 as a sign that the Spirit "takes up and transforms the usual societal implications of gender, and renders them both labile and cosmic" (cf. Gal 3:28). *God, Sexuality, and the Self*, 115.

10. This phrase is that of Pseudo-Dionysius, *Mystical Theology*, 1; cited in Coakley, *God, Sexuality, and the Self*, 323.

11. See Sarah Coakley, "Prayer, Politics and the Trinity: Vying Models of Authority in 3rd–4th Century Debates on Prayer and 'Orthodoxy,'" *Scottish Journal of Theology* 66 (2013): 379–99.

tant, Coakley claims, since the church is again facing a "crisis" regarding sexuality and gender.[12]

While more should be said of Coakley's fascinating project, we have now done enough to note why her apophatic and experiential version of the *Spirituque* can be described—with a nod to Abbott and Costello—as "'I Don't Know' is on first." To be in mystical relationship with an invisible God is to engage in what Coakley refers to as "a love affair with a blank."[13] The divine life, like Sinai's peak, is cloaked in "thick darkness" (Deut 5:22; Ps 97:2). Thus Coakley's conclusion is not that the Father's place as "source" should be rejected but that it should be "quer[ied]."[14] "'I Don't Know' who is first," she might be heard to say, since to claim this privileged knowledge would be to peer too deeply into the "dazzling darkness"[15] and replace one form of hierarchal false certainty with another. Hers is an apophatic *Spirituque.*

In response to Coakley's pneumatology, several strengths stand out. First, her reading of Romans 8 is insightful, and ample biblical support exists for the contention that the Spirit is, in some sense, "first" in our experience of God and salvation. No one says "'Jesus is Lord,' except by the Holy Spirit" (1 Cor 12:3). The Spirit convicts of sin (e.g., John 16:8), bears witness in our hearts, and enables the prayer by which we call to God as "Abba, Father" (e.g., Rom 8). To speak of the Spirit as "first" in these capacities is appropriate since for those "dead" in sin the first breath of life comes by the prevenient work of the Spirit.[16]

Second, Coakley's gesture toward the Spirit's particularizing power is also helpful. In her view, the Spirit enables us to say, "three persons," while simultaneously affirming, "one God." And this particularizing point could even be strengthened with reference to the post-Pentecost way in which the Spirit brings oneness in the church not by bland homogeneity but by redeemed particularity: "hands" and "feet," Jews and gentiles, slave and free, men and women in a unity that is not uniformity.[17]

---

12. This is the first sentence in Coakley's volume, *God, Sexuality, and the Self*, 1.

13. Coakley, *God, Sexuality, and the Self*, 342. Coakley notes that this "wonderful" phrase is that of Dom Sebastian Moore, "Some Principles for an Adequate Theism," *Downside Review* 95 (1977): 201–13.

14. See Coakley, *God, Sexuality, and the Self*, 332.

15. Coakley, *God, Sexuality, and the Self*, 96.

16. For the recasting of "prevenient grace" as the "prevenient work of the Spirit," see Joshua M. McNall, *The Mosaic of Atonement: An Integrated Approach to Christ's Work* (Grand Rapids: Zondervan, 2019), 303–5.

17. See McNall, *Mosaic of Atonement*, 305–8. This point builds on the work of *doctor particularis* Colin Gunton.

Third, a measured apophaticism is praiseworthy, especially with regard to the Trinity. Coakley is attuned to the overconfident projectionism that attended the so-called twentieth-century renaissance of Trinitarian theology.[18] And her apophaticism helps avoid the radicalizing of Rahner's Rule, in which any claim about the persons in the economy is taken as an absolutist assumption about the Trinity *in se*.[19]

But these strengths are accompanied by potential problems for the Coakleyan *Spirituque*. First, the biblical basis for her proposal is rather thin. The vast majority of exegetical support is based on just a few verses from Romans 8, and even this work is confined to around four pages in a lengthy monograph. Earlier portions of Paul's letter are ignored, perhaps because they (along with the gospel of John and Acts, according to Coakley) might seem to highlight a "linear" and "patriarchal" model of God that is focused on the Father and the Son.[20]

Second, Coakley's tendency toward apophatic excess runs the risk of replacing the clarity of biblical revelation with the "I Don't Know" of a "love affair with a blank." To be sure, there is mystery in God and mystical experience, yet the Scriptures (and Paul in particular) hold together the "dazzling darkness" that clouds our fallen perceptions (1 Cor 13:12) with the "light" that enlightens us (2 Cor 4:6), so that our worship does not devolve into an Athenian apophaticism that pays homage "to an unknown god." Such reverential ignorance was condemned in Paul's encounter with the actual (as opposed to the "Pseudo-") Dionysius (Acts 17:23, 34).[21] And rightly so, since one may project onto a "blank" God even more easily than with a graven image, and since one may "find in that blank a *carte blanche* to fund one's sociopolitical interests."[22]

Finally, and most directly to the *Spirituque*, Coakley's methodological move from the economic to the immanent Trinity is also shot through with "rays of darkness." The rationale for the precise correspondence between temporal *prayer* and the eternal *processions* is underdetermined. It needs to be asked: *Why* must Spirit-leading prayer result in the "radical ontological

18. See *God, Sexuality, and the Self*, xiv, 270, 272, 309, 321n22.

19. "Even though we stand by the insistence that 'the economic Trinity *is* the immanent (or 'ontological') Trinity,' the latter (the 'ontological') clearly cannot simply be *reduced* to God's manifestation to us. And hence the speculation that follows here." Coakley, *God, Sexuality, and the Self*, 332n33. Italics hers.

20. See Van Kuiken, "'Ye Worship Ye Know Not What,'" 408.

21. See McNall, "Shrinking Pigeon," 305. Quote from Acts 17:23 uncapitalized.

22. Van Kuiken, "Ye Worship Ye Know Not What," 415–17. See the similar point by John Webster, *Holiness* (Grand Rapids: Eerdmans, 2003), 44.

conclusion" that the Spirit also "sources" the Son's eternal generation? Coakley provides no answer, except to admit that her proposal remains in the realm of "speculation."[23] For this reason, Christopher Holmes notes rightly that the "force" of her pneumatology remains largely "on the economic level."[24] To merely "query" the meaning of "first" and "source" is ill-fitted with a simultaneous dogmatism that there can be "no Sonship" apart from the *Spirituque*.[25]

"WHAT" IS ON SECOND: THOMAS WEINANDY'S SPIRIT-MEDIATING TRINITARIANISM

Coakley's affirmation of the *Spirituque* includes her qualified endorsement of Thomas Weinandy's treatise on the subject, *The Father's Spirit of Sonship*.[26] While Coakley starts with the Spirit in first place, Weinandy focuses on the Spirit as the second or mediating term between the Father and Son. His thesis is that "the Father begets the Son in or by the Holy Spirit, who proceeds then from the Father as the one in whom the Son is begotten."[27] The generation of the Son is not logically prior to the procession of the Spirit.[28] Rather, in generating the Son, the Father gifts his life, love, truth, wisdom, power, and glory—in sum, the divine nature—to the Son, yet that gift is not the divine nature generically or abstractly but is concretely the Spirit of Life, Love, Truth, and so on. To his Son, the Father communicates his holy, spiritual nature as particularized by the Holy Spirit.[29] In being thus communicated, the Spirit particularizes or "persons" the Father as Father and the Son as Son.[30] This personalizing activity signals that the Spirit is an agent, hence truly a person,[31] not the "shrinking pigeon" of Coakley's critique or a passive "birdie" served between Father and Son in a heavenly badminton match.

Weinandy commends his model as producing a more perfect correspondence between the immanent and economic Trinity without collapsing

23. See Coakley, *God, Sexuality, and the Self*, 332n33.

24. Christopher R. J. Holmes, *The Holy Spirit*, New Studies in Dogmatics (Grand Rapids: Zondervan, 2015), 42.

25. Coakley, *God, Sexuality, and the Self*, 332.

26. Coakley, *God, Sexuality, and the Self*, 332–33.

27. Thomas G. Weinandy, *The Father's Spirit of Sonship: Reconceiving the Trinity* (Edinburgh: T&T Clark, 1995), ix.

28. Weinandy, *Father's Spirit of Sonship*, 71–72.

29. Weinandy, *Father's Spirit of Sonship*, 46–49, 72; cf. 8–9n16.

30. Weinandy, *Father's Spirit of Sonship*, 73–74, 97.

31. Weinandy, *Father's Spirit of Sonship*, 8.

the former into the latter.[32] He spends two chapters tracing the biblical data regarding the Son's dependence on the Spirit in his conception and baptism, passion and resurrection, along with Christians' dependence on the Spirit for regeneration, adoption, and sanctification.[33] Thus Christian experience follows the pattern of Christ's experience in the economy of salvation, which in turn suggests an eternal pattern within the immanent Trinity.

The major challenge to Weinandy's proposal, he knows, is its lack of traction in church tradition. Historically, both Eastern and Western theologians have concluded that the Spirit's procession is logically posterior to and so derivative from the Father-Son relationship. Weinandy blames this conclusion on theologians' projection onto the Godhead of unbaptized philosophical notions such as Platonic emanationism and Aristotelian epistemology. Emanationism yields a unilateral sequence in which the Spirit originates from the Father (and, in the West, from the Son, too, albeit as from a single source) and so cannot act causally upon either. Aristotelian epistemology informs Thomas Aquinas's psychological model of the Trinity in his principle that rational knowledge must precede volitional love, and so the Son, who is God's Logos, must precede (logically, not chronologically) the Spirit, who is God's Love.[34] Weinandy agrees with the tradition that the Father is the primary source of the other two divine persons; still, he stresses the reciprocity of Trinitarian relations of origin, a key expression of which is the Spirit's involvement in the Son's begetting.[35]

Weinandy's work has won qualified sympathy even from some scholars predisposed to traditional pneumatology.[36] His understanding of the *Spirituque* as *per Spiritum* or *in Spiritu* should soothe worries of the Spirit's becoming another Father in the Trinity.[37] His extensive exegesis grounds his proposal in biblical data rather than egalitarian sociopolitical ideology[38]

32. Weinandy, *Father's Spirit of Sonship*, 4–5, 22.

33. Weinandy, *Father's Spirit of Sonship*, chs. 2–3.

34. Weinandy, *Father's Spirit of Sonship*, 9–14, 20–22. Coakley, *God, Sexuality, and the Self*, 332n34, demurs from Weinandy's "latter-day 'Harnackian' suspicion of 'Platonism' (or Thomist 'Aristotelianism')."

35. Weinandy, *Father's Spirit of Sonship*, 71–74, 78–83, 97.

36. Lewis Ayres, review of *Father's Spirit of Sonship*, *Journal of Theological Studies* 50, no. 1 (1999): 429–32; Holmes, *The Holy Spirit*, 123–24, 126, 129.

37. A concern expressed by Photius, *Myst.* 3, 9–10, and, as noted below, Barth. Does Weinandy's proposal make the Spirit a heavenly Mother? Weinandy himself never uses such language, though *Father's Spirit of Sonship* (81n44) includes a quotation on "the maternal-virginal womb of the Holy Spirit" from Leonardo Boff, *Trinity and Society* (New York: Orbis, 1988), 147. The notion of Spirit as Mother fits ill with Weinandy's presentation of the Spirit as the hypostasized forth-flowing of the Father's power in begetting the Son, not as the recipient of that action. Biblically, only two familial terms condition the Spirit: Fatherhood and Sonship, for the Spirit is the Spirit of both.

38. See Karen Kilby, "Perichoresis and Projection: Problems with Social Doctrines of the Trinity," *New Blackfriars* 81 (2000): 432–45.

or an aesthetic of tidy Trinitarian symmetry.[39] His nested analogies of the Spirit's role in Christian experience, the economic Trinity, and the immanent Trinity trace praxis and revelation to their headwaters in ultimate reality while in turn mapping that reality's practical, historical outflow.[40]

Nonetheless, the most substantial objection to *Spirituque* arguments comes from the tradition. Thus we must take a slight detour from our three interlocutors to face this critique head on. In what follows, we will revisit the complaint of theological novelty and supplement Weinandy's rebuttal. We also will weigh Karl Barth's unfavorable evaluation of the *Spirituque*. Lastly, we will lodge our own caveat concerning Weinandy's handling of the Spirit's whatness so as to guard the personhood of the Spirit when occupying second place in the triune *taxis*.

EXCURSUS: THE OBJECTION FROM TRADITION

We start by returning to tradition. In the thirteenth century, Aquinas raised the hypothetical possibility that "the Son is from the Holy Ghost . . ." only to dispatch it: ". . . which no one says."[41] Already in the fifth century Augustine had dismissed the same hypothesis as "absurd."[42] What made the *Spirituque* inconceivable? Whatever one makes of Weinandy's claim that these theologians' philosophical presuppositions blinded them, other factors suggest themselves: To begin with, already in the second century the church faced the heresies of adoptionism and Montanism. Adoptionists interpreted Christ's earthly reliance on the Spirit as a case of a mere man anointed with the divine Spirit. Montanists relativized the authority of the bishops and their Bible in the name of the prophets and their Paraclete. The church responded to both heresies by subordinating the Spirit to Christ and his apostles (as represented by their inspired writings and ordained successors). This economic subordination made it unthinkable that the Son should depend on the Spirit in eternity.[43]

---

39. In the question-and-answer session following Fred Sanders, "Eternal Procession and the Complicated Name of the Spirit" (unpublished paper, annual meeting of the Evangelical Theological Society, Denver, November 13, 2018), he rightly warned against theological innovation for the sake of a more symmetrical diagram of the Trinity. Of course, one may employ a diagram simply to *illustrate* a theological proposal rather than *establish* it.

40. For a similar two-way movement between the Trinity and ecclesiology, see E. Jerome Van Kuiken, "Transpositions: The Notes of the Church in Trinitarian and Wesleyan Keys," *Wesleyan Theological Journal* 53, no. 1 (2018): 79–91.

41. Thomas Aquinas, *Summa Theologiae* 1.36.2, quoted in Weinandy, *Father's Spirit of Sonship*, 21.

42. Augustine, *De Trinitate* 15.37, quoted in Weinandy, *Father's Spirit of Sonship*, 20.

43. Gary D. Badcock, *Light of Truth and Fire of Love: A Theology of the Holy Spirit* (Grand Rapids: Eerdmans, 1997), 38–41, 160–61; cf. Coakley, *God, Sexuality, and the Self*, 115–26; John A.

The Trinitarian terms themselves are another factor in the traditional rejection of the *Spirituque*. The name Father implies both antecedence and a Son as its consequence; the name Holy Spirit bears no clear relation to either of the other names, so it was relegated to last place as the odd left-over term.[44] A further factor was the Trinitarian sequence of Father first, Son second, and Holy Spirit third in the church's dominant baptismal formula. This formula became the framework for the creeds,[45] so that when the Arian crisis forced the church to make official pronouncements about the Trinity *ad intra*, it seemed only natural to read the creedal order as the order of processions (Son logically prior to Spirit).[46] Related to this factor was the early universal acceptance and influence of Matthew's gospel, which contained the familiar baptismal formula.[47] By contrast, in the Eastern churches John's Apocalypse remained canonically and liturgically marginalized for centuries,[48] along with its Father-Spirit-Son sequencing (Rev 1:4–5; chs. 4–5) and its portrayal of Christ's divine omniscience and omnipotence as due to the Spirit's presence upon him (Rev 5:6).[49]

A RESPONSE TO THE REBUTTAL FROM TRADITION

Our claim is that these factors do not decisively rule out the *Spirituque*. Sergei Bulgakov has noted that the patristic period did not thresh out a

---

McGuckin, "The Book of Revelation and Orthodox Eschatology: The Theodrama of Judgment," in *The Last Things: Biblical and Theological Perspectives on Eschatology*, ed. Carl E. Braaten and Robert W. Jenson (Grand Rapids: Eerdmans, 2002), 113–14, 122–23; Michael F. Bird, *Jesus the Eternal Son: Answering Adoptionist Christology* (Grand Rapids: Eerdmans, 2017), ch. 5.

44. Herwig Aldenhoven, "The Question of the Procession of the Holy Spirit and Its Connection with the Life of the Church," in *Spirit of God, Spirit of Christ: Ecumenical Reflections on the* Filioque *Controversy*, ed. Lukas Vischer, Faith and Order Paper 103 (London: SPCK; Geneva: World Council of Churches, 1981), 123–26; Sergius Bulgakov, *The Comforter*, trans. Boris Jakim (Grand Rapids: Eerdmans, 2004), 36, 51, 54, 56–57. Both Aldenhoven and Bulgakov trenchantly critique this factor.

45. Jaroslav Pelikan, *Credo* (New Haven, CT: Yale University Press, 2003), 376–83.

46. This despite the fact that the Nicene Creed makes no mention of Pentecost but only of the Spirit's preparatory work for Christ in Mary's womb and Israel's prophets! Cf. Bulgakov, *The Comforter*, 39–40.

47. Manlio Simonetti, ed., *Matthew 1–13*, Ancient Christian Commentary on Scripture (Downers Grove, IL: InterVarsity, 2001), xxxvii–xxxviii; cf. Pelikan, *Credo*, 376–77. Bulgakov, *The Comforter*, 73, cautions, "With reference to the *taxis* this formula does not have absolute significance; it is one of its possible expressions."

48. McGuckin, "The Book of Revelation," 114–15, 120–34.

49. Richard Bauckham, *The Theology of the Book of Revelation* (Cambridge: Cambridge University Press, 1993), 109–13, notes that the seven eyes, horns, and spirits of Rev 5:6 symbolize the Holy Spirit and allude to Zech 4:1–14. But he interprets them as simply symbolizing the Spirit's universal application of the Lamb's work. In Bauckham, *pace*, Zech 4 promises the Spirit's power to Zerubbabel (Zech 4:6–10), Jesus's ancestor (Matt 1:12–16; Luke 3:23–27) and the seven spirits also allude to Isa 11:1–3, in which the ideal Davidic king is anointed with the sevenfold Spirit of wisdom and power. Thus in Rev 5 the Spirit not only *applies* Christ's work but *empowers* Christ with omni-attributes.

thorough, ecumenically accepted pneumatology as it did with Christology, instead deferring that task to the contemporary church.[50] What Aquinas heard nobody saying is now proposed by significant Catholic, Orthodox, and Protestant theologians.[51] What Augustine thought absurd seems more plausible to those impacted by the charismatic movement;[52] modern biblical studies' recovery of the reciprocity of Son and Spirit in the scriptural data;[53] and intellectual climate changes toward nonlinearity as found in, for instance, personalism, complexity theory, and quantum mechanics—a climate in which the title *Being as Communion* is equally apt for a book on Trinitarian theology and another on the philosophy of science.[54] We do not claim that because of these factors the *Spirituque* is *right*, only that it is *ripe* for reconsideration.

That ripeness becomes even more apparent when we give church tradition a second look. Once the presumption of the Son's logical priority over the Spirit is bracketed, the Christian East is especially rich in precedents for the *Spirituque*. Gregory of Nyssa played on the *double entendres* in Greek of the Trinitarian titles *Logos* (reason, word) and *Pneuma* (spirit, breath) to explain that God's Reason comes to verbal expression through God's Breath/Spirit.[55] This analogy hints at not only the dependence of the outwardly spoken word upon the breath by which it is uttered but also the reliance of one's inward reasoning upon one's innermost being or mind, that is, one's spirit. This outward/inward distinction corresponds to the economic and immanent Trinity. Gregory of Nazianzus and John of Damascus both illustrated the Trinity by means of Adam (God the Father), Eve, who proceeds from him (God the Holy Spirit), and Abel or Seth, whom he begets (God the Son). Regardless of the illustration's merit, Yves Congar has pointed out that since Adam begot his son by means of Eve, pressing this illustration produces the *Spirituque*.[56] Lastly, Eastern Orthodox tradition permits the transposition of Christ's temporal dependence on the Spirit into eternity by speaking of

50. Bulgakov, *Comforter*, 40, 50–51, 144–45.

51. Weinandy, *Father's Spirit of Sonship*, 18–19, lists as *Spirituque* proponents Catholics F. X. Durrwell, Leonardo Boff, and Edward Yarnold; Orthodox Olivier Clément and Paul Evdokimov; and Protestants Jürgen Moltmann and the Church of England Doctrinal Commission.

52. Weinandy, *Father's Spirit of Sonship*, x, 4.

53. Weinandy, *Father's Spirit of Sonship*, 2; Badcock, *Light of Truth*, 229–30.

54. John D. Zizioulas, *Being as Communion: Studies in Personhood and the Church* (Crestwood: St. Vladimir's Seminary Press, 1985); William A. Dembski, *Being as Communion: A Metaphysics of Information* (Farnham: Ashgate, 2014).

55. Gregory of Nyssa, *Cat. Or.* 1–2; behind this analogy lies Ps 33:6.

56. Yves M. J. Congar, *I Believe in the Holy Spirit* (trans. David Smith; New York: Seabury, 1983), 33, 158, citing Nazianzen, *Or.* 30.32 (using Seth) and Damascene, *De duabus Christi* 18.30 (using Abel), respectively. See, however, our caveat above about viewing the Spirit as a heavenly Mother.

the Spirit's resting on or abiding in the Son within the immanent Trinity.[57] All that remains is similarly to read the Spirit's formative role in Christ's earthly begetting back into his heavenly generation.

THE BARTHIAN BLOCK TO SPIRITUQUE

Precisely here Karl Barth balked, despite recognizing that the *Spirituque* would seem to follow from his theological method of basing the doctrine of the Trinity strictly on its revelation in the economy of grace. He objected that the Son's eternal generation is solely from the Father's essence. But in the Spirit-wrought begetting of Christ in his birth, baptism, and resurrection, as well as in the analogous case of Christians' regeneration, what transpires is a change in an already-existing human essence. In regeneration a human acquires a new manner of being, not being itself. In Christ's birth and baptism, "it is this man Jesus of Nazareth, not the Son of God, who becomes the Son of God by the descent of the Spirit." His resurrection, too, merely changes Christ's manner of being. The Holy Spirit is not the father of either the Son's humanity or his deity, Barth insisted.[58]

Let us first take up Barth's last point. As we have seen, Weinandy's understanding of the *Spirituque* as *per Spiritum* or *in Spiritu* removes any danger of the Spirit's encroaching on the Father's uniqueness. Secondly, Barth's statement that "this man Jesus of Nazareth, not the Son of God, . . . becomes the Son of God by the descent of the Spirit" seems to distinguish a divine Son from a human Son in Christ—a distinction associated with the heresies of Nestorianism and Spanish adoptionism.[59] Barth's language is at least incautious. It also means that the Spirit's son-making activity in relation to both Jesus's humanity and ours has no roots in God's inner life, thus widening once more the breach Barth was seeking to close.

Finally, Barth's claim that the Spirit only brings sonship to preexisting persons ignores biblical counterexamples. Isaac did not exist before his

---

57. This tradition stretches from John of Damascus through Photius, Gregory of Cyprus, and Gregory Palamas to contemporary Orthodox theologians. See the chapters by Markos A. Orphanos, Boris Bobrinskoy, and Dumitru Staniloae in *Spirit of God, Spirit of Christ*, 21–45, 133–48, 174–86, respectively; Andreas Andreopoulos, "The Holy Spirit in the ecclesiology of Photios of Constantinople," in *The Holy Spirit in the Fathers of the Church: The Proceedings of the Seventh International Patristic Conference, Maynooth, 2008*, ed. D. Vincent Twomey and Janet E. Rutherford (Dublin: Four Courts, 2010), 151–63.

58. Barth, *Church Dogmatics*, I/1:485–86 (quotation from former page).

59. For cogent sketches of these heresies, see "Adoptionism" and "Nestorianism" in Justo L. González, *Essential Theological Terms* (Louisville: Westminster John Knox, 2005), 2, 120–21, respectively. For an exegetical case that Mark's gospel does not present Jesus's baptism as the point at which he became God's Son, see Bird, *Jesus the Eternal Son*, ch. 4. Bird's arguments apply *a fortiori* to the other three Gospels.

conception.[60] Paul's Galatian letter attributes Isaac's origin to the Spirit as a foreshadowing of Christians' Spirit-enabled sonship (4:28–29), which in turn echoes Christ's Sonship (4:4–7).[61] Likewise, Adam did not exist before God formed him from virgin soil and breathed into him the breath or spirit or Spirit of life (Gen 2:4–7). Luke's gospel labels Adam "the son of God" (3:38) and links him to Christ immediately following Jesus's adult reception of the Holy Spirit and designation as God's Son (3:21–38), an event that recalls Christ's Spirit-enabled conception (1:31–37).[62] Likewise, John's gospel blends allusion to Adam's origin in Genesis 2 with Ezekiel 37's vision of the valley of dry bones in describing Christ's resurrection and breathing on his disciples so that they may receive the Holy Spirit (John 20:1–22),[63] making them God's children after the pattern of the *monogenēs* Son (John 1:12–14; 3:3–8, 16).[64] Barth was metaphysically correct that the person of God the Son antedated his incarnation and that sinners are persons (albeit dysfunctional) before regeneration. But if Scripture uses Adam's and Isaac's Spirit-wrought sonship *ex nihilo* as a heuristic device for Christ's and Christians' sonship, then this suggests that indeed, as Coakley and Weinandy claim, *all sonship is the Spirit's doing*—even within the eternal Trinity.

Underlying Barth's rejection of the *Spirituque* was his determination to keep the Spirit firmly subordinate to Christ, lest liberalism, mysticism, and Nazism run amok.[65] This fear animated his full-throated defense of the *filioque* in its strongest form—no half-measured "through the Son" would do!—against Eastern Orthodoxy.[66] It also surfaced in his idiosyncratic reading of Genesis 1:1–3. The Bible's opening verses could lend support to the *Spirituque*,[67] for the sequence is first God (1:1), secondly the Spirit (1:2),

60. Unless one assumes with Origen and the early (and perhaps later?) Augustine the preexistence of souls. See Dominic Keech, *The Anti-Pelagian Christology of Augustine of Hippo, 396–430* (Oxford: Oxford University Press, 2012).

61. Lest "sonship" be read gender-exclusively, note that Paul explicitly extends this status to women (Gal 3:26–4:7).

62. These Adam-Christ parallels draw from Irenaeus, *Adv. Haer.* 3.21.10; 3.22.3.

63. Craig S. Keener, *The Gospel of John: A Commentary* (Peabody: Hendrickson, 2003), 2: 1204–5; Brian Neil Peterson, *John's Use of Ezekiel: Understanding the Unique Perspective of the Fourth Gospel* (Minneapolis: Fortress, 2015), 167–76.

64. For an argument that John 1:12–13 refers not to believers' regeneration but to Christ's virginal conception, see Thomas F. Torrance, *Incarnation: The Person and Life of Christ*, ed. Robert T. Walker (Milton Keynes: Paternoster; Downers Grove: InterVarsity, 2008), 89–92.

65. For critical analyses, see Badcock, *Light of Truth*, 160, 217–19 (who finds Barth's rejection of the *Spirituque* inconsistent with his mature doctrine of election); Gregory Collins, "Three Modern 'Fathers' on the *Filioque*: Good, Bad or Indifferent?," in Twomey and Rutherford, *Holy Spirit in the Fathers of the Church*, 173–76 (who finds Barth's allegations against nonfilioquist praxis unsubstantiated).

66. Barth, *Church Dogmatics*, I/1:477–84, 486–87.

67. As Bulgakov, *Comforter*, 72, acknowledges and embraces.

and thirdly the Word (1:3) that John's gospel identifies with Christ (John 1:1–4, 14). But Barth advocated a sharp contrast between verses 2 and 3. He scorned verse 2 as a mythological picture of the Spirit brooding impotently over chaos. This is a possible world to which God says no. Verse 3 begins the account of the world to which God says yes: an orderly realm in which *mythos* yields to *Logos*.[68] Unlike Barth's zero-sum game of verse 3 over verse 2, pro-*filioque* West over anti-*filioque* East, and Christ over Spirit, we prefer a harmonizing approach open to the *Spirituque*.

If neither church tradition nor modern objections from so influential a theologian as Barth offer insuperable obstacles to Weinandy's proposal, then what is to hinder it? The answer is that it is just the "What" that hinders it. Weinandy thinks his *Spirituque* clearly makes the Spirit a "Who" by giving the Spirit something to do in the immanent Trinity. But the activity of personalizing the Father and Son does not ensure the Spirit's personhood. One could conceptualize the Holy Spirit as simply a holy field of force, a principle of personalization, the dynamism of the divine nature—a what, not a who.[69] This ambiguity springs from Scripture itself. From Genesis 1 to Jesus's ministry, the Spirit as the second or middle term between God and God's sons (Adam, Israel, the Davidic kings, Jesus) appears to be merely God's power or disposition. As we shall see, the Spirit's whoness only becomes obvious when coming third in the triune *taxis*.

"WHO'S" ON THIRD: SERGEI BULGAKOV'S SPIRIT-COMPLETING TRINITARIANISM

When Lewis Ayres reviewed Weinandy's book *The Father's Spirit of Sonship*, he noted the precedent set for Weinandy's proposal by Russian Orthodox theologian Sergei Bulgakov.[70] Bulgakov's magisterial *The Comforter* concludes that the Old Testament attests the Spirit's activity everywhere but the Spirit's personhood nowhere. Not until Jesus's Upper Room Discourse (John 13–16) and the post-Pentecost church is a full-fledged person revealed: the Paraclete, of whom personal pronouns are used (John 14:16, 26; 15:26; 16:7, 13–14); the one who speaks (Acts 13:2) and grieves (Eph 4:30), prays

68. Barth, *Church Dogmatics*, III/1:106–8.

69. See Theodore James Whapham, "Spirit as field of force," *Scottish Journal of Theology* 67, no. 1 (2014): 15–32 on Wolfhart Pannenberg's use of field theory in pneumatology. As the article explicitly notes, Pannenberg affirms the Spirit's personhood (22). But one could easily modify his proposal in a binitarian direction. Badcock, *Light of Truth*, 68–73, 78, detects this danger in Augustine.

70. Ayres, review of *Father's Spirit of Sonship*, 431.

and groans (Rom 8:26), knows and seeks (1 Cor 2:10–11), and wills to distribute differing gifts (1 Cor 12:11).[71] Thus, in the economy of salvation, the Holy Spirit's hypostatic identity emerges only after the Father's and the Son's. The question of the ontological freight this fact carries has divided the church for centuries. Under Augustine's influence, the West radicalized the Spirit's status as the third person by teaching that the Spirit owes origination to both the first and the second persons of the Trinity as from a single principle: in the language of the Nicene Creed's Western recension, the Spirit "proceeds from the Father and the Son [*filioque*]." As the Spirit of both Father and Son, the Spirit serves as the "bond" (*vinculum*) of their mutual love.[72] Byzantine Patriarch Photius reacted against the *filioque* by issuing a one-sided statement of monopatrism: the Spirit proceeds from the Father *alone*, with no indication of any eternal relationship to the Son. Both these positions read only part of the data of the Trinitarian economy back into the immanent Trinity. Augustinian filioquism left the Son's dependence on the Spirit at the economic level, while Photian monopatrism seemed to do likewise with the Spirit's dependence on the Son.[73] Yet a more sophisticated Eastern stance has allowed for the Spirit to eternally rest upon the Son and manifest through him, thus transposing their mutual interdependence in the economy into the immanent Trinity.[74]

Bulgakov inherited this nuanced Eastern perspective and developed it creatively in dialogue with the West. From Augustine he took the model of the Trinity as Lover (Father), Beloved (Son), and their shared Love (the Spirit), adding that the Spirit is likewise their mutual Joy (cf. Luke 10:21). The Father eternally delights in his Son in the outgoing Spirit, who then passes through the Son and returns as the reciprocal delight of the Son in his Father to complete the "ring of love."[75] Within this model is room for the *filioque* "in a certain sense," without the Western

71. Bulgakov, *The Comforter*, ch. 3. Cf. Anthony C. Thiselton, *The Holy Spirit—In Biblical Teaching, through the Centuries, and Today* (Grand Rapids: Eerdmans, 2013), 3–160, with two qualifiers: First, *pace* p. 20, God's grieved spirit in Isa 63:10–14 is not early evidence of the Spirit's personhood; here "spirit" suggests God's inner disposition (cf. Ps 73:21), not a distinct divine hypostasis. Second, Thiselton neglects the implications for the Spirit's personhood of Acts 5:3; 13:2; 15:28.

72. Augustine, *De Trin.* 6.5.7; cf. 15.27.50. As David T. Williams, *Vinculum Amoris: A Theology of the Holy Spirit* (Lincoln: iUniverse, 2004), 15–16, notes, the exact phrase *vinculum amoris* does not appear in Augustine's *De Trinitate* but only in his *Liber de Spiritu et anima* (PL 40:820).

73. Bulgakov, *The Comforter*, 95–149, reviews the entire *filioque* controversy and condemns both sides as missing the truth about the Spirit due to pursuing it in a situation of schism, hence apart from the very Spirit of love about whom they quarreled.

74. Holders of this more sophisticated stance include Photius himself in his less lopsided comments. See Andreopolis, "The Holy Spirit in the ecclesiology of Photios of Constantinople," 158–60.

75. Bulgakov, *The Comforter*, 66–67, 70, 88, 142 (quotation from p. 67).

single-principle-of-origination theory:[76] the Spirit who proceeds from the Father passes through the Son and so is hypostatically conditioned by him. Bulgakov coupled this modified *filioque* with a complementary *Spirituque*, for the Spirit also conditions the Son by reposing upon him.[77]

For a visual illustration (though not one used by Bulgakov), one might consider the famous lithograph entitled *Drawing Hands* by Dutch artist M. C. Escher.[78] Like the two hands in the drawing, the Son and Holy Spirit each condition the other's identity, while the Father is like Escher himself, who serves as the unseen "source" of both. Like any Trinitarian analogy, this one fails if pressed too far.[79] It does, though, possess a certain patristic pedigree. Irenaeus spoke famously of the Son and Spirit as the two "hands" of God at work within the world.[80]

For Bulgakov, the Spirit's active conditioning of the Son in eternity preserves the Spirit from being a "barren hypostasis" as in the Western schema, in which the Spirit's intra-Trinitarian passivity seems subordinationistic, if not depersonalizing.[81] Thus within the immanent Trinity the Spirit is not merely the bond but the binder—less *vinculum* than *vinculator.* This hypostatic activity in eternity sets the precedent for the Spirit's economic agency as counselor, gift-giver, and (as Coakley has emphasized) intercessor.

The Spirit, then, completes the Trinity by binding Father and Son into communion, while they both in turn complete the Spirit's hypostatic profile as their common Spirit. Moreover, the Holy Spirit completes the personalization of the Godhead by hypostasizing the holy, spiritual nature shared lovingly and joyously between the other two persons. There is no divine residue that remains impersonal.[82] This giving and receiving of completeness within the Trinity warrants the Spirit's association with thirdness, the number that completes the triune life. But Bulgakov grants that the *Spirituque* relativizes this enumeration. From the standpoint of the Son's eternal reception of the Spirit, the Father is first, Spirit second,

---

76. Bulgakov, *The Comforter*, 66–67, 142 (quotation from p. 66).

77. Bulgakov, *The Comforter*, 70–73, 142, 150.

78. Before reading further, we urge readers to view this lithograph. An image is easily accessible by performing an online search using the phrase "Escher drawing hands."

79. E.g., (1) Escher's lithograph is not homoousial with him as the Son and Spirit are with the Father. (2) His two hands' agency in *Drawing Hands* is merely illusory (only Escher does any actual drawing), while within the Godhead all three persons are really active in the undivided divine agency. (3) In Escher's piece, the two hands are identical, differing only by position, whereas in the Trinity the Spirit and Son are more particularized (with the incarnate Son especially being more "fleshed out").

80. See Irenaeus, *Adv. Haer.* 4.20.1.

81. Bulgakov, *The Comforter*, 68.

82. Bulgakov, *The Comforter*, 64–67, 156.

and Son third. While the Father's primacy stays stable, the ordinals of the other two persons vary with one's angle of approach.[83] Here too the analogy of *Drawing Hands* is instructive. For though Escher remains "first" as the source of his drawing, the question of which drawn hand is second or third depends on how one "reads" the picture (e.g., from left to right or from right to left).

CONCLUSION

Having surveyed our three proponents of the *Spirituque* as well as the major objection from tradition, we are now prepared to render some conclusions on how our three interlocutors might mutually inform one another so as to commend a more biblically driven and theologically coherent version of the *Spirituque.*

Bulgakov's pneumatology clearly overlaps significantly with Weinandy's proposal while complementing it by providing both an exegetical basis for the Spirit's personhood and an Eastern adaptation of the *filioque.*[84] For his part, Weinandy outstrips Bulgakov by crediting the Spirit with conditioning not only the Son but the Father as well, yet without denying the Father's priority as the Beginning or *Archē* of the Trinity.[85] To return a final time to our *Drawing Hands* illustration: as with God the Father, the drawn hands also condition Escher since he receives his identity as the artist of *Drawing Hands* precisely by drawing these two hands that mutually condition one another. On such an understanding, the Spirit's hypostatic agency appears not only in binding but also in loosing—as Love, the Spirit unifies Father and Son, but the Spirit is also the Liberty (2 Cor 3:17) that preserves each one's unique personhood.[86] Finally, we have noted the utility of Coakley's biblical argument (selective though it is) for acknowledging the Spirit-leading nature of Christian experience, as well as the particularizing power of the Spirit within the post-Pentecost church.

By way of analogy, though not of any Rahnerian absolutism, one might infer that the Spirit fulfills a particularizing role within the Trinity itself.

83. Bulgakov, *The Comforter,* 70–73.

84. Space constraints forbid further grasping of the *filioque* nettle. For recent ecumenical reflections, see Myk Habets, ed., *Ecumenical Perspectives on the* Filioque *for the Twenty-first Century* (London: Bloomsbury T&T Clark, 2014).

85. Weinandy, *Father's Spirit of Sonship,* 73–74, 97.

86. See Colin E. Gunton, *The One, the Three and the Many: God, Creation and the Culture of Modernity* (Cambridge: Cambridge University Press, 1993), 190; likewise, McNall, *Mosaic of Atonement,* 305–08.

If that is so, then it is appropriate to entertain the idea that the Spirit participates with the Father in the Son's eternal generation, even as the Father is conditioned precisely *as* the eternal *Abba* by a Son who cries perfect, everlasting love in the power of the Spirit. In this qualified sense, the *Spirituque* remains a live option for Christian theology.

CHAPTER 7

HOLY PEDAGOGUE, PERFECTING GUIDE

The Holy Spirit's Presence in Creation

DANIEL LEE HILL

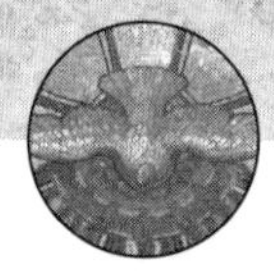

"WHERE SHALL I GO FROM YOUR SPIRIT? Or where shall I flee from your presence?" the psalmist wonders, "if I ascend to heaven, you are there! If I make my bed in Sheol, you are here" (Ps 139:7–8).[1] In these brief sentences, the Psalmist confesses that the Lord's presence and nearness is a source of great comfort for his people. Yet in so doing, the Psalmist also raises significant questions regarding the *meaning* of divine presence. What does it mean for God to be present in his world? Moreover, how can such language be meaningfully applied to the Holy Spirit, the one whom we confess as Lord and life-giver?

Traditionally, the church has affirmed that the triune God is omnipresent. And if what is true of the essence is indeed true of the Trinitarian persons, then the Holy Spirit must be omnipresent as well. Yet, at the same time, the church has affirmed that there are unique "sites" of the Spirit's presence in the temple, church, and believer. How can we conceive of these latter instances without predicating spatial categories to God? Put differently, what are we to make of the language of divine presence throughout the Scriptures, particularly as it relates to the third person of the Holy Trinity? This paper will attempt to move toward an answer through a dialogue with Basil of Caesarea. In it I will argue that a retrieval of Basil's account

1. Unless indicated otherwise, Scripture quotations in this chapter come from the ESV.

of conceptualization and his particular pneumatological points of emphasis provides a helpful resource for responding to questions of divine presence. More specifically, *I will argue that the Spirit's presence should be understood predominantly as an articulation of the Spirit's role in inscribing creation with its telos, training creation in wisdom, and guiding creation toward its ultimate end: reconciliation in Christ.* This essay will consist in three parts. First, I will give an overview of the problem of divine presence as it is raised in the work of Robert Jenson. From there, I will explore Basil's view of the Holy Spirit, focusing specifically on his approach to theological language and his emphasis on the Spirit's work as an active participant in the work of creation and sanctification, wherein the Spirit not only inscribes creation with its telos but also works within the creature to realize its true end. Finally, I will retrieve Basil's insights, arguing that language of the Spirit's presence is perhaps best understood as description of how God uses space to train creation in wisdom and providentially direct it toward reconciliation in Christ.

THE QUESTION OF SPACE

The question regarding divine presence is perhaps uniquely raised when we consider the person of Jesus Christ and the mission of the Spirit. While the church has traditionally confessed that spacetime is a creation of the triune God, it has also affirmed that God is uniquely present on earth in the incarnation. But if Jesus Christ is the condition for the possibility of the knowledge of God as well as the perfect revelation of the Godhead, and Jesus Christ exists in space, does this not then require us to conceive of God in spatial terms? After all, it is in Jesus Christ and not in Peter or Pilate that God is uniquely present.[2] Furthermore, how are we to make sense of notions of the temple and church as unique loci of the Holy Spirit's presence? Scripture seems to describe the Holy Spirit as uniquely present in the church and believer (cf. 1 Cor 6:19; Eph 2:22), at least in a way that appears to be dissimilar to his presence in the rest of creation. In order to make sense of these doctrinal commitments, are we not required to appeal to spatial categories to articulate cogently how God can be more present or uniquely present in certain locations as opposed to others?

2. This conundrum is perhaps heightened when we consider the theophanies of the Old Testament. To consider just a few examples, it is near the oaks of Mamre, the burning bush at Mount Horeb, and in the clefts of Mount Sinai that God appears to Abraham and Moses respectively (cf. Gen 18:1–5; Ex 3:4–6; 33:18–23). These texts certainly seem to indicate that God's presence is localized in these three locations on these three occasions in a way that God was not present in the clefts of Kilimanjaro, near the oak trees of Ann Arbor, or the depths of the Mariana Trench.

Robert Jenson, for his part, wonders if traditional accounts of divine omnipresence and timelessness have much to offer in response to these questions. He writes, "So we may say that God transcends space, meaning perhaps that if he is present in one place he is not necessarily absent from any other. But this tells us very little about God's actual relation to space, certainly far from enough to form any decisive part of the distinction between Creator and creature."[3] Jenson worries that such interpretations either completely divorce God from the created order or subsume the world within the divine essence in a way that obliterates creaturely integrity. Instead, Jenson proposes that we reconstruct our understanding of the Creator's relationship to creation so as to avoid obfuscating the distinctiveness of creation. "For God to create is for him to open a place in his triune life for others than the three whose mutual life he is. . . . He *makes room*, and that act is the event of creation. If creation is God's making room in himself, then God must be *roomy*."[4] This room or space is a "conversational space," since the triune persons of the Godhead and creation itself are constituted by a communal conversation.[5] Consequently, time, and by extension space, are not things that differentiate the Creator and creature; they are that which the Creator shares in common with his creature.

For Jenson, then, the Spirit is present within creation as its liberator, freeing it for a future life with God.[6] As it relates to the questions of the believer and the church, Jenson argues that the Spirit is present within the ecclesial community as *its* spirit—that is, he is its animating principle and the center of its polity.[7]

---

3. Robert Jenson, "Creator and Creature," in *Theology as Revisionary Metaphysics: Essays on God and Creation*, ed. Stephen John Wright (Eugene, OR: Cascade, 2014), 157. Jenson is not alone in this. Jürgen Moltmann writes, "In order to create a world 'outside' himself, the infinite God must have made room beforehand for a finitude in himself. It is only a withdrawal by God into himself that can free the space into which God can act creatively." Jürgen Moltmann, *God in Creation: A New Theology of Creation and the Spirit of God*, trans. Margaret Kohl, The Gifford Lectures 1984–1985 (Minneapolis: Fortress, 1993), 86. For Moltmann, God carves out space in creation, and then returns to preserve it in virtue of the Spirit's presence, preventing creation from returning to the *nihil* from whence it came and preparing it for Sabbath rest (150). See also Richard Bauckham, *The Theology of Jürgen Moltmann* (Edinburgh: T&T Clark, 1995), 184–85.

4. Robert Jenson, "Aspects of a Doctrine of Creation," in *The Doctrine of Creation: Essays in Dogmatics, History, and Philosophy*, ed. Colin E. Gunton (London: T&T Clark, 2004), 24. Elsewhere Jenson writes, "We arrive at the idea of *envelopment*: to be a creature is to be in a specific way bracketed by the life of the triune persons. . . . For God to create is for him to *make accommodation* in his triune life for other person and things than the three whose mutual life he is. In himself, he *opens room*, and that act is the event of creation." Robert Jenson, *Systematic Theology*, vol. 2, *The Works of God* (Oxford: Oxford University Press, 1999), 25. See also Robert Jenson, "Does God Have Time?," in *Essays in Theology of Culture* (Grand Rapids: Eerdmans, 1995), 190–201.

5. Paul Cumin, "Robert Jenson and the Spirit of It All: or, You (Sometimes) Wonder Where Everything Else Went," *Scottish Journal of Theology* 60, no. 2 (2007): 169.

6. Jenson, *The Works of God*, 28.

7. Jenson, *The Works of God*, 197. Earlier, Jenson writes, "The spirit of the church is the Holy

While Jenson desires to avoid appeals to substance ontology, one cannot shake the feeling that he still depicts the Godhead as the larger container that surrounds the created order. If this is the case, it seems that we quickly transition from discussing God's *mode of being* to exploring the mysteries of the divine essence itself. And it is unclear to me how such claims do not presume to possess an essential knowledge of God. Moreover, there is the worry that such spatial metaphors commit the error of projection, pushing us down the Feuerbachian rabbit hole into a land where God truly is beholden to the creature's imagination.[8]

BASIL, THE HOLY SPIRIT, AND DIVINE PRESENCE

However, in exploring Basil's Trinitarian theology with special reference to his pneumatology, it seems that we are presented with another option. But first we must stop to engage Basil on account of how language functions in relation to the divine essence. From there, we will turn to articulate his particular points of emphasis vis-à-vis the mission of the Holy Spirit before appropriating it in the task of theological retrieval.

BASIL AND THEOLOGICAL LANGUAGE

In order to understand Basil's Trinitarian theology and his approach to theological language, it is helpful to begin with his dispute with Eunomius of Cyzicus. Eunomius, in his *Apology*, claimed to possess knowledge of the very essence of God and in so doing concluded that only the Father, as the unbegotten one, was truly God. "God is the only true and only wise God because only he is unbegotten."[9] For Eunomius, the logic is rather clear. Since God is not composed of parts, we cannot claim that only part of God is unbegotten, nor can we state that there is anything else within God other than unbegottenness. Moreover, God cannot be both begotten and unbegotten, because God is one. In Eunomius's understanding, then, a commitment to both divine simplicity and unity precludes the Son,

Spirit himself" (182). For a discussion of Jenson's pneumatology and ecclesiology, see Michael Mawson, "The Spirit and the Community: Pneumatology and Ecclesiology in Jenson, Hütter and Bonhoeffer," *International Journal of Systematic Theology* 15, no. 4 (2013): 454–59.

8. Karen Kilby, "Perichoresis and Projection: Problems with Social Doctrines of the Trinity," *New Blackfriars* 81, no. 956 (2000): 442. See also Alan J. Torrance, "Creatio Ex Nihilo and the Spatio-Temporal Dimensions, with Special Reference to Jürgen Moltmann and D. C. Williams," in *Doctrine of Creation: Essays in Dogmatics, History, and Philosophy*, ed. Colin E. Gunton (Edinburgh: T&T Clark, 1997), 90–91.

9. Eunomius, *Eunomius: The Extant Works*, trans. Richard P. Vaggione (Oxford: Clarendon Press, 1987), 62–63.

who is begotten, from being divine. Divinity *qua* divinity just is essentially unbegottenness and, as a result, the Son differs from the Father on the level of being.[10]

It is important to note that a quest to stabilize theological epistemology fuels Eunomius's project: he wants to ensure that we can have true knowledge of God. Eunomius posited that our knowledge of God is immediate and that this enables theological language to be predicated of him univocally. As Andrew Radde-Gallwitz explains, "The only way theology can be meaningful is if the ontology of simple divine being is perfectly reflected in our speech about it."[11] For Eunomius, then, names grant us actual contact with essences they represent, and so to know God's name is to have God's actual essence present in one's mind.[12]

According to Basil, Eunomius errs in that he has claimed access to a kind of knowledge that is not readily available: essential knowledge. For Basil, neither unbegottenness nor any other name can exhaust the knowledge of God. Rather, the essence of God is fundamentally beyond us, and names contribute to our knowledge of God.[13] Basil argues that "unbegottenness" and "begottenness" are properties of the Father and Son, but that neither defines the divine essence *en toto*.[14] Consequently, the divine substance is something we can describe but is beyond our ability to define.[15]

So how then do we apply the names and concepts of Scripture to God in

---

10. Eunomius, *The Extant Works*, 46–47. Gregory Lee provides a helpful summary of Eunomius's argument. He writes, "On [Eunomius and Aetius'] account, the essence of God is to be unbegotten. But the Son is begotten of the Father and not unbegotten. Therefore, the Father alone is God, and the Son is not. The Son is, moreover, of a different essence (*ousia*) from the Father, which means he is actually 'unlike' the Father." Gregory Lee, "The Spirit's Self-Testimony: Pneumatology in Basil of Caesarea and Augustine of Hippo," in *Spirit of God: Christian Renewal in the Community of Faith*, ed. Jeffrey W. Barbeau and Beth Felker Jones (Downers Grove, IL: IVP Academic, 2015), 41. For an excellent discussion of Eunomius's argument in favor of limiting divinity to the Father, see Michel René Barnes, *The Power of God: Dynamis in Gregory of Nyssa's Trinitarian Theology*, repr. ed. (Washington, DC: Catholic University of America Press, 2016), 173–219.

11. Andrew Radde-Gallwitz, *Basil of Caesarea, Gregory of Nyssa, and the Transformation of Divine Simplicity* (New York: Oxford University Press, 2009), 114.

12. Richard Paul Vaggione, *Eunomius of Cyzicus and the Nicene Revolution*, Oxford Early Christian Studies (Oxford: Oxford University Press, 2000), 254. For an explanation of the origin and reasoning behind Eunomius's theory of names, see Mark DelCogliano, *Basil of Caesarea's Anti-Eunomian Theory of Names: Christian Theology and Late-Antique Philosophy in the Fourth Century Trinitarian Controversy*, Supplements to Vigiliae Christianae, (Boston: Brill, 2010), 49–134.

13. Radde-Gallwitz, *Basil of Caesarea*, 152.

14. Alco Meesters, "The Cappadocians and Their Trinitarian Conceptions of God," *Neue Zeitschrift für systematische Theologie und Religionsphilosophie* 54, no. 4 (2012): 404. DelCogliano notes, "In Basil's notionalist theory of names, all names—including proper and absolute names—do not communicate substance, but properties, often called distinguishing marks. Different kinds of names simply disclose different kinds of properties" (DelCogliano, *Basil of Caesarea's Anti-Eunomian Theory of Names*, 221).

15. Radde-Gallwtiz, *Basil of Caesarea*, 157.

a way that avoids Eunomius's error while still granting us true knowledge of the triune God? Due to our proclivity to project creaturely categories onto God, Basil suggests that we must undergo a process of "conceptualization" where our creaturely knowledge of God is refined. Basil writes, "Godly thoughts about God must be pure so far as is possible for the human mind."[16]As Dragos Giulea observes, conceptualization is "the intellectual process of identifying the distinct attributes (ἰδιόματα) of a certain class of realities."[17] For example, Basil recognizes that in ordinary language "to beget" refers to either the process of procreation or affinity of nature.[18] Instead of assuming that such language has to do with degrees of greatness or priority of existence, "begottenness and unbegottenness are distinctive features that enable identification."[19] As Radde-Gallwitz notes, "Basil is clear . . . that we need to 'purify' certain concepts, like the concepts of Fatherhood and generation or begetting, in order to grasp them rightly in the case of God. On the one hand, we apply ordinary language to God without altering its basic meaning; on the other, we must modify ordinary language to avoid problematic connotations."[20] According to Basil, we can indeed have positive knowledge of God, but this knowledge is always chastened by the reality that we can only know God, who is simple, in a piecemeal fashion.[21]

Bringing this issue to bear on our question of divine presence in general and the Spirit's presence in particular, it seems that Basil would charge us to "purify" the concept of space in a way not dissimilar from his purification of the term *begottenness*. The question we must ask is: What then is the language divine presence intended to communicate? Is such language intended to give us *essential* knowledge of God? Or something else? T. F. Torrance avers that space is perhaps better understood as the place where God meets and interacts with his world.[22] Just as Basil argued that a commonality of

16. Basil, *On Faith*, 3.94.

17. Dragos A. Giulea "Divine Being's Modulations: *Ousia* in the Pro-Nicene Context of the Fourth Century," *St. Vladimir's Theological Quarterly* 59, no. 3 (2015): 331.

18. Basil, *Against Eunomius*, 2.24.

19. Basil, *Against Eunomius*, 2.29.

20. Andrew Radde-Gallwitz, *Basil of Caesarea, Gregory of Nyssa, and the Transformation of Divine Simplicity* (Oxford: Oxford University Press, 2009), 117–18.

21. As Radde-Gallwitz observes, Basil predicates a number of terms as common to the divine substance as a whole, including but not limited to life, light, and goodness (*Basil of Caesarea*, 157–62). For example, Basil writes, "For we claim to know the greatness, the power, the wisdom, the goodness of God, as well as the providence by which he cares for us and the justice of his judgments, but not the very essence. For the one who claims that he does not know the essence does not admit that he does not know God, since our notion of God is drawn together from many things which we have enumerated" (*Ep.* 234.1.5–12).

22. Thomas F. Torrance, *Space, Time, and Incarnation* (Edinburgh: T&T Clark, 1997), 13.

power between the Son and Father presupposed a commonality of essence, so too we might argue that divine activity presupposes divine presence.[23] In other words, the language of divine presence in Scripture is intended to draw our attention to what God is *doing*, and if God is *doing* something, then he is present. Accordingly, our inquiry into the Spirit's presence in creation will turn to focus on the question of the Spirit's activity in the created world, a question that takes us back to Basil, who depicts the Spirit as the giver of life and sanctification.

THE ONE WHO GIVES LIFE

One of the primary ways that Basil describes the Spirit's presence in creation is in virtue of his activity of creating and sustaining the created world. In his defense of the deity of the Holy Spirit, Basil argues that the Holy Spirit shares in the work of creation and is therefore divine. For Basil, there is a sharp distinction differentiating the Creator from creation. He writes, "Either [the Holy Spirit] is a creature and therefore a slave . . . or else he is above creation and shares in the kingship."[24] According to Basil, if the Spirit is not numbered among the creatures, then he stands on the "Creator" side of the dividing line, sharing in the kingship and power of the Godhead.[25] However, Basil not only argues that the Spirit is to be identified with the Creator, but he also posits that the Spirit was active in the very act of creation.[26]

What then is the Spirit's particular contribution to the creative process? On the one hand, Basil affirms the inseparable operations of the Trinity, especially vis-à-vis the act of creation.[27] The triune God, Father, Son,

---

23. Basil writes, "Christ is the power of God, therefore, he is called the Unicorn on the ground that he has one horn, that is, one common power with the Father" (Basil, *Hom.*, 13.5). Michel Barnes helps to clarify Basil's reasoning, which is rooted in exegesis of Jn 5:19 and 1 Cor 2:24. Barnes explains that Basil makes "explicit the link between Christ's actions and the power that produces these actions. . . . The similarity of action testified to in John 5:19 is thus witness to the identical power that must exist to produce the common actions. And the common power means common essence." Michel René Barnes, *The Power of God: Dynamis in Gregory of Nyssa's Trinitarian Theology*, repr. ed. (Washington, DC: Catholic University of America Press, 2016), 164.

24. Basil, *On the Holy Spirit*, 20.51.48–50. Hildebrand notes that for Basil "all human beings . . . are *homotimoi*, sharing the rank of slaves before the creator. But there is no mediating rank between creator and creature, and the Spirit cannot be ranked with creatures—he is not *homotimos* with creatures." Hildebrand, *The Trinitarian Theology of Basil of Caesarea* (New York: Routledge, 2018), 96.

25. Basil, *Ep.,* 105.

26. Basil, *Hexaemeron* 2.6.

27. Basil writes, "Since, then, the Savior is the Word of the Lord, and the Holy Spirit is the Spirit from His mouth, both joined with Him in the creation of the heavens and the powers in them" (Basil, *Hom.,* 15.4). Elsewhere, we see Basil argue in a manner similar to his argument on behalf of the deity of the Son: if the Spirit shares in the creative power of God, he must also share in the essence of God (cf. Basil, *Ep.,* 105).

and Spirit, is the maker of heaven and earth. At the same time, Basil appropriates the acts of sustaining the created order and inscribing each creature with its proper telos to the Holy Spirit. As the sustainer of the created order, the Spirit "quickens" living creatures and works together with the Father and Son to ensure creation's continued existence.[28] For Basil, the Spirit gives the waters the power to produce life and "bestows firmness and steadfastness upon the heavenly powers."[29] However, not only does the Spirit sustain creation, but he also inscribes each creature with its respective telos, which is essential to the identity of each creature. Timothy McConnell avers that Basil's description of the Spirit as the perfecting cause of creation is rooted in an argument from teleology. The Spirit inscribes a telos into each creature, and this telos is essential to the substantial identity of each created thing. McConnell writes, "Following Aristotle, Basil is confident in saying that this purpose is constitutive of the essence of the cosmos. There is no essence without a purpose, no *ousia* without a *telos*."[30] Moreover, Basil argues that God's pronouncement of creation's goodness in Genesis 1 is a reflection of creation's fulfillment of the purposes that God has given to it.[31] And for Basil, the inscription of this telos is appropriated to the Holy Spirit.[32]

THE ONE WHO SANCTIFIES

However, the Spirit is present to creation not only as its creator and sustainer but also as its perfecter, drawing it into communion with God.[33] Perhaps the most lucid portrait of the Spirit's perfecting work appears in

28. Basil writes, the Spirit "quickens together with God, who produces and preserves all things alive, and together with the Son, who gives life" (*On the Holy Spirit*, 24.56).

29. Basil, *Hexaemeron*, 2.6; *Against Eunomius*, 3.4. Elsewhere, Basil describes the Spirit as the "life-giving Power" (Basil, *Ep*. 105). Timothy McConnell writes, "Basil's theology includes the Spirit in the divine act of creation and gives the Spirit a divine role in the continuous sustaining of the created order." McConnell, *Illumination in Basil of Caesarea's Doctrine of the Holy Spirit* (Minneapolis: Fortress, 2014), 98.

30. McConnell, *Illumination in Basil of Caesarea*, 103. This is not intended to imply, however, that Basil was a thoroughgoing Aristotelian. As David Robertson observes, in Basil's time the distinction between Stoic and Aristotelian had dissolved. "Basil is somewhere in between the Stoic and Aristotelian doctrines of substance, while his mind is also guided on these matters by his theological predecessors and contemporaries." Robertson, "Stoic and Aristotelian Notions of Substance in Basil of Caesarea," *Vigiliae Christianeae* 52, no. 4 (1998): 417.

31. Basil writes, "It is not to the eyes of God that things made by him afford pleasure, nor is his approbation of beautiful objects such as it is with us; but, beauty is that which is brought to perfection according to the principle of art and which contributes to the usefulness of its ends" (*Hexaemeron* 3.10). Notice here that Basil connects the "perfection" of creaturely realities with their specific telos, a perfection that is brought about through the work of the Spirit.

32. McConnell, *Illumination in Basil of Caesarea*, 104.

33. Basil, *On the Holy Spirit*, 9.23.

Basil's discussion of the Spirit's role in the sanctification of believers. Basil argues that the Spirit "teaches us who were blinded, and guides us to the choice of what profits us."[34] On the one hand, Basil repeatedly accentuates the Spirit's work in advancing the believer in piety.[35] Whether it is from dispositions of gluttony, greed, anger, or lust, the Spirit works to "liberate creation," cleansing us from vice and lifting our eyes away from corruptible things so that we might "behold the 'Brightness of the glory' of God."[36] Consequently, one's growth in piety cannot be disconnected from the Spirit's work of illumination, as he grants us the ability to contemplate God in Christ. For Basil, the Spirit "shows the glory of the only begotten, and on true worshipers He in Himself bestows the knowledge of God. Thus the way of the knowledge of God lies from One Spirit through the One Son to the One Father."[37] We might say, then, that the Spirit is the one who guides us and shapes us so that our lives are molded in the wisdom of God.

But we must remember that the Spirit is not merely the perfecter of humanity but the perfecting cause of *all of creation*. In other words, if creation is to become holy—whatever that might entail—it can do so only on account of the Spirit's presence and work. Admittedly, Basil is less interested in delineating the exact details of the perfection of nonangelic and nonhuman creatures. However, it seems that his logic must run strongly in this direction since "nothing is made holy, except by the presence of the Spirit."[38]

Traces of Divine Presence

One cannot help but notice that, for Basil, discussion of God's presence focuses predominantly on God's activity in the world. It begins with a focus on divine action, that is, the Spirit's activity in the world, and reasons backward to the reality of divine presence. In other words, we can affirm that the Spirit of God is present within the created order by paying attention

34. Basil, *On the Holy Spirit*, 19.50.

35. Basil, *Hom.*, 17.2. As Christopher Beeley notes, "Basil identifies the Holy Spirit primarily with the work of sanctification and the Christian's progress in virtue. In Basil's view, human beings fulfill their purpose to become fully the image and likeness of God chiefly through the mastery of the passions." Beeley, "The Holy Spirit in the Cappadocians: Past and Present," *Modern Theology* 26, no. 1 (2010): 96.

36. Basil, *On the Holy Spirit*, 26.64; cf. *Hom.*, 14. Elsewhere, Basil describes piety as "the groundwork and foundation of perfection (*Hexaemeron* 1.5).

37. Basil, *On the Holy Spirit*, 18.47. In wonderfully poetic language, Basil posits that Ps 45:2 refers to the Holy Spirit "because he is wise and apt teacher of all" (*Hom.*, 17.3). In another homily, he writes, "The common Director of our lives, the great Teacher, the Spirit of truth, wisely and cleverly set forth the rewards, in order that, rising above the present labors, we might press on in spirit to the enjoyment of eternal blessings" (*Hom.*, 10.3).

38. Basil, *Hom.*, 15.4.

to what God is doing in the world he created as the Spirit sustains, orders, and directs creation to the fulfill the purposes God assigned to it.

RETRIEVING AND EXTENDING BASIL'S PNEUMATOLOGY

It seems to me that Basil provides two primary goods for a theological understanding of the Spirit's presence in all of creation. First, his process of conceptualization should chasten our proclivity to predicate spatial or local language of God. Simply put, we must recognize the significant dissonance that ideas such as "space" and "locality" will retain when referring to the God who is "before all things." For our purposes, we might say that the Spirit's presence in creation does not mean that God or the Spirit "occupies space" but that the Spirit is *present to* and *active in* creation. The second emphasis builds on the first: our focus must shift from *what* to *how* in regards to the Spirit's presence in creation. In virtue of the Spirit's presence, how is he relating to the created order? Extending Basil's thought, we can describe the Spirit's presence in creation in two regards. First, the Spirit is present to creation as the one who trains and marks creation with the wisdom of God. Second, the Spirit is present to creation as the one who sustains as he directs creation to its ultimate telos: reconciliation in Christ.

HOLY PEDAGOGUE

First, then, the Spirit is present in creation as its pedagogue, training and forming creation in wisdom. In confessing that the Spirit is present in creation, we confess him as the one who inscribes creation with the wisdom of God and trains it to reflect the wisdom of God. "Observe well, [the psalmist] says, the creation, and, aided by the order in it, thus ascend to the contemplation of the Creator."[39] While Basil is clear that humans are rational animals, he seems to suggest that creation itself is marked with the wisdom of God.[40] Whether it is in the gnats, bees, ants, or stones, Basil argues that "frequently in the smallest objects the wisdom of the Creator shines forth."[41] He argues that the created world "is really the school where reasonable souls exercise

39. Basil, *Hom.*, 17.10.

40. Basil, *Hexaemeron*, 6.10. Matthew Levering is helpful here as he notes that for Basil, "Genesis focuses upon the wisdom and goodness of creation, and upon the multitudes of diverse creatures that give glory to the creator in all sorts of ways." Levering, *Engaging the Doctrine of Creation: Cosmos, Creatures, and the Wise and Good Creator* (Grand Rapids: Baker Academic, 2017), 128.

41. Basil, *Hom.*, 15.3. Earlier in this same homily Basil writes, "If you see the heavens . . . and the order in them, they are a guide to faith, for through themselves they show the Craftsmen; and if

themselves, the training ground where they learn to know God; since by the sight of visible and sensible things the mind is led, as by a hand, to the contemplation of invisible things."[42] Elsewhere, Basil notes that to hear the voice of God is to "entertain noble thoughts of God, contemplating sublimely the reasons for creation, and being able to comprehend to a certain extent at least the goodness of God's providence."[43] Creation, in a sense, is inscribed with the very wisdom of the "supreme Artificer."[44] It is for this reason that Basil encourages the saints to contemplate "the Creator in relation to the created world" in order to grow "in knowledge and praise of the Creator."[45] While Basil seems to be primarily emphasizing an anthropological point, it has clear implications for our understanding of how the Spirit is present in creation. It is the Spirit's task to communicate the knowledge of God in Christ to the believer.[46] Furthermore, for Basil, the end and final purpose of perfection is ingrained into the very fabric of creation. Consequently, if this wisdom is not merely subjectively perceived, albeit in virtue of the Spirit's aid, but *actually* present, then it stands to reason that the Spirit is writing the wisdom of Christ in the created world.

However, Basil also seems to hint that things may be taken a step further. Not only is creation intended to direct us in praise of God and is thereby indelibly marked by the presence of the Spirit, all created things, inanimate and animate, are to join in praise of God. He writes, "If there should be the noise of waters breaking against some barrier, and if the sea, thrown into confusion by the winds, should seethe and send forth a mighty sound, these inanimate creatures have voice from the Lord, since Scripture shows that every creature all but cries out, proclaiming the Creator."[47] However, we must remember that, for Basil, the Spirit enables any creature—angelic, human, or otherwise—to offer praise to God.[48] The Spirit is present in

---

you see the orderly arrangement about the earth, again through these things also your faith in God is increased."

42. Basil, *Hexaemeron*, 1.6.

43. Basil, *Hom.*, 13.4.

44. Basil, *Hom.*, 1.11. Stephen Hildebrand sees a similar theme in Basil's work, arguing that for Basil, "The behavior of animals . . . is designed by God to instruct men in the way of virtue and awe them with divine wisdom" (Stephen M. Hildebrand, *Basil of Caesarea*, Foundations of Theological Exegesis and Christian Spirituality [Grand Rapids: Baker Academic, 2014], 39).

45. Paul Blowers, "Beauty, Tragedy and New Creation: Theology and Contemplation in Cappadocian Cosmology," *International Journal of Systematic Theology* 18, no. 1 (2016): 12.

46. Basil, *On the Holy Spirit*, 9.23. See also Lee, "The Spirit's Self-Testimony," 45.

47. Basil, *Hom.*, 13.3. Later, after discussing the doxological vocation of the angels, Basil again highlights the task of both inanimate and animate creatures in offering praise to God: "Every creature, whether silent or uttering sound, whether celestial or terrestrial, gives glory to the Creator" (13.7).

48. Basil, *On the Holy Spirit*, 18.46.

creation, teaching it to offer praise to God. Admittedly, Basil does not elaborate much on this point. In fact, he could be simply stating that inanimate creation glorifies God in virtue of its being.[49] And this certainly does seem to be a theme throughout Basil's corpus. However, I believe there are grounds to think that creation's glorification of God entails more than that when viewed through the lens of wisdom. Wisdom, at least in part, involves the ability to navigate one's proximate contexts. Ephraim Radner writes, "Wisdom . . . is precisely the fruit of the life, at least one that is well ordered. Thus, the shape of a life over time is one aimed at wisdom."[50] Concerning creation, there does seem to be a grain that it *ought* to follow and a particular way that its existence *ought* to be shaped, even while it remains subjected to decay. If this is the case, the Spirit is present in creation, directing, guiding, and sustaining it in its proximate contexts. Just as the Spirit is the teacher of those who believe in Christ, we might also say that the Spirit is present in creation, training it in the wisdom of Christ.[51]

Yet, after a second glance, this only seems to be applicable to rational and semirational living creatures or, at the very least, those creatures endowed with some semblance of agency. After all, it is difficult to ascertain how a piece of granite or pile of sand might grow in wisdom. What then does it mean for nonliving creatures to be inscribed and trained in wisdom? While the Scriptures do seem to indicate that nonliving creatures offer praise to God (cf. Ps 65:11–13; Isa 44:23), we may be hard pressed to elucidate the mysteries such texts connote. After all, as Robert Spaemann notes, our understanding of the internal life of other living creatures is constrained by the limits of anthropomorphism.[52] So how then can we account for the Spirit's work in leading all of creation to glory in the wisdom of God?

---

49. Richard Bauckham writes, "All creatures bring glory to God simply by being themselves and fulfilling their God-given roles in God's creation. . . . Frogs praise God by their jumping, their feeding, their mating, and whatever else belongs to being a frog, just as much as by their croaking." Bauckham, "Joining Creation's Praise of God," *Ecotheology* 7, no. 1 (2002): 47–48. Levering makes a similar observation. Arguing from the *analogia entis*, he posits that all of creation, from rocks to dinosaurs, glorifies God in virtue of its existence. He writes, "Rather than being useless, dinosaurs and galactic systems are *theophanic*: in their finite actuality, they point to the creator who is pure act. . . . Everything points to God, participates in God, and glorifies the wondrous activity that God is" (Levering, *Engaging the Doctrine of Creation*, 138).

50. Ephraim Radner, *A Time to Keep: Theology, Mortality, and the Shape of the Human Life* (Waco, TX: Baylor University Press, 2016), 125.

51. Basil, *Against Eunomius*, 3.4

52. Robert Spaemann posits, "We can, of course, never know what it is like to be a bat. We can only understand the question by analogy, from knowledge of what it is like to be a human being, or, more precisely, what it is like to be *this* human being." Spaemann, *Persons: The Difference between "Someone" and "Something"* (Oxford: Oxford University Press, 2006), 30. Paul Griffiths is also helpful here in calling into question our sentimental proclivities to project our mental states

For our purposes, it might be helpful to think of nature's participation in the glorification of God along symphonic lines. Consider, for example, a snare drum, consisting of a rawhide covering stretched across and latched to a wooden shell. When the rawhide is struck with a hand or drumstick, a series of sounds ring forth, sounds which are ordered and measured to make music. However, those sounds, and the subsequent performance that they will comprise, do not seem to be reducible to either the drumstick, the hand, or the snare drum. Rather, the sound emerges from the encounter between the wood of the drumstick and the canvas of the drum. Additionally, in order for a *proper* sound to emerge from the drum, it is not enough for the drummer to merely *perceive* the instrument in a particular way. Switching sections, from percussion to strings, a cello's strings must be properly tuned and the appropriate amount of rosin must be applied to the bow in order for the instrument to realize its telos. It is not enough for the cellist to subjectively appreciate the instrument, but a change must take place in the objects themselves. Recognizing the limits of analogy, then, it seems that we can say that the Spirit is the one who affects this change; he "tunes" the animate and inanimate objects that comprise the creaturely orchestra so that starry hosts and limestone alike can in fact "declare the glory of the Lord" (Ps 19:1). And for those galaxies and comets which blink in and out of existence without being perceived by the human eye, we would do well to remember how the angels themselves offer a "Spirited" praise, as the diversity of creation leads them to worship the wisdom of the Creator (cf. Rev. 4:11). In the event that any such praise is taking place, we recall from Basil that it is only in virtue of the Spirit's work that any creature, living or otherwise, is given a voice whereby it might rightly participate in the praise of God. In essence, the Spirit is creation's maestro, enabling it to become "well-pleasing to God" and leading it in worship of its Creator.[53]

---

onto the inner life of non-human creatures. He writes, "It is a mistake because we have no idea what that inner life is like even where there is, or may be one, and we deceive ourselves if we think we do. Even those nonhuman animals most physiologically like us . . . are still deeply different from us physiologically, so different that we can imagine little or nothing of the quality of their sensory experience, and still less of their affective or intellectual life, should they have one." Griffiths, *Decreation: The Last Things of Creatures* (Waco, TX: Baylor University Press, 2016), 284.

53. Basil, *Against Eunomius*, 3.2. Colin Gunton is helpful here, in noting that while creation is currently able to praise God, it awaits its glorification and it is only in that glorification that creation can offer its maker the right kind of praise. "Creation praises its maker, as it is; yet without healing it cannot praise its maker as universally as it should do." Gunton, "The Spirit Moved Over the Face of the Waters: The Holy Spirit and the Created Order," *International Journal of Systematic Theology* 4, no. 2 (2006): 197.

PERFECTING GUIDE

Second, the Spirit is present in creation as its perfecting guide. Here, we extend Basil's discussion of the Spirit's role as the agent of sanctification to describe how he works to cleanse and purify creation from corruption, readying it for eschatological rest. In other words, in stating that the Spirit of God is present in creation, Christians confess that the Spirit is providentially at work in his world, directing creation toward its telos: reconciliation in Christ (cf. Col 1:20). For Basil, creation is teleological and can only be understood teleologically.[54] This is evident in Basil's discussion of the goodness of creation in Genesis 1. Throughout the creation account, God repeatedly observes that his creative work "is good." For Basil, this communicates a divine affirmation of creation's suitedness to accomplish the ends for which it was created.[55] However, the realization of the creature's purpose and telos is fundamentally dependent upon the work of the Spirit. As McConnell notes, "Human beings, like the rest of creation of which they are a part, are measured in goodness by their orientation toward their proper end. They are helpless in being directed toward their proper end, as in fact all of creation is helpless in being oriented toward its proper end, without the Spirit of God."[56] All of creation is intended to experience reconciliation with God, and it is the Spirit of God who enables this telos to be realized. While, as Ian McFarland rightly cautions us, we must maintain a healthy level of agnosticism regarding the degree to which God's glory is manifested in the perfection of mayflies, cicadas, and echidnas, we do see glimpses throughout the Scriptures of creation lamenting the futility and corruption to which it has been subjected (cf. Rom 8:20–21) and ultimately rejoicing in the consummated victory of God in Christ (cf. Isa 55:12).[57] The Spirit actively sustains creation in being and directs it toward this future consummation, the end for which it was created. Gunton writes, "We must say that through his Son and Spirit . . . the Father both prevents creation from slipping back into the nothingness from which it came and restores its teleology, its movement to perfection."[58] The Spirit of God guides creation toward the realization of its telos and ensures that it can be what God has created it to be.

The Spirit, as creation's perfecting cause, is the one who works to bring

54. Blowers, "Beauty, Tragedy, and New Creation," 16.
55. Basil, *Hexaemeron*, 3.10; cf. McConnell, *Illumination in Basil*, 118.
56. McConnell, *Illumination in Basil*, 120.
57. Ian McFarland, *From Nothing* (Louisville: Westminster John Knox, 2014), 135n1.
58. Gunton, "The Spirit Moved," 198.

creation into a place of eschatological rest. On the one hand, the Spirit works to communicate the blessings of divine providence, as God actively upholds the integrity of the created order and directs it in faithful care.[59] Yet more than that, the Spirit leads creation onward, directing it toward the realization of its telos. Robert Wilken notes that for Basil the work of God's creation *ex nihilo* implies that there is a particular telos toward which creation is intended. He writes, "Beginning also implies end, not only in the sense that the world will come to an end, but that its created was directed to a 'useful end.' Basil recognizes . . . that creation is an ongoing work of God, and the world is providentially ordered by God's guiding hand."[60] While the providence of God in the present is a confession of faith and seems to be clouded in mystery, particularly in a world that appears to swarm with chaos, Basil reminds us that created things are headed in a particular direction and it is the Spirit's presence that both undergirds the creature's existence and ensures the realization of this telos. Ultimately, the Spirit is creation's guide and his presence testifies to the fact that God has not abandoned his world and is committed to faithfully caring for it.

DIVINE PRESENCE AS COMMUNICATIVE PRESENCE

As John Webster reminds us, "The centre of theological concern, we might say, is less the physics of space or the poetics of space than the 'economics' of space, its significance in God's ordered administration of created reality."[61] Questions regarding the nature of divine presence ought to be developed with an eye and ear toward the communication of the blessings of divine providence to his creatures. With Basil, then, we can restrain any proclivities to capture divine presence with the creaturely categories of space and time. Rather, in saying that God's is present in creation, we focus on a much more fundamental claim: God the Father, with his two hands of Son and Spirit, is providentially sustaining the created world as he prevents it from slipping into nothingness, directs it toward eschatological rest, and trains and conforms it in divine wisdom. Creaturely space, as Webster reminds us,

---

59. John Webster writes, "Indeed, providence is in a certain way the special dimension of Christian belief in God the creator, because it specifies the act of creation as the beginning not simply of contingency but also of faithful care." Webster, "Providence," in *Christian Dogmatics: Reformed Theology for the Church Catholic*, ed. R. Michael Allen and Scott Swain (Grand Rapids: Baker Academic, 2017), 157.

60. Robert Louis Wilken, *The Spirit of Early Christian Thought: Seeking the Face of God* (New Haven, CT: Yale University Press, 2003), 142.

61. John Webster, "The Immensity and Ubiquity of God," in *Confessing God: Essays in Christian Dogmatics II* (New York: T&T Clark, 2016), 105.

serves as the realm in which the omnipresent Creator affirms the distinction of his creation while enabling the creature to be confronted with the saving reality of God in Christ. "In him all creaturely places are reordered, by being claimed with the full authority of the one who is Lord of heaven and earth, as the spaces in which we are to discover the presence of God."[62] It seems, then, following Webster, that when the Christian confesses the Spirit's presence among creation she is affirming a form of communicative presence, that is, the Spirit of God's active communication of the blessings of redemption and providence to the created world.[63] The Spirit directs creatures in wisdom so that they can navigate their proximate contexts and reach their intended ends. The Spirit brings creatures into being, inscribes them with their telos, and trains them in wisdom. But more than that, the Holy Spirit is also the Spirit of perfection, that is, the Spirit guides the created world away from corruption and away from futility to a place of rest, enabling it to participate in its ultimate purpose: the worship of God.

62. Webster, "The Immensity and Ubiquity of God," 106.

63. There are some similarities here with Michael Horton's observation that the concepts of divine presence and absence are less focused on ontological categories, and more on ethical or relational categories. See Michael Scott Horton, *Lord and Servant: A Covenant Christology* (Louisville: Westminster John Knox, 2005), 12.

CHAPTER 8

". . . AND THE FELLOWSHIP OF THE HOLY SPIRIT"

The Relational Nature of the Spirit in God and Humans

ESTHER E. ACOLATSE

SOMETIMES I THINK WHATEVER Christians may conceive and debate about what constitutes "the sin against the Holy Spirit," surely it must be or include the fact that the communion-forming, relationship-desiring aspect of the Godhead is thought of as one who strikes dread and portends division among Christians. It was not so long ago that Christians could easily pass for "Binitarians," a notch above Unitarians in the way they think of and speak about God. In ecclesial settings Christians talk about God the Father, express gratitude to and for Jesus our Savior, and then shuttle between the two in worship. Even when at Pentecost we bid the Spirit come, he seems a third wheel. It is almost as if the third person of the Trinity, the eternal gift and giver and of the gifts of God's people, was not from the beginning. Even now I fear that he has moved from the margins of our afterthoughts to the foreground in a most inappropriate way. He has become the "new show" in the theological town.

If I am honest, my presentation is probably one more attempt to do inadequate pneumatology. But perhaps there is a sense in which our inabilities to capture and frame what should be a proper theological aesthetic of the Holy Spirit is in order. It is rather difficult to paint an adequate picture of the Holy Spirit and perhaps appropriately so because the seeming elusiveness of the third person of the Trinity is forewarned in the Scriptures. The Spirit blows where it wills and shows up in various ways shape and form in the Scriptures. But at least we can try not to misrepresent the Spirit and thus do bad theology, and I am afraid that some of the works on the Spirit in our day is veering in that direction. In exploring the relational nature of the Holy spirit in God and humans, I am attempting to call attention to the ways in which we might already be doing some bad theology because we paint a false picture of the Spirit, especially in our account of how the Spirit works in and relates to human beings.

First I will explore the relational nature of the spirit within the triune God in Scripture by attention to aspects of Trinitarian and christological thought arguing for a Trinitarian pneumatology and christocentric pneumatology in tandem as the properly way to understand and speak about the relational nature of the Spirit in God. I will then ask questions of how that relationality allows us, if at all, to know how the Spirit relates to human beings. In this my primary conversation partner beyond Scripture is John Levison, who has written comprehensively about the Holy Spirit and the human spirit and about the Spirit's presence in the world. Levison is also my theologian of choice because he speaks from and to many sides of the theological aisles and has been engaged, especially by Pentecostal theologians,[1] which is key to locating him on any and everything pneumatological.

Before I continue to lay out what I hope to share in our time together, or better still what I hope you will hear and come to know, I want to borrow from Augustine, whose language—or attempts to put into language—about the nature and substance of the triune God speak to my own attempts. *Condiffidence* (at the border of confidence and diffidence) is the operative word here. This is what Augustine says:

> From now on I will be attempting to say things that cannot altogether be said as they are thought by a man—or at least as they are thought by me. In any case, when we think about God the Trinity we are aware that our thoughts are quite inadequate to their object, and incapable of grasping him as he is; even by men of the caliber of the apostle Paul he can only be seen, as it says *per speculum in aenigmate* (I Cor 13:12). Now since we ought to think about the Lord our God always, and can never think about him as he deserves; since at all times we should be praising him and blessing

1. See conversations between John Levison and Pentecostal theologians on the Spirit in *Pneuma* 33, no. 1, Brill (January 2011).

> him, and yet no words of ours are capable of expressing him, I begin by asking him to help me understand and explain what I have in mind and to pardon any blunders I may make. For I am keenly aware not only of my will but of my weakness. And I also ask my readers to forgive me, wherever they notice that I am trying and failing to say something which they understand better, or which they are prevented from understanding because I express myself so badly; just as I will forgive them when they are not able to understand on account of their tardiness.[2]

NATURE OF GOD IN TIME AND SPACE

Time, space, and essence/substance is how we refract relationship and relationality, and it makes sense to think of God from whom we acquire personhood and relationality as occupying time and space and having essence.[3] In the beginning we observe this time and space as the bookends within which God operates even if we think of eternal time and limitless space. One cannot say anything substantive about the nature of God without speaking about God as person and what is meant by persona and substantia. Thankfully we have two chapters that have fleshed out this concept at length.[4]

In both the Old and New Testaments, there is a sense that no real conversation about "the spirit," whether in relation to God or to humans, is without the three, so we cannot talk about the Spirit without reference to the Trinity. I begin this conversation, or conversation starter, then with a recap of what I think the church from millennia has been teaching about the Trinity. For the church, God is three persons, and the third person, the Holy Spirit, might be seen as the third term that holds the relationship of the Godhead together. What does it mean or look like when the church declares in her creedal statements that we believe in God the Father Almighty and in his Son, and then we add on belief in the Holy Spirit? How is the Holy Spirit related to the Father and Son within the one Godhead? What does it mean when we say that the Spirit is gifted to the world or the

---

2. Augustine, *De Trinitate* 5.1.1 (Corpus Christianorum Series Latina 50, p. 207; Edmund Hill translation, p.189), cited in F. B. A. Asiedu, *From Augustine to Anselm: The Influence of* De Trinitate *on the* Monologion (Turnhout: Brepols, 2012), 265.

3. Theologically, to speak of God *in se* is to speak of a being outside and above time. The immanent God, the God we know, however, has shown himself to us in time, "In the beginning" (Gen 1:1), and then in a particular time and place in the Son in the fulness of time.

4. The chapters in this volume by Fred Sanders and Lucy Peppiatt give attention to what can be known about God as triune persons.

church from the Father and the Son? How are we to read Jesus's words to the disciples about the Spirt he will send, who at the same time is himself coming back to them to be with them. If this is the salvific presence of the second person, we might be speaking about the Son again, and maybe practically speaking (and you might throw your Bibles at me if you like), we are, as I have already suggested, "Binitarians" rather than "Trinitarians," but that is for another time.[5] These are legitimate questions that hide in the corners of our ecclesial psyches that we may elide for now because we also know the scriptural testimony is of Father, Son, and Spirit. How they are related, especially how the Spirit relates to the two and even what we mean by "spirit" of God, may continue to exercise our theological muscles.

Reading the Spirit in the Triune God: Pitfalls and Fallacies Along the Way

Approaches to the study of the Holy Spirit in the past have been fraught with two problems. One problem has to do with ignoring a deep Trinitarian basis of the work of the Spirit in the world. This omission is, I think, usually an attempt to accommodate religious pluralism and to understand the work of the Spirit beyond ecclesial spaces and beyond the Christian religion. But in doing so, we almost elide the Christian notions of God as "triune" and as "person." We come dangerously close to panentheism in a bid to see the Spirit of God everywhere often collapsing the divide between Creator and creation. I'll say more about this later.

The second problem that we have in how to understand the Holy Spirit is that we forget that we cannot properly speak about the Spirit without grounding the work of the Spirit christocentrically—that is, a strong Christology is required for a good pneumatology.

While I invite us to ground pneumatology in both the Trinity and Christology, I am aware of the questions that such a move can raise. For instance, the whole church[6] does not agree on the understanding of the Godhead as three in one, recall here unitarians as well as strands of the apostolic denomination, which are yet a part of the church if we are not to dabble in the murky waters of the "invisible and visible church."

5. Unitarians and some strands of Apostolic tradition come to mind in this regard.

6. I note here the old understanding of the "visible and invisible" church in Augustinian theology and ecclesiology and even the push back against this way of viewing the church by people like Collin Gunton who situate the doctrine of the church in the communion of the Trinity. See his *Theology through the theologians: Selected Essays 1972-1995* (Edinburgh: T & T Clark, 1996).

Secondly, our Christologies are also not so clean cut—we are still those who debate and divide over the nature of Jesus, whether he is one or two natures.[7] Additionally, even when we have overcome the tensions between Logos Christology[8] and Spirit Christology[9] and see both in tandem as the properly way to conceive the relation of the Son to the Father, our theology still stalls. The very notion of the Son as birthed of the Spirit, from the Spirit, undergirded by the Spirit in his earthly life and ministry, troubles the idea of the procession of the Spirit from the Father and the Son "worshiped and glorified," as our creedal statement stands. Never mind that now we have the Spirit here in the world, the Son a glorified body with the Father where . . . well, where God is, which is also everywhere. But we will not linger here. For now I just raise the issues to suggest that even when we speak about God and God's inner relationality from what we assume to be the perspective of true and tried orthodoxy (whatever that may be), and when we do so with faithful persuasion, we intuit that we do so as those who indeed see through a glass dimly, until we see and are seen face to face.

Yet we probe these ideas as an act of obedience as those who seek after God, to know and to love and to serve. So we keep searching and speak tentatively yet courageously. What I share is part of what and where I have been excavating. The terrain is large, so I draw insights largely from Scripture and how the Scriptures have been utilized to uncover the relationship among the Godhead and how the Holy Spirit relates to humans and operates in the world. In this task I speak as an African Christian who has lived half my life in Africa and the other in the West—Ghana and North America in particular. I speak thus from and to the theologies of these ecclesial spaces with an eye to what we can learn about life in the Spirit and the work of the Spirit in the world and in our day. In spite of these many caveats offered about the limits of Trinitarian and christological basis of the relationality of the Spirit in God and humans, however, I reiterate, the way to avoid the double pitfalls of pneumatology mentioned earlier is to ground pneumatology in Trinity as well as in Christology. Let me explain.

---

7. For example the Eastern and Western churches differ on how they see how the divinity and humanity of Christ coinhere.

8. Here we conceive the Son as proceeding in the eternal Word of the Father.

9. The Son emanates from the Spirit: "For us and for our salvation he came down from heaven: by the power of the Holy Spirit he became incarnate from the Virgin Mary, and was made man". (Nicene Creed)

THE RELATIONALITY OF THE TRIUNE GOD IN THE SCRIPTURES

There is a Trinitarian concept of the work of the Spirit in the world throughout the Scriptures. The work of the Spirit in the world is seen in both creation and incarnation. Long before the church, the relationality of the Spirit with the Father and the Son is circumscribed by the work of creation and redemption. The Spirit of God is from the beginning seen birthing the cosmos out of chaos and is at one with the triune God as the world is called forth into being with the Word without whom nothing was made that was made. We need to understand that the Trinitarian basis of the work, according to the Scriptures, transcends the bounds of Israel and the church. Yet we have to be careful that in our bid to accommodate a theology of religions and pluralism, we do not speak in ways that circumvent Christ, undercut the Trinity, and make nonsense of our pneumatology.

The procession and mission of the Spirit in the world is in the incarnation, in salvation and sanctification, and in final consummation. So when we speak from a Trinitarian basis about the work of the Spirit in the world in time and space, which is our starting point according to the Scriptures, we see the work of the triune God in its cooperation and in appropriation.[10] In creation and salvation and transformation of the whole world, it is the Spirit of God and of the Son "gifting" the creation with life and new life, respectively and together.

The relationality of the triune God is seen in God's relationship with the material world.[11] The Spirit of God has always been in cooperation with the material, never repudiated nor set aside but always with.[12] But this "withness" is, in the same way as the inner relationality of the triune God, present with yet distinct from. Father, Son, and Spirit are always present with each other and yet distinct in function from each other in their work and their relation to the world.

As Catholic theologian Jacques Dupuis notes, when we ground the work

10. We allude here to the Thomist Doctrine of Appropriation in which all three persons are involved in the acts within the economy while cognizant of the personal mode of each Trinitarian act by a particular person of the Trinity.

11. When Paul speaks of the resurrection and describes the one and the other as a sowing in the ordinary body but rising as spiritual body, he places spirit and body together not in opposition.

12. It is in Gnostic thought that we find the break between God, conceived as spirit, and the world not in Hebraic thought. Even in indigenous religions such as African Religions, the Supreme Being and the spirits are almost at one with all creation.

of the Spirit in the world in the Trinity, we avoid three common errors.[13] Two are pertinent to our discussion. The first is that which puts Christ and God in opposition, thus rendering either a theocentric or christocentric approach to pneumatology, and the second, a pneumatology that valorizes the role of the Holy Spirit over that of Jesus Christ as if the Holy Spirit is not, in Johannine theology, the salvific presence of the risen Christ. One only has to attend to the liturgy of much charismatic/Pentecostal worship to encounter this anomaly. Thus not only do we require a pneumatology grounded in the Trinity, but we also need to ground it in Christology. When we do, we uncover the relational nature of the Spirit in the Godhead.

A CHRISTOCENTRIC PNEUMATOLOGY

The relational nature of the spirit in the Godhead is not only embedded in the Trinity but in many ways a matter of the relationship between the Son and the Spirit. The incarnation is the primary point of the relationship between the Son and the Spirit. The Spirit of God, not an independent spirit, overshadows Mary. In our creedal statement, conception takes place of the Holy Spirit. God thus through God's Spirit incarnates the Son, and even when we try to speak of the relationship of the Spirit to the Son, it is impossible to do so without thinking and speaking Trinitarian language. From birth to the resurrection and beyond, Jesus is both the gift and giver of the Holy Spirit. The inseparable unity of the Father and the Son is also with the Son and the Spirit. At the same time the incarnate Son was also spirit so that we have a relation of Son and Spirit. The insights of *The Shepherd of Hermas* are helpful here:

> The Holy Spirit which pre-exists, which created all creation, did God make to dwell in the flesh which he willed. Therefore, this flesh, in which the Holy Spirit dwelled, served the Spirit well, walking in holiness and purity and did not in any way, defile the spirit . . . for the conduct of this flesh pleased him, because it was not defiled while it was bearing the Holy Spirit on earth. (Herm. Sim V, 6:5–6)

Clearly what we see here is an intimate and inseparable union between the Son and the Spirt fashioned by God. Notice that the Spirit dwelt in the

13. Jacques Dupuis, *Toward a Christian Theology of Religious Pluralism* (Maryknoll, NY: Orbis, 1997), 206.

flesh, the spirit enfleshed in the incarnation. This concept of the unity of Son and Spirit is extended in the work of Bishop Theophilus of Antioch (c.169) in his three books to Autolycus.

For Bishop Theophilus, Logos—the eternal Word that in the beginning (John 1)—combines with the Spirit of God (Gen 1) and Sophia (Prov 8:22) together with the power of the Most High (Luke 1:35) imbue and speak through the prophets about God's acts in creation.[14] Thus in God, *pneuma* and *logos* exist in inseparable unity, and this *pneuma* is also *sophia*, the Spirit of wisdom, and in Johannine theology, the Spirit of truth who returns to the church and the world the truth who is Jesus. Always the Spirit and the Logos eternally coexist, the Son incarnate by the power of the Spirit, the same Spirit in turn is the gift from the Father whom the Son requests for us, and at the same time the Spirit is for the Son to give to us. So how are they related again?

The Relational Nature of the Spirit in Humans

So far, we have indicated the proper way to understand the relational nature of the Holy Spirit in the Godhead is to think both in terms of Trinity and Christology. Our explorations indicated that if we are wise, we speak with muted tones and never dogmatically about this inner relationality because we know only in part. As Anselm ponders, speaking of the relation of Father and Son,

> For the Father and the Son are so distinct that when I speak of both I see that I have spoken of two yet, what the Father and the Son are is so identical that I do not understand what I have called two. For although the Father, considered distinctly, is completely the supreme spirit, nevertheless the spirit who is Father and the Son are not two spirits but one. Thus, just as the properties which are unique to each do not admit of plurality because they do not belong to both, so what is common to both constitutes an individual oneness even though the whole of it belongs to each.[15]

14. Theophilus of Antioch, *Ad Autoclycum*, trans. Robert M Grant (Oxford: Clarendon, 1970), 39ff (2:10).

15. Anselm, *The Monologion* 1.59–60, in *A New Interpretative Translation of the Monologion*, trans. Jasper Hopkins, pp. 157–59, cited in F. B. A. Asiedu, *De Trinitate in From Augustine to Anselm: The Influence of the Trinitate on the Monologion* (Turnhout: Brepols, 2012), 359.

In this regard, we are in the realm of mystery, notes Anselm.

The same Trinitarian and christological considerations need to be brought to bear on the relationship of the Holy Spirit in humans, including the idea that even here we might be in the realm of mystery. And yet not mystery in the sometimes opaque way that it presents in the relationship with the Godhead. We are not in the same semidarkness about how God relates to human beings, and we can take the existence of such relationship for granted, as well as take for granted that the Spirit of God communes with humans since we have various proofs.

First, if we know anything about God and the inner workings of the Godhead laid out in Scripture by the prophets and apostles, we owe it to the inspiration of the Holy Spirit. And we understand inspiration regarding the Scriptures and their reception as emanating from the corporation of the Holy Spirit and the human spirit. If we can have knowledge *ad extra* from the Scriptures about the Godhead as explored and taught by the abbas and ammas of the faith—and even as we gathered here at the conference seek—we owe it to the presence and fellowship of the promised Holy Spirit to lead into truth. (John 14ff)

Second, what we have is based on promise. Jesus promises the Holy Spirit to his disciples before his death and underscores. If we read John correctly, this in fact was himself in Spirit (John 16:12–24). Pentecost ushers in the Holy Spirit and by doing so the inception of the church as we know it. Acts 2 sets the tone to envision what the presence of the Holy Spirit and his relationship with humans would be. A powerful and active spirit that collapses hierarchies (unlike what is depicted in the Old Testament where he graces kings, priests, and prophets) and binds all humans together as recipients of God's grace. At the least we come to understand that everyone can be addressed by God and respond to God. The Spirit is not an exclusively Christian possession as we well know (there is no such thing as Christian flesh; flesh is flesh), for "the Spirit blows where it wills." But in what way is the Spirit of God in relation with humans, Christians or otherwise, and should such a distinction be even considered? What is the nature of that relationship? To ponder . . .

If to date we are still finding our way in the terrain of the relationality of the Holy Spirit in the Godhead via the Scriptures and theological explorations, at least we are not scratching our heads as we do so. I find that it is an entirely different matter to walk the terrain of how we talk about the nature of the relationship between the Holy Spirit and humans. Some of the pneumatology in our day and seeing how the relationship of the Spirit with the human spirit is to be construed makes for rather troubling reading. The kind of ineffable plurality we find in the relationship of Father and Son and in Son and the Spirit, where we cannot quite tell where one begins and the other ends, which can be ascribed to mystery, becomes almost confusion bordering on idolatry in how we speak of the relational nature of the Spirit in humans. Some of our pneumatology, whether in popular culture, church, and the theological academy, both in Africa and the West, lacks a thoroughgoing biblical perspective. What we have, across the board among the numerous "theologies of the Spirit" in our day, describes anything but the Holy Spirit of God. In many instances the conversation runs along denominational lines and theologies or along North-South lines,[16] a signal that we are talking about anything but *the* communion forming Spirit of God. The expression of what is assumed to be the presence of the Spirit of God operating in humans, under the guise of "led by the Spirit," goes beyond biblical literalism to bizarre behaviour that causes harm to self and others.[17]

THE SPIRIT IN POSTMISSIONARY AFRICAN CHRISTIANITY

Nowhere more than in the church in Africa, where church historians valorize numerical growth and the church celebrates the explosion of Christianity, do we encounter what amounts to a divisive spirit of divination touted as the Spirit of God. The emphasis is on signs, sounds, and wonders. And since congregants seek this, the need of pastors to supply what seems more like voyeurism accounts for some of the growing numbers. There is a demand for what amounts to divination, in the form of "visions" and "word of knowledge" from individual members to indicate that the pastor (often referred to as the "man of God") is filled with and operates with the "Spirit of God." There is insatiable demand for pastors who can indicate a direct line to God. Many of them act as covert comediators with Jesus, and sometimes may wield more power than him for access to God. We need to sound a cautionary note and ask that people hold the "Hallelujahs!" on the explosion of Christianity on the continent. In our day, the turn to pneumatology in the theological guild may be a sign of hope for a needed

16. See a fuller account in Esther Acolatse, *Powers, Principalities, and the Spirit: Biblical Realism in Africa and the West* (Grand Rapids: Eerdmans, 2018).

17. Appalachian snake handlers come to mind here.

corrective (this conference is one such sign), but how do we ensure that it does not become one more academic exercise where we dabble in theologology (talking about talking about God) rather than talking about and relating to God and, in this instance, the Spirit? I find it amazing and quite lamentable that in Africa, where life is refracted theologically and everything operates at the level of "spirit," little has been written about pneumatology of or for the church. On the other hand, all over the place on the Western academic front we see theologies of the Holy Spirit abound with hyperattention to the third person of the Trinity, even when the need or evidence of such attention is not indicated in our ecclesial spaces.

In a recent book, Anthony Thistleton has given us a useful sketch of pneumatology from various authors ranging from biblical times through the epochs of the church to today.[18] While his comprehensive survey covers numerous authors and themes about the Holy Spirit, I think the scholar who has attended most to the spirit in the twenty-first century is John (Jack) Levison. He paints for us what I see as a new aesthetics of the spirit.

The New Theological Aesthetics of the Spirit: Engaging the Work of Levison

Everything we know about the Spirit of God in the Scriptures indicates that there can be no exact description of who he is and no way to paint an adequate picture of the acts and signs of his presence for all time.[19] The Spirit blows where it wills (John 3:8) and shows up in various ways, shapes, and forms both in the Scriptures and in the work of various theologians today. Some theologians, however, suggest that they have down pat what and who he is and how one should think about the Spirit, while noting the ineffableness of the Spirit and his work. John Levison is one theologian who has written extensively on the spirit and has engaged theologians across the ecclesial aisles as he tries to help people grasp what the spirit is doing at the personal private and corporate public spheres. This makes his work available to many and one can easily see him as the go to modern theologian for all this on the Spirit, and rightly so.

Levison is to be commended for wresting the Holy Spirit from Pentecostalism and its ecclesial expression, where sometimes pneumatology

---

18. Anthony Thiselton, *The Holy Spirit—In Biblical Teaching, through the Centuries, and Today* (Grand Rapids: Eerdmans, 2013).

19. In much of this section, I draw on my previously published work, *Powers, Principalities, and the Spirit.*

is freighted to the point of making Jesus otiose. His careful exegetical work on the language of the Spirit and spirits, including the relationship of the Holy Spirit to the human spirit, spans Old Testament, New Testament, and intertestamental periods. It is rather troubling that with such laborious exegetical work, his insights and conclusions leave us wondering whether the Spirit he offers us bears any real resemblance to the Holy Spirt, the third person of the Trinity. In spite of how close he stays to the biblical narrative in his analysis of the Spirit, which covers Israelite, Jewish, and early Christian ideas, and has received acclaim from Pentecostals and non-Pentecostals alike, he demonstrates that he is a product of his time. Excavating the foundational, postfoundational, nonfoundational, and postmodern approaches to analysis and interpretation of the Scriptures, many of us land right back at the large feet of modernity, with its insistence on weeding the supernatural from biblical accounts.[20] Such is the case with Levison's aesthetic of the Holy Spirit.

At first blush, Levison's description of the Holy Spirit, which he offers through painstaking exploration of both Old Testament and New Testament Scriptures and extra biblical historical data as presented in *Filled with the Spirit*, helps us overcome the extreme dualism of the Holy Spirit especially as it is conceived in the churches in the Global South. Yet the way he refracts the work of the Spirit in and through us ultimately conflates the two moments of the work of the Holy Spirit and eventually conflates the human spirit and the Holy Spirit.

Since Levison's analysis on this important theme of the Spirit and the relational nature of the spirit in human beings (and it is not quite clear to what he refers here, whether human spirit or Holy Spirit as in the third person of the Trinity) has had acclaim from Pentecostals and non-Pentecostals alike, he deserves careful consideration because his work could have far reaching consequences for the whole church in their understanding of the Spirit, I think, in the way that the long arm of Bultmann's demythologizing tugs at how we hear and interpret Scripture today.

His exegesis and interpretation of the work of the spirit in humans draws on key biblical antecedents as in the examples of characters like Daniel and Joseph and their rare gift of dreams and dream interpretation, as well as the differing but great prophetic gifts of Micah and Isaiah, to name a few. We know these characters and their stories—I don't have to fill you in. The presence of the spirit in these characters, Levison avers, is not something

20. Acolatse, *Powers, Principalities, and the Spirit*, 216.

that comes from outside of them. It is rather a reifying of what always existed in them when the occasion called for it.

There is no doubt that humans are spiritual beings, have spirits though they are not spirit as in the third component of their being, and that God's Spirit undergirds humans as embodied souls. This spirit thus allows for facility in how humans live. Additionally, there are charisms, and in both theological and psychological parlance we speak of grace-given gifts, some of which certain individuals wield to perfection. Levison gives us examples from well-known characters in the Bible as evidence of this point: Daniel and Joseph in their gift of dream and interpretation are notable examples. For Levison, what is going on with Joseph and Daniel in their giftedness is definitely the work of the spirit, but it is not the working of the spirit that comes upon them from outside of them and who then exits the scene and returns, it is not an imbuing with but a residing in. The difference between Daniel and Joseph (and he would later refer to some prophets) and other humans, it seems, is the extent to which individuals have allowed for the cultivation of the particular skill with which they have been gifted and which the spirit (sometimes holy spirit in all lowercase letters) stirs in them. The question we need to ask is whether the breath of God in humans is the same as the Holy Spirit, the third person of the triune God? What exactly is this spirit sometimes described as holy with a lowercase *h*? Levison is clear that Israel's literature does not make any such distinctions, so we should not either.

When one carefully examines Levison's work, one is left wondering about several holes in his argument and exegeses of key passages, as well as his exploration of events dealing with the spirit. Of special concern is his understanding of Luke's account of Pentecost in Acts as well as the meaning and evidence of what being filled with the spirit entails or what is going on with the slave girl with whom Paul has a confrontation and out from whom he subsequently casts a spirit of divination. While most mainstream Evangelicals and Pentecostals would see two differing spirits and powers at work in this confrontation, Levison sees the same spirit at work in different ways in the two key players and eventually interprets the imbuing with power at Pentecost and the glossolalia through the lenses of the Delphic cult.[21] For him it is mainly ecstatic behavior not uncommon to the region. At the end, we are left with a Holy Spirit that is not supernatural and that we cannot distinguish from the human spirit. Of course,

21. John R. Levison, *Filled with the Spirit* (Grand Rapids: Eerdmans, 2009), 321, 325–35.

he is right in cautioning against the tendency toward both rationalism (West) and extreme supernaturalism (Global South). We have to be vigilant against falling into either of the traps set for navigating the hermeneutical issues attendant to what the Scriptures mean by the work of the Spirit. Yet the way Levison is framing the questions, and the vision he is casting for theological engagement with the world picture painted in the strange world of the Scriptures, is in real danger of expelling the supernatural completely from the character and account of the Holy Spirit. He is thus in some ways closer to Durkheim than to Bultmann, whom we can be certain most evangelical theologians would normally critique and blame for the legacy of demythologizing the Scriptures, which still dogs biblical interpretation to date.

Part of the problem lies in the fact that the way we do systematic theology has left us thinking quantitatively about the Godhead; the Trinity as three persons in one has us in a bind. So whether we are doing Christology or pneumatology, we find ourselves stuttering around how to say what we mean because the terminology is bound up in the doctrine of God, which we have already parsed quantitatively. That problem and its ramifications loom large in Levison's account of the Holy Spirit in *Filled with the Spirit*. It is such that while his analysis and insights that cover this important theme in Christian theology is intriguing, he assimilates things that are not there as such, and in the end we are offered at best an ordinary mysticism of the Holy Spirit in association with the human spirit. But this offering is not adequate to the biblical data in which the Holy Spirit, or the Spirit in the Old Testament (that is, the Spirit of God), breaks in upon people and gives them power to do extraordinary things, such as the apostles' miracles, exorcisms, and the preaching of the gospel with signs and power after Pentecost in Acts. Indwelling and miraculous acts still accompany the work of many a preaching of the gospel in the Global South.[22]

Ultimately, as I argued and articulated earlier,

> Levison's account offers us an ordinary notion of the Spirit, at once common, real and indefinable and what leads to a domesticated ordinary mysticism, generic and thus problematic. It seems appealing and gentrified to fit the mood of the age. This account of the Holy Spirit seems appealing and updated to fit the mood of the age: a Spirit that bothers no one

22. This is indicated with a caveat that there are many charlatans and much Simonism going on that plagues Christianity in the Global South.

> and whom no one really need bother with if they do not want to—even though always somehow present.[23]

It allows people to be spiritual and not religious and especially to eschew Christianity and the demands of the gospel in their lives yet hold themselves out as Christian in the public sphere if need be. The real far-reaching implication of his conclusion is that refining the human spirit with the presence of the Spirit at work in humans is all that is required to fulfill God's purposes.[24] It would imply then that redemption is not really necessary. A stretch maybe, but perhaps not. It is for this reason that an inadequate pneumatology ultimately makes for bad theology, because we would not have the Son. How then do we account for the Father in the economy and therefore speak of the God we know?

The Fellowship of the Holy Spirit: General and Particular

If the way Levison narrates the relationship of the Holy Spirit with the human spirit is not theologically adequate, what is the nature of the relationship between the Holy Spirit and humans? No doubt there is Trinitarian theology of the Spirit at work in the world, and Levison is right in calling our attention to the ways in which God acts through peoples across time to fulfills God's purposes. We note that in the Scriptures even across religions if we are paying attention.

There is legend about a Sufi mystic: Rabe'a al-Adiwiyah, a great woman saint of Sufism, was seen running through the streets of her hometown, Basra, carrying a torch in one hand and a bucket of water in the other. When someone asked her what she was doing, she answered, "I am going to take this bucket of water and pour it on the flames of hell, and then I am going to use this torch to burn down the gates of paradise so that people will not love God for want of heaven or fear of hell, but because He is God."[25]

23. Acolatse, *Powers, Principalities, and the Spirit*, 6.

24. I think part of the problem with our understanding of the nature of the relationship of the Spirit in humans may be due to a faulty anthropology. The concept of the tripartite being inherited perhaps from Hellenistic thought is peripheral to the New Testament, but we have erroneously given it a central place in our theology. When we talk about the human spirit, we talk as though it were a tangible reality on its own, as the Spirit is a tangible person of the triune God. This is a large issue with the notion of the human spirit and the Spirit in African Christianity as well, which I have tried to address elsewhere. See Acolatse, *For Freedom or Bondage? A Critique of African Pastoral Practices* (Grand Rapids: Eerdmans, 2014).

25. Cited in Patrick J. Ryan, SJ, *Amen: Jews, Christians, and Muslims in Dialogue* (Washington, DC: Catholic University of America Press, 2018), 40.

But why would a theologian like Levison, who might be assumed to be even bibliocentric, draw the kind of conclusions he comes up with, those which seem to go against the Scriptures. I think there are likely two reasons: one is modernity and the critical method of interpretation of Scripture. In this regard we have all drank the Bultmannian Kool-Aid (or draft of beer). Embedded in Levison and approaches like his is the problem of modernity. While we eschew the extreme supernaturalism of the Global South, there is the loathing to acknowledge that there is another spirit in the world opposed to the Holy Spirit. There is the loathing to own and account for personal evil or sin for which atonement and therefore the Son was necessary. It is to refuse to acknowledge as that there are four dramatis personae in the theatre of the world's stage. Somehow it may even mean that the Spirit won't have much to do. But is not the Spirit to cause us to fall in love with Jesus and thereby to be drawn to God because of the Son's task to draw us to the Father? Is it also possible there is a fuller desired end of the work of the Spirit in humans that is more than the sanctification of believers for their sake but for the ultimate end of returning all peoples to Edenic communion anticipated in the second creation account?

Second, in our day, diversity and pluralism has birthed a political correctness and civility that I think is hurting the church. Sure, we need to pay attention to the religious other and even learn from them, but we cannot tiptoe around the clarity of the Scriptures about chosenness and election and God's personal relationship with specific groups and peoples within larger groups. Not even the failure of the nineteenth- and twentieth-century Western missionary enterprises should cause us to cower and not say that there is an intimate, promised fellowship between the Holy Spirit and the called people of God to which others are not and cannot be privy and that their relationship is predicated on mutual giving and receiving of love emanating in obedience on the part of the believer (John 14:23). So while there is the general Trinitarian work of the spirit in the world, there is a particular communion of the Holy Spirit, an intimate supernatural fellowship of the Spirit with believers. The nature of this relationship looks like everything the Son the giver promised. If we follow the promise of the Johannine farewell discourse, we know that he is both comforter and sanctifier and that his life in us separates us from the world. He convicts us of sin, of righteousness, and of judgement so that we do not do these on our own and act more harshly with ourselves than God would. He is sanctifying to ease the way of recovering sinners so they can raise their eyes Godward. He is the one who carries us in prayer when we cannot know even how to pray aright (Rom 8:26). Above all, he is our seal (2 Cor 1:21–22; Eph 1:13–14) for the day when we are drawn finally into God. Our life with him now is practice time for eternal presence of God. Meanwhile, the in-filling, as Jesus promised, is like a well that can last us for the long haul. Our spiritual hunger and thirst organs are attached to a wellspring that is self-generating. Our work is simple: get close, drink deep, and find it true. Now that's a doxological moment.

CHAPTER 9

THE SPIRIT OF THE LORD

Reflections on a Christomorphic Pneumatology

LUCY PEPPIATT

ANYONE FACED WITH THE TASK of writing on the Holy Spirit will immediately be confronted with the challenge of where to start, which direction to go in, and how to shape their thinking. It is no longer true to say that pneumatological reflections among theologians are few and far between or that the Spirit has been dismissed as the lowest, the least, or the last. Work on the Spirit abounds. There is now a wealth of literature and hundreds of resources on the Spirit representing a profusion of perspectives on pneumatology.[1] Theologians reflect on the Spirit in creation, in culture, in the arts, in science, in other faiths, in the workplace, in the public square, and in the search for the common good.[2] But how we

1. There are too many works to mention here, but it is worth noting that theologians working on the Spirit come from a huge variety of perspectives and denominational commitments. Work on the Spirit is being done in both theology and biblical studies, from Pentecostal, Orthodox, charismatic, and Roman Catholic perspectives, among others. At times this springs out of a commitment to a greater understanding of the Trinity, at others it is linked to an exploration of Spirit Christology, and with still others it comes out of an interest in how a theology of the Spirit might inform Christian life and understanding both inside and outside of the church.

2. Again, publications are now numerous. For a few examples of this, see Daniela C. Augustine, *The Spirit and the Common Good: Shared Flourishing in the Image of God* (Grand Rapids: Eerdmans, 2019); Sigurd Bergmann, *Creation Set Free: The Spirit as Liberator of Nature* (Grand Rapids: Eerdmans, 1995); Luke Bretherton, *Christ and the Common Life: Political Theology and the Case for Democracy* (Grand Rapids: Eerdmans, 2019); Steven R. Guthrie, *Creator Spirit: The Holy Spirit and the Art of Becoming Human* (Grand Rapids: Baker Academic, 2011); Kirsteen Kim, *Mission in the Spirit: The Holy Spirit in Indian Christian Theologies* (Delhi: ISPCK, 2003); Jürgen Moltmann, *The Spirit of Life: A Universal Affirmation* (London: SCM, 1992); Eugene R. Rogers Jr., *After the Spirit: A Constructive*

identify this or that specifically as a work of the Spirit in all these spheres is a challenge. It might be claimed that signs of life, renewed life, order out of chaos, sacrificial love, joy, and peace are always signs of the Spirit. Or forgiveness of an enemy, reconciliation, or liberation of the enslaved or oppressed may be signs of the Spirit. Could we claim, perhaps, that the Spirit is at work when we see creativity in any form, truth-telling, discovery, medical breakthroughs? We might be able to do so, but none of the aforementioned are the preserve of the church or Christians *per se*. So one might struggle to prove that this or that is the work of the Spirit of the triune God where the Holy Spirit is never acknowledged and/or there is no mention of the Father and the Son in or behind the work. However, one might also be hesitant to *deny* that a certain thing is the work of the Spirit in the world on the grounds that the Spirit is at work, upholding life in all of creation. If "the earth is the Lord's, and all that is in it, the world and those who live in it" (Ps 24:1), then it should not surprise us that theologians seek evidence of God's involvement in what properly belongs to him. Thus, perhaps unsurprisingly, pneumatology can be a somewhat general and nebulous topic.

In this paper, however, I wish to focus on a specific New Testament claim that the Spirit at work in the world is the Spirit of Christ, whose mission is to bear witness to Christ in order that those who believe in Jesus would also witness to him as Lord and Savior. Jesus promises his disciples, "When the Counsellor comes, whom I shall send to you from the Father, even the Spirit of truth who proceeds from the Father, he will bear witness to me." He goes on, "And you also are witnesses, for you have been with me from the beginning" (John 15:26–27). In reflecting on the work of the Spirit from this perspective, I am not sure there is a lot to add that is new as such. I do, however, think that there is something about this claim that bears continual reflection in service of the process of discerning what it means for the church to be filled with the Spirit, to walk in the Spirit, to pray in the Spirit, and to follow the leading of the Spirit if this is, indeed, the Spirit of Christ. If the Spirit that we are speaking of is "another" who is not Jesus Christ but is also one with Christ, and whose mission is to follow after him, to witness to him, to speak of him, to lead to him, to glorify him, and to unite humanity to him, incorporating human beings into his

Pneumatology from Resources outside the Modern West (Grand Rapids: Eerdmans, 2005); Michael Welker, ed., *The Spirit in Creation and New Creation: Science and Theology in Western and Orthodox Realms* (Grand Rapids: Eerdmans, 2012); Amos Yong, *Hospitality of the Other: Pentecost, Christian Practices, and the Neighbour* (Maryknoll, NY: Orbis, 2008).

body, then what do we expect this might look like and what are some of the implications of this for church life and practice (John 14:12, 26)? There is, thus, a two-fold orientation of the Holy Spirit: the Spirit of truth, who witnesses to the truth of the Son, and the Spirit within humanity, who bears witness to the individual that she too is a child of God in the Son and so is united to the body of believers in one new humanity. The one who is witnessed to from within by the Spirit then becomes a witness to the world as to what she has seen and now knows to be true. Reflections on the relation of Christ and the Spirit inevitably lead us to anthropology in some form or other.

Up until this point, I have spent much of my time researching Spirit Christology—Christologies in which the Spirit is constitutive of the person and work of Jesus of Nazareth. I am persuaded that the gospel narratives compel us to give an account of how Christ, who promises the sending and baptism of the Spirit once he has been glorified (John 7:39), is also the one who is conceived by the Spirit, grows in the Spirit, is baptized in the Spirit, and is thus himself the bearer of the Holy Spirit. It is this Spirit who anoints him, sends him, comforts him, leads him, and empowers him throughout his earthly ministry. And even beyond that, the resurrected Christ teaches the disciples "through"' the Holy Spirit before he is taken up (Acts 2:1). Yves Congar is correct, therefore, to remind us that there should be no Christology without pneumatology. However, he famously completed this maxim with the plea that there should also be no pneumatology without Christology. Thus I welcome the opportunity to attempt to think through the Spirit-Christ relation from the other direction, as it were.

As I have noted, there are multiple ways we can approach the subject of the Holy Spirit. In this paper I first examine how we might understand some of the New Testament claims regarding the relation of Christ and the Spirit before turning to the task of exploring how this relation then shapes our understanding of the work of Christ and the work of the Spirit in the world. As an exercise in how Christology might shape pneumatology, I examine how particular modern perspectives on Christology affect our understanding of the work of the Holy Spirit and argue that only a Christic pneumatology characterized by the unity and distinction of Christ and the Spirit will prevent us from a one-sided or reductionist account of God at work in the human condition.

On the question of how we speak of the Spirit, I wish to say in the beginning, as a disclaimer, that I am uncomfortable both with gendered and neuter pronouns for the Spirit. Neither *he*, *she*, or *it* is adequate, and none of them expresses exactly what I would like to say of the Spirit. But as Augustine pointed out many years ago, the language of persons is there so that we are able to say something rather than nothing, and so for the sake of communicating the personal nature of the Spirit I will sometimes use *she* and sometimes *he* with the caveat that neither is correct as such.

THE SPIRIT OF CHRIST

The New Testament clearly bears witness to the Spirit as the one who belongs to Christ. We read of the Spirit of Jesus (Acts 16:7), the Spirit of Christ (Rom 8:9; Phil 1:19; 1 Pet 1:11), the Spirit of the Lord (where clearly referring to Jesus; Luke 4:18; 2 Cor 3:17), and the Spirit of the Son (Gal 4:6). By focusing specifically on the relation of Christ and the Spirit in this paper, it is not my intention to ignore the place or role of the Father. Jesus speaks to the disciples of the Spirit of "your Father" (Matt 10:20). The discourses in John's gospel communicate the unity of the Father and the Son who both are also one with the Spirit (John 15:26; 16:12–15). And Paul's letters tell the story of a triune God in Christian experience and prayer (Rom 8; 1 Cor 12:4–6; 2 Cor 1:21–2; 13:14; Gal 4:6; Eph 2:20–2; 5:18–20). There is, in Scripture, the basis for the inseparable operations of the Father, Son, and Spirit, and to some extent all reflection on Christ and the Spirit has the Father in view, although time and space will limit this discussion to the second and third person. Similarly, there is much to add in relation to the Spirit in the Hebrew Bible, but again this too is for another time. For the sake of brevity, therefore, I just take one aspect of the triune life presented to us in the New Testament, namely, the coinherent missions of the Son and the Spirit to the world, how the persons who are sent relate one to another in the creaturely realm, and what that tells us of the nature and work of God.

That the Spirit referred to in Acts and the Epistles is the Spirit of Jesus Christ is not really a contested claim and has even led some to see the two as coterminous in some way. James Dunn famously argues for the closest possible identification of the post-Pentecost Spirit with the risen Christ. He writes, "For Paul christology becomes a controlling factor in pneumatology. Paul takes it for granted that the Spirit of God is known now only by reference to Christ—'The Spirit of Sonship' voicing Jesus's prayer, 'Abba Father' (Rom. 8:15), the Spirit known by the confession 'Jesus is Lord' (1 Cor 12:3), the Spirit who transforms us into the image of Christ (2 Cor 3:18)." He concludes, the "Spirit can now be defined as 'the Spirit of Christ' (Rom 8:9; Gal 4:6; Phil 1:19)." And out of this close identification of the Spirit and Christ goes on to claim that this Spirit "must be measured against the pattern of Christ crucified (2 Cor 4:7–5:5; 13:4; Phil 3:10–11)." He extends this identification of Christ and the Spirit to Christian experience where he sees a "strong degree of synonymity . . . (particularly Rom. 8:9–11 and 1 Cor. 12:4–6); it is in Christian experience of the divine that Christ and the Spirit are one; Christ experienced not independently of the Spirit but through and *as the Spirit*."[3]

Dunn's work raises the question of how closely exactly we identify the Spirit with Christ. *That* Paul identifies the Spirit with Christ, however, is largely uncontested and leads to various conclusions. Victor Pfitzner draws out two positive aspects of identifying Christ and the Spirit in relation to soteriology and Christian experience with reference to Pauline Christology. First, he writes that a Christic understanding of the Spirit prevents pneumatology "degenerating into vague spiritism that is divorced from the Gospel and the triune God who creates, redeems and sanctifies." Second, in relation to experience, he makes the point that "Paul's emphasis on the communal reception of the Spirit will provide a hedge against the absolutization of individual experience, and against any temptation to divorce individual charism from communal good."[4]

NAVIGATING UNITY AND DISTINCTION

Exegetically then, we are propelled in the direction of the identification of the Spirit with Christ in a way that will speak of the unity of the Son and the Spirit, perhaps particularly in relation to Christian life and experience. However, in addition to this, it is also in the economy (i.e. how God is revealed to us and how we come to know him) that we see a distinction of Son and Spirit in the second and third persons. The Spirit is not united to flesh, is not also fully human, is not the image of God, is not the firstborn over all creation. The Spirit is not crucified, is not resurrected, is not at the right hand of the Father, and will not come again in glory. This is the work of the Son. The Spirit is Lord but is not the Messiah, the Anointed One, the Savior—though the Spirit's work in humanity is a saving work.

---

3. James D. G. Dunn, *The Christ and the Spirit*, vol. 1, *Christology* (Edinburgh: T&T Clark, 1998), 17 (italics added).

4. Victor C. Pfitzner, "'The Spirit of the Lord': The Christological Focus of Pauline Pneumatology," in *Starting with the Spirit*, ed. Stephen Pickard and Gordon Preece (Hindmarsh: Australian Theological Forum, 2001), 116.

It is not the Spirit who is our pattern for Christian living, nor the prototype of humanity. The Spirit is not the Son. Similarly, there are aspects of the Spirit's work that are peculiar to the Spirit. The Son is not like the wind that blows where it wills, does not come as a dove and tongues of fire, is not poured out on all flesh. Of course, the inseparable operations of the Trinity allow us to claim that all the works of Christ and the Spirit are perichoretically the work of the one God in the world. But what we know of the economic distinctions of the Son and the Spirit matter. They tell us something profound of the nature of God, how he communicates with humanity, and how we come to know him, and of the destiny of humanity as ones who will participate in the divine nature as adopted children of God through the Son in the power of the Spirit.

Early reflections on the Trinity emphasize both the one essence of God as three persons and resist an overemphasis on the synonymity of the Spirit with the risen Christ that we find especially in Dunn's work. They consistently make the point that in the Spirit we are confronted with one who is "another" with the Father and the Son. Just as the Word *is* God and is *with* God, the Spirit is *one* with the Son and *another* with the Son. Irenaeus articulates this with a picture of the Spirit as one of the two hands of the Father, thus evoking a sense of the equal and coordinated but distinguishable work of the Spirit and the Son.[5] Basil writes in defense of the divinity of the Spirit, a task which would clearly not be necessary unless the Spirit had been perceived to be "another" (in this case, by those who saw the Spirit as another unlike the Father and the Son).[6] The amendments to the creed in 381 add the third article; the Spirit is also the Lord, the giver of life, worshiped and glorified together with the Father and the Son. And Hilary and Augustine write extended reflections on the three-in-one God. In all these early theological deliberations we see that christologically and Trinitarianly there is always a delicate balance between unity and distinction in descriptions of the Godhead, and I imagine there will always be a temptation to emphasize one more than the other.

Comparatively recently there have been a number of voices calling for a recognition of the person and work of the Spirit as distinguishable from the Son. In this, the Western tradition is often cited as a culprit in diminishing the personhood of the Spirit and collapsing distinction into unity. It is well known that Augustine is sometimes fiercely criticized, in my view unfairly,

---

5. Irenaeus, *Against Heresies*, 5.6.1.
6. Basil the Great, *De Spiritu Sancto*.

as not only diminishing the hypostatic individuation of the Spirit himself but also then handing this down as a Western legacy.[7] Vladimir Lossky, among others, criticizes the Western church for what he sees as a lopsided and detrimental ecclesial Christomonism attributable, in his view, to both Augustine and the *filioque*.[8] I am aware, of course, in discussing the relation of Christ and the Spirit, of the shadow of the *filioque* disagreement; however, I would prefer to bracket the debate for now.[9] The historical marginalization of the person and work of the Spirit no doubt has multiple causes. However, whether primarily attributable to dogmatic commitments or other factors, it is worth mentioning the hazards associated with a strong account of the identification of the Spirit with Christ and why there is some nervousness on the part of those who wish to maintain a distinction.

If one of the problems is the swallowing up of the personhood of the Spirit, another might be the instrumentalizing of the Spirit's work in relation to Christ, a criticism which is again levelled at the Western tradition. Hendrikus Berkhof criticizes certain Reformed accounts as instrumentalizing the Spirit, where the Spirit's task is limited merely to the application of "the salvation obtained by Christ to [hu]mankind."[10] With reference to Calvin's *Institutes* (3.1), Berkhof writes, "The Spirit is customarily treated in noetical, applicative, subjective terms. He is that power that directs our attention to Christ and opens our eyes to his work. The main result of his work is the awakening of faith in Christ."[11] In one sense, there is nothing

---

7. Colin Gunton is known for his criticism of Augustine and his legacy in what he sees as a diminished understanding of the Spirit as "person" in the West. See also Thomas Weinandy, *The Father's Spirit of Sonship: Reconceiving the Trinity* (Edinburgh: T&T Clark, 1995) in which he criticizes both Western and Eastern traditions for obscuring the personhood of the Spirit. Lewis Ayres addresses this and rebuts this critique in *Nicaea and its Legacy: An Approach to Fourth-Century Trinitarian Theology* (Oxford: Oxford University Press, 2004).

8. See Vladimir Lossky, *The Mystical Theology of the Eastern Church* (Crestwood, NY: St Vladimir's Seminary, 1976), 64. Also Lossky, "The Procession of the Holy Spirit in Orthodox Trinitarian Doctrine," in *In the Image and Likeness of God* (Crestwood, NY: St Vladimir's Seminary, 1985), chapter 4. D. Lyle Dabney also identifies the *filioque* as a culprit of the subordination of pneumatology to Christology in Reformed theology attributing this as the cause of the failure of the Reformers to articulate the role of the Spirit in the life of Christ as well as in the life of the Christian post-Pentecost. See D. Lyle Dabney, "Naming the Spirit: Towards a Pneumatology of the Cross" in *Starting with the Spirit*, ed. Stephen Pickard and Gordon Preece (Hindmarsh: Australian Theological Forum, 2001), 28–58, 33.

9. Despite criticisms of the Western tradition, I am not fully persuaded that a doctrinal commitment to the *filioque* on its own led to the neglect of the Spirit in doctrinal and ecclesial life in the West. Augustine's insistence on the coequality and coeternality of the Spirit is clear, affirming as he does, the full divinity of the Spirit. He also emphasizes the material manifestation of the Spirit (as the dove who alights on Jesus and the tongues of fire that alights on the disciples), which I see as laying the foundations for a unique mission. So I imagine there are many forces at play when the church fails to recognize one aspect of the truth that has been handed down from previous generations.

10. Hendrikus Berkhof, *The Doctrine of the Holy Spirit* (London: Epworth, 1965), 21.

11. Berkhof, *The Doctrine of the Holy Spirit*, 23.

wrong with identifying this as a primary work of the Spirit. This appears to be where the New Testament data leads us. I agree with Berkhof, however, that one of the ramifications of these initial claims is a subsequent assumption that the work of the Spirit is thus "merely instrumental." Berkhof summarizes this Reformed characterization of the Spirit in the following: "[The Spirit] himself wants to step back and to remain hidden in order to give way to the encounter between Christ and man. So the Spirit is a second reality beside Christ, but entirely subordinate to him, serving in the application of his atoning work, in the realization of justification by faith."[12]

So in working out how the Spirit is the Spirit of Christ, there are some things I would want to avoid: (1) the modalism associated with the synonymity of the Spirit with the risen Christ, (2) the instrumentalization of the Spirit as simply a function of God's salvific act in Christ, (3) any subordinationist accounts that ignore the Spirit's coequality and codivinity with the Son and the Father, including those that emphasize the "hiddenness" of the Spirit in favor of the prominence of Christ.[13] I do not see any evidence in the New Testament for the claim that the Spirit is hidden and self-effacing, always only pointing away from himself as is sometimes claimed. Jesus teaches his disciples that they are to wait for another who will clothe them with power from on high. The coming of the Spirit is not hidden but occurs in plain view, causing Peter to have to explain to the ones who see the ensuing chaos that those who have received the Spirit are not drunk! Just as the Spirit descended on Jesus as a dove, he now descends again on the gathered disciples, only this time with tongues of fire signifying cleansing, refining, power, and the presence of God in an unprecedented way. The Spirit fills the disciples, empowering them from that moment forward to obey the Great Commission with courage and boldness. The Spirit speaks and inspires speech, in tongues, praise, prophecy, and preaching. There are healings and miracles as well as martyrdom, persecution, imprisonment, and conflict. Neither the Spirit *nor* the disciples

12. Berkhof, *The Doctrine of the Holy Spirit*, 23.

13. Lossky writes, "Roman Catholic and Orthodox theologians agree in recognizing that a certain anonymity characterizes the Third Person of the Holy Trinity. While the names 'Father' and 'Son' denote very clear personal distinctions, are in no sense interchangeable, and cannot in any case refer to the common nature of the two hypostases, the name 'Holy Spirit' has not that advantage. Indeed, we say that God is Spirit, meaning by that the common nature as much as any one of the persons." Lossky, *Image and Likeness*, 74. Lossky himself gives a nuanced account of the hiddenness of the Godhead in relation to Orthodox apophaticism and the ineffable nature of God. I find, however, that this theme of the "hiddenness" of the Spirit is often adopted in relation to the idea that the Spirit points away from himself to Christ reminiscent of the instrumentalization of the Spirit referred to above.

are very hidden or self-effacing. The Spirit of Christ who is sent after the Son has ascended appears to be far more troublesome than that.

There is a hiddenness in the Godhead in a different sense that not only applies to the Spirit but also is seen most clearly in the incarnation, where the presence of God is so veiled that only those given eyes to see can see what is in front of them. The eyes of faith are a gift from God, and all those who believe have to believe without "seeing" as it were. God as Father, Son, and Holy Spirit is both veiled and made manifest in this world, but this is not a property peculiar to one person of the Trinity (John 20:29).

So as Berkhof points out, the Spirit is more than "an instrumental entity, the subjective reverse of Christ's work." His "coming to us is a great new event in the series of God's saving acts." In favor of this reading, John Barclay makes the point that although Paul presents an inseparable connection between Christ and the Spirit, he (Paul) also coins the phrase *pneumatikos* and *pneumatikoi* as a distinctively Pauline expression to describe the people of God. This term occurs fifteen times in 1 Corinthians and nine times elsewhere, more than the term *Christians*. Christ's people are not just Christians, they are "spiritual" or the "Spirit-people." Thus Barclay brings out the uniquely Christian meaning of this term, which is not "in origin an anthropological but an eschatological term: it describes people not through analysis of their human constitution but in relation to their new status as graced by the Spirit of God." It is a status conferred on them by the reception of the Spirit. "Thus the term is self-consciously new . . . in the sense that Paul employs it to designate a reality not hitherto attested because it describes a state of affairs believed to be wholly without precedent."[14]

THE WORLD OF THE SPIRIT

What we see in the New Testament witness are two narratives of the Spirit. In one, the work of the Spirit is a continuation of the work of Christ, and Christ is always present. The Spirit points to Christ, leads to Christ, and witnesses to him. In the other, there is more to say about the Spirit than that the Spirit is merely Jesus Christ in another mode of existence. There is a unity and a distinction that somehow we need to articulate. For this, I will borrow from Berkhof. Berkhof first brings out the inextricable connection

14. John M. G. Barclay, "Πνευματικός in the Social Dialect of Pauline Christianity," in *The Holy Spirit and Christian Origins: Essays in Honour of James D. G. Dunn*, ed. Graham N. Stanton, Bruce W. Longenecker, and Stephen C. Barton (Grand Rapids: Eerdmans, 2004), 157–67, 161.

between Jesus and the Spirit in the economy with the claim that the "work of *Jesus* is the *content* of the Spirit's work."[15] He goes on, however, with a further claim that the Spirit "creates a world of his own." I understand that this latter phrase might be the cause of a worry that the Spirit is deemed to be some kind of "free agent," for want of a better expression. However, if we hold the two claims together, then the world that the Spirit creates cannot be separated from the work of Christ. It must be an instantiation of the kingdom inaugurated by the King, Jesus. Furthermore, what I like about this phrase is that it does capture something of Jesus's claim in John 3 that the Spirit "blows where he wills" and the statement in Acts 13:2 where Luke tells us that the disciples heard the Spirit say, "Set apart for *me* Barnabas and Saul for the work to which *I* have called them." The Spirit creates the world that shapes the church, the body of Christ, and this is work properly appropriated to him.

Berkhof describes this world in the following: "a world of conversion, experience, sanctification; of tongues, prophecy, and miracles; of mission; of upbuilding and guiding the church, etc. He appoints ministers; he organizes; he illumines, inspires, sustains; he intercedes for the saints and helps them in their weaknesses; he searches everything, even the depths of God; he guides into all truth; he grants a variety of gifts; he convinces the world; he declares the things that are to come."[16] This is all the work of the Spirit—more than an instrument and more than just a function of the risen Christ. This is the Spirit who is not really hidden at all but who nevertheless extends the mission of the Son in the world, which has now become the Spirit's mission. This work is extended so that there will be greater works done throughout history than those done through the Messiah in first-century Palestine, but works, nevertheless, done in the name of Jesus and with the stamp of his character upon them (John 14:12). On the experience of the Spirit among the early Christians, Barclay writes, "Once the new and overwhelming experience of God in early Christianity was interpreted as the presence of 'the Spirit,' it was natural that this term [*pneumatikos*], and its adjectival derivative, would play a prominent role in Christian discourse. Since Paul places particular emphasis on 'the Spirit' as the source of eschatological life, the medium of knowledge, and the criterion of morality, it is not surprising that he, and those influenced by his thought, should find themselves speaking of things which characterize

15. Berkhof, *The Doctrine*, 22.
16. Berkhof, *The Doctrine*, 23.

their new life as πνευματικά."[17] In terms of the economy then we could take these two complementary phrases from Berkhof: the work of Jesus (and one could add the Father) is the content of the Spirit's work as the Spirit also creates a world of his own emerging from this work that is peculiar to the Spirit. In the second half of the paper, I wish to explore how these two ideas together might form the basis of a rich and complex pneumatology in relation to the human condition.

A Christomorphic Pneumatology

If the work of Jesus is the content of the Spirit's work, then what does that tell us of where and how we might see the Spirit at work in the world? How might the person and presence of the Son shape the post-Pentecost person and presence of the Spirit? It becomes immediately obvious that linking the work of the Spirit so closely to Christ does not necessarily limit the conversation in very meaningful ways as much as it merely raises the questions of "Whose Christ?" and "Which Christ?" for which, of course, there are multiple answers. We could take this pneumatological principle in many directions; the fact that there are endless Christologies that could then inform a given pneumatology means that narrowing the field is a challenging task.

I do, however, want to explore a particular example of how Christology and pneumatology might be mutually constitutive and thus have chosen to focus on kenosis in relation to Christ, examining how well this can be mapped on to pneumatology. In addition, I will explore how a focus on the Spirit might inform our view of kenosis. I have chosen this theme for a number of reasons. First, because kenosis appears to be a persistent theme in modern Christologies, and while I appreciate some of the insights of those committed to a kenotic Christology, I see some problems of definition and method that I think bear further discussion.[18] Secondly, for the most part, kenotic Christologies appear to be worked out with little reference to the Spirit. However, where a kenotic theme has been applied to pneumatology, because of initial problems with the christological accounts, I am not convinced that this works well, so I wish to consider this move.

17. Barclay, "Πνευματικός in the Social Dialect of Pauline Christianity," 165.

18. There are a number of prominent theologians who have taken up the cause of kenotic Christology/theology including C. Stephen Evans, Stephen Davis, Ronald Feenstra, and David Brown among others. For a collection of essays on the topic from different perspectives, see C. Stephen Evans, ed., *Exploring Kenotic Christology: The Self-Emptying of God* (Oxford: Oxford University Press, 2006).

Some kenotic Christologies are much more nuanced than others, and it is impossible to do justice to them all, so I will attempt to sketch out some of the predominant themes of kenotic Christology under which most of the accounts coalesce with a view to exploring how this gives shape to Congar's maxim. I hope that introducing a kenotic perspective on pneumatology and a pneumatic perspective on kenosis will give us a more balanced view that will succeed in retaining some of the gains of a kenotic account while addressing certain weaknesses and presenting a faithful account of the New Testament data.

KENOSIS AND THE SPIRIT

In my view, there are some positive developments coming out of the modern emphasis on kenosis. The term is now used in a much broader sense than just "self-emptying" and appears to encompass a wide range of themes from the renunciation of power, to humility, self-sacrifice, self-giving, nonviolence, preferring others, submission, and the like. It seems to me that there is a great need for the church to embrace the kind of humble, serving posture that is enshrined in kenosis. In relation to pneumatology, however, there are ways in which kenosis is interpreted and applied that remain problematic, and some elements of what comes under broader themes of "self-emptying" are not easily applicable to the Spirit and the world that he creates. In other words, I do not wish to deny the impact of the narrative of the self-giving of God in Christ and how that speaks to our conceptions of power, but knowing that this also has to be explained in the light of the post-Pentecost Spirit, and the world around her, confronts us with a need to accommodate a much more complex picture in which we encounter a world of tension and contrasts that are not easily explained solely by the language of kenosis.

The term has its roots in the hymn of Philippians 2 where we read that the Son "emptied himself" (RSV/NRSV), "made himself nothing" (NIV), or "gave up his divine privileges" (NLT). What Paul's term *ekenosen* precisely means is unclear. We read further that Christ did not consider equality with God something to be "grasped," "seized," or "taken advantage of." But again this is a disputed term. As Bruce Fisk writes, the word *harpagmos* has "singlehandedly fuelled a cottage industry in New Testament Studies."[19]

19. Bruce N. Fisk, "The Odyssey of Christ: A Novel Context for Philippians 2:6–11," in *Exploring Kenotic Christology: The Self-Emptying of God*, ed. C. Stephen Evans (Vancouver: Regent, 2006), 63.

Fisk advocates translating the verse as "Did not regard equality with God as something to be exploited."[20] Kenotic Christologies do not simply rely on this one Philippians reference. Scholars also cite 2 Corinthians 8:9 and the book of Hebrews in favor of the view of an impoverishment and self-emptying of the Son, and possibly also self-emptying in or of God himself.

That the debate continues among Bible scholars and theologians over what Paul meant by the self-emptying of the Son, let alone what this means for Christian living, tells us that there is no simple solution. I sometimes feel the discussion around the meaning of the self-emptying of Christ has distracted us from the strong themes in Philippians 2 in relation to Paul's exhortation to renounce vainglory and selfish ambition that precedes the hymn and for which it stands as a powerful illustration. The theme here is obedience, to Christ and even to Paul. In other words, it seems Paul intends Christ's example to be employed within the body so that we understand what it means to forego self-aggrandizement to prefer and serve others.[21] However, rather than simply being applied in an exemplarist fashion, these verses have given rise to all sorts of claims as to what the ontological "self-emptying" of the Son entails in relation to the nature of God. C. Stephen Evans writes, "I would argue that if the incarnation is revelatory of God and involves a kenosis, then this must reflect something deeply true of the nature of God."[22] His intuition is that the kenotic movement of the Son is not temporary but reflects something of God's essence. Michael Gorman writes, "God is, in other words, a God of self-sacrificing and self-giving love whose power and wisdom are found in the weakness and folly of the cross."[23]

Strong accounts of kenosis posit that the Son divests himself of divine attributes in one form or another to embrace the human condition in its entirety. Others argue that Christ forgoes divine prerogatives, either as a temporary divestment or as some kind of eternal and continuous self-emptying. There are those who eschew the stronger accounts but still wish to emphasize the self-sacrificial and self-giving nature of Christ and thus focus on the continuous self-emptying as a self-giving that flows from the

---

20. Fisk writes, 'I find myself drawn to the trajectory of interpretation charted by C. F. D. Moule, Roy W. Hoover and N. T. Wright, according to which Christ 'did not regard equality with God as *something to be exploited*.' Fisk, "The Odyssey," 64.

21. Michael Gorman, with reference to Phil 2 writes of the "self-renouncing, others-regarding pattern of slavery, with Christ as the paradigm and the Philippians as the 'reincarnation.'" *Cruciformity: Paul's Narrative Spirituality of the Cross* (Grand Rapids: Eerdmans, 2001) 258.

22. C. Stephen Evans, "The Self-Emptying of Love: Some Thoughts on Kenotic Christology" in *The Incarnation*, ed. Stephen T. Davis, Daniel Kendall, SJ, Gerald O'Collins, SJ (Oxford: Oxford University Press, 2002), 247.

23. Gorman, *Cruciformity*, 16.

Godhead into the world. Those who have become alert to the problems of what it might mean for the Son to divest himself of any aspect of divinity sometimes explain that the self-giving does not "empty" the Godhead as such but instead carries with it the idea of emptying out into, just as a spring acts as a source pouring out to become a river but is never emptied as it does so.

There is no doubt that kenosis has caught the modern imagination. Evans talks of the "religious power of God's self-giving love and full humanity" that he sees behind kenotic theology.[24] There must be multiple reasons for this development. It seems, in the 1970s, there was fertile soil for Moltmann's groundbreaking *The Crucified God*, and this has been picked up as an attractive account of a God who is able to suffer with suffering humanity, who knows the pain of abandonment and forsakenness, and whose nature is defined by self-emptying and sacrifice.[25] In many circles, at a grassroots level, this narrative has been adopted unquestioningly and emerges in sermons, songs, pastoral care, and prayer. It certainly does have a religious power.

Moltmann, of course, cut across the carefully drawn lines of classical Christology where it was understood that the Son suffered *in the flesh* and where patripassianism was ruled out as a feature of the Godhead. In my view, the early bishops were right to draw the lines and to hold to them; however, the fact that a Moltmannian view is seen to be such an appealing option by so many who have probably never even read Moltmann's work should cause us to reflect on why this is the case and how we might be able to renarrate the classical position in a way that will be equally compelling. Rightly or wrongly, it must have something to do with the fact that God was deemed to be too distant, impassible as one who is unmoved by suffering, and therefore uncaring in the face of tragedy, loss, fear, and pain.

If people are expressing such a need for a human God, surely something must have gone wrong in our telling of the story of the God-man who assumed and embraced humanity for our sakes. In addition to this, as I noted, kenosis has, I think, become a catch-all term that includes various descriptors: self-emptying, self-sacrifice, self-giving, the willingness to suffer for the good of others, voluntary self-humiliation, moving aside to allow others to flourish, and the renunciation of power and privilege. It is also often understood to be synonymous with cruciformity, or at least often used synonymously, and these converge to form the basis of an ethical

24. Evans, *Exploring*, 6.
25. Jürgen Moltmann, *The Crucified God* (London: SCM, 1974).

account of the Christian life.[26] All of this together paints a picture of God through the incarnation that in many ways is compelling and truthful. This picture of God in Christ is a judgement that stands over a church that allies itself with worldly power, abuses the weak and the poor, distances itself from the marginalized, and excludes the outsider.[27] These narratives that question worldly power so deeply are not ones we want to lose, especially now. However, certain problems persist with kenoticism.

PROBLEMS WITH KENOSIS

There are the manifest difficulties with strong accounts of kenosis in relation to soteriology and revelation (in that if the Son is not fully divine, then he can neither save humanity nor be the "image of the invisible God"), but these arguments are well rehearsed, so I will refer to more nuanced kenotic accounts. First, I turn to the question of method and the reading of the nature of the Godhead through kenosis. Despite my commitment to the centrality of the Christ in theological reflection, I remain cautious about the emphasis on self-emptying or even cruciformity as the *sole* lens through which to understand the Godhead.[28] In my view, this rests on a misstep regarding the nature of the revelation of God and our reception of it. Ian McFarland writes, "Jesus is the unique and unsubstitutable touchstone against which all talk about the nature and character of God (that is, all claims to know God) must be tested."[29] This is a key claim. He goes on to make the point, however, that this is very different from saying that "he is

26. Michael Gorman believed that he had coined the term *cruciformity*, until he discovered that Eric W. Gritsch had used this term twenty years before. Nevertheless, Gorman has popularized this term and brought it into common parlance. He defines it as "conformity to the crucified Christ," and employs it primarily in the ethical sphere. Gorman, *Cruciformity*, 4.

27. Gorman writes, "Centering on the cross was also an inherently anti-imperial posture that unashamedly challenged the priorities and values of the political, social, and religious status quo." Gorman, *Cruciformity*, 5.

28. Gorman is careful not to speak of the crucified God but writes, "*The cross is the interpretive, or hermeneutical, lens through which God is seen; it is the means of grace by which God is known.*" Gorman, *Cruciformity*, 17. Another example of this approach can be found in Brad Jersak, *A More Christlike God: A More Beautiful Gospel* (Pasadena, CA: CWR, 2015). One of the themes that recurs throughout kenotic accounts of the Godhead is noncoercion. On the topic of coercion and noncoercion, Colin Gunton writes, "There is much talk of the non-coercive love and power, and indeed, the cross is a sign that in one respect God indeed does not coerce. But that is not the whole story, for the resurrection of Jesus from the dead is an act of power of another kind and, although in no way to be divorced from the divine action on the cross, is coercive of reality in a strong sense. As John Donne's great sonnet celebrates, death the coercer is coerced." Gunton, *The Christian Faith: An Introduction to Christian Doctrine* (Oxford: Blackwell, 2002), 16, quoting John Donne, "Death Be Not Proud."

29. Ian A. McFarland. *The Divine Image: Envisioning the Invisible God* (Minneapolis: Augsburg, 2005), 51.

the *only* source of such knowledge."[30] We have the revelation of God through the Son, through the Scriptures in their entirety, and through the ongoing work of the Spirit including the work of the Spirit through the church. In addition to this, we will continue to be confronted with the unknowability of God on the one hand, and our tendency to create him in our own image on the other, both of which pertain to our human frailty.[31] We will ever only know in part and there will always be more to say that we do not know how to articulate. Thus, while knowing God through the crucified Christ is the essence of our faith, claiming that we can know *all* there is to know of God through the crucified Christ seems to me to be problematic in some ways. Kenosis narrates the story of the condescension of the Son and his identification with the lowest of the low in his society. Paul reminds the Philippian church that his crucifixion carried with it the ignominy of a slave's death.[32] It is a powerful and haunting picture. However, rather than imagine that God limits or empties himself of power in order to suffer, I would contend that an even more compelling picture can be seen in God in the Son, forever the holy, powerful, and transcendent one, found on the cross for our sakes. Aquinas focuses on this in particular in relation to the Son as Mediator: "Weakness is assumed by strength, lowliness by majesty, mortality by eternity, in order that one and the same Mediator of God and men might die in one and rise in the other—for this was our fitting remedy."[33] He goes on, "By taking flesh, God did not lessen His majesty; and in consequence did not lessen the reason for reverencing Him, which is increased by the increase of knowledge of Him. But, on the contrary, inasmuch as He wished to draw nigh to us by taking flesh, He greatly drew us to know Him."[34]

If kenosis is read back into the Father or God as a controlling metaphor to describe the essence of God, it is also mapped onto the Spirit with claims that the Spirit too undergoes some kind of "self-emptying." D. Lyle Dabney extends the Moltmannian abandonment motif to the Spirit also, so the Spirit as the Spirit of Sonship is abandoned with the Son.[35] Lossky

30. McFarland. *The Divine Image*, 52.

31. These themes are discussed in some detail in McFarland's *The Divine Image*.

32. This is a real, humiliating, and brutal death. Bruce Fisk makes the point that Paul is emphatic that Jesus suffers a real death, not a near-death from which he is snatched away. Fisk, "The Odyssey," 69.

33. Aquinas, *Summa Theologiae* 3.2, ans.

34. Aquinas, *Summa Theologiae* 3.2, ad 3.

35. D. Lyle Dabney speaks of the negation of both the Son and Sonship itself on the cross which also means the abnegation of the Spirit on the grounds that the Spirit is the Spirit of Sonship. Dabney,

writes that the person of the Spirit is "hidden from us by the very profusion of the Divinity which He manifests. It is this 'personal kenosis' of the Holy Spirit on the plane of manifestation and economy which makes it hard to grasp His hypostatic existence."[36] Building again on Moltmann, Jane Linahan explores the Holy Spirit as the bearer of suffering, speaking of the vulnerable, grieving Spirit who inhabits creation's "tortured, fragile, endangered, unfinished history."[37] This, it seems to me, is where we end up if we take Dunn's principle that we should now measure the Spirit against the cross and then view the cross through a Moltmannian lens, where no other perspective is admitted as revelatory of the nature of God. This is not necessarily where I see the New Testament account of the Spirit leads us. Gorman has a much more careful account of what he calls "the Spirit of cruciformity," which is more in line with what I am arguing in this paper. However, one of his key concerns is also to prioritize cruciformity as the dominant hermeneutical lens, something I am questioning here.[38]

There is a trenchant feminist critique of kenosis as a controlling lens for human relations that posits that "women are socialized to be inordinately self-sacrificing" and that the last thing women need is to be told to be self-emptying and in submission.[39] The picture of the kenotic Christ can be and is used as a weapon against any powerless group to keep them in subjection and subordination and should be treated with caution. I appreciate that there is some resistance to the idea that this characterization of women applies *tout court*. Ruth Groenhout reminds us that "women throughout history have been capable of strength and purposiveness, and if we define women's nature in terms of oppression we lose sight of the accomplishments women have achieved in the past as well as the accomplishments they may be capable of

"Naming the Spirit: Towards a Pneumatology of the Cross," in Pickard and Preece, *Starting with the Spirit*, 28–58, 56.

36. Lossky, *Image and Likeness*, 92.

37. Jane E. Linahan, "The Grieving Spirit: The Holy Spirit as Bearer of the Suffering of the World in Moltmann's Pneumatology" in *The Spirit in the Church and the World*, ed. Bradford E. Hinze (Maryknoll, NY: Orbis, 2004), 28–48, 43. This is also a theme in Daniela Augustine's work mentioned above. She speaks of the askesis and kenosis of the Trinity instantiated in the life of the church through the Spirit. Daniela Augustine, *The Spirit and the Common Good*, 48.

38. See Gorman, *Cruciformity*, chapter 3. Gorman presses the point that Paul sees his ministry as "the renunciation of power, rights, and self-interest for the good of others (1 Cor 9; 10:33). . . . He makes this self-denying, others-regarding edification the hallmark of love (1 Cor 8:1; 13:5)" (59–60). Gorman subordinates the "charismatic" narrative to this lens which is, no doubt, what Paul is wanting to communicate to the Corinthian church. I feel, however, that Gorman is nervous of the strong exhortation from Paul that also comes out in this letter to "eagerly desire the spiritual gifts," especially that they might prophesy, but including tongues, healing, etc.

39. Ruth Groenhout, "Kenosis and Feminist Theory," in Evans, *Exploring Kenotic Christology*, 291. See also Valerie (Goldstein) Saiving, "The Human Situation: A Feminine View," *Journal of Religion* 40 (April 1960): 100–112.

achieving in the future."[40] It does not help any group to be cast only as the powerless and vulnerable; however, proponents of kenosis as the controlling christological paradigm should be aware of how the narrative of submission and even subjection can play out in real lives and alert to the dangers of how this might be employed in the service of control, manipulation, and abuse. My three worries with kenosis then are (1) how it is employed in an ontological sense to describe the essence of the Godhead when it properly applies to the work of the Son, (2) how it is mapped on to the Spirit, and (3) how it may be misused as a means of control. That said, it forces us to focus on aspects of God's revelation that touch something deep in the heart of the human condition while challenging our conceptions of power, and for this I wish to hold on to some of these insights.

KENOSIS/PLEROSIS

I chose kenotic Christology because I think the prevalence of kenotic rhetoric reminds us of a contemporary plea that we should forget neither the true humanity of Christ nor the challenge to conceptions of worldly power that confront us in the incarnation and the cross. Kenotic Christologies are, I think, a response to docetic trends in Christology where it is felt that there is no proper account of the fully human Jesus who truly lived a life like ours in every respect (Heb 2:17). Thomas Thompson writes about "creating a greater space for Christ's true, full, even radical humanity offered by a kenotic construal."[41] It is thought, then, that kenotic Christologies fill this gap—that they account for the human conditions of Christ's life, his visible lack of omnipotence, omniscience, his growth in wisdom and knowledge, his dependence on the Father, his suffering and death. It is one answer to the question of how we can say he lived a life just like ours. It is my opinion that John Owen's Spirit Christology gives the best account in answer to this question, but I have discussed this elsewhere, so I will not refer to this in detail. However, I would say that a robust pneumatology accentuates rather than attenuates the true humanity of Christ, highlighting the mode of Christ's existence as fully human in dependence upon the Spirit in relation to the Father. Thus a robust pneumatology would aid rather than undermine the ultimate aims of the kenotic project in this regard.

---

40. Groenhout, "Kenosis and Feminist Theory," 295.

41. Thomas R. Thompson, "Nineteenth Century Kenotic Christology: The Waxing, Waning, and Weighing of a Quest for a Coherent Orthodoxy," in Evans, *Exploring Kenotic Christology*, 74–111, 106.

Be that as it may, I suggest that what is so often missing with kenosis is the dynamic of the filling, or plerosis, of the Spirit and all that this entails, and if kenosis is held together with an account of plerosis, that this will tell a better story of the work of God in the world and the complexity of the Christian life. (By *plerosis* here I am not referring to the self-fulfillment or exaltation of Christ as a corresponding movement to kenosis but to the filling of humanity by the Spirit at Pentecost and beyond.) From this perspective, there are two concurrent narratives in the New Testament: one of emptying and one of filling—that is, of weakness and power, absence and presence, suffering and healing, and death and life. If we see the missions of the Son and the Spirit as coinherent, then we are, I think, compelled to hold these two narratives together, which means accommodating various opposing concepts in a simultaneous tensive relation without collapsing one into the other or seeing the first as a means to the second only in this life (i.e. first the cross then fulfillment, healing, victory, etc.). Seeing the missions of the Son and the Spirit as intertwined and as equally informative of the nature of God invites us to resist the temptation to resolve the tension or to argue that there is a simple trajectory from one to the other. Emptying and filling, weakness and power, suffering and healing, absence and presence, and death and life coexist as signs of both the life of Christ and the presence of the Spirit in the church. There is not a simple trajectory from weakness to strength in a given life or community. In my view, holding this all together better describes the tensive existence of those who have put their faith in Christ living in the power of the Spirit. It opens up a rich and complex world of definitions when it comes to how we understand God's work in creation, and it will be a better way of construing the Christ-centred and Spirit-filled world.

The Emptying and Filling of the Saints

The incarnation tells us a powerful story of a God who humbles himself in the Son, experiences life exactly as we experience it, sin excepted, which makes the story even more poignant and horrific. He, the innocent Son of God, suffers an unbearable death in shame and agony for our sakes. He embraces the whole of the human condition to restore humanity to the Father and to share the riches of his inheritance with us. Kenosis is a feature of the incarnation, cruciformity a feature of the cross, but the two are linked. It is in this context that Paul makes reference to the "emptying" of the Son as the means of salvation for humanity and a sign of the deep love of Father, Son, and Holy Spirit, that the Son was sent and came to suffer of his own accord and die for our sakes. We know then that God is capable of inhabiting our suffering, the suffering that is part of the human condition, even our despair, our loneliness, our destitution, our horrors, and our tragedies.

> He was despised and rejected by others;
> a man of suffering and acquainted with infirmity;
> and as one from whom others hide their faces
> he was despised, and we held him of no account. (Isa 53:3)

As the kenoticists say, one of the manifestations of God's almighty power is his power to embrace weakness. We also know that those who follow Jesus will participate in his suffering (Col 1:24), and that this is an inevitable pattern for those incorporated into his body (John 15:18–20).

As someone from the charismatic tradition, I see this narrative as a welcome corrective to so much of the charismatic and Pentecostal lived theologies that all of us on the inside recognize. It seems to me that we constantly focus solely on the positive outcomes (i.e. filling, power, presence, healing, and life). We are prepared only to give our testimonies once we have a good end to the story.[42] We are much less willing to tell stories of when we are powerless, vulnerable, sick, or dying. These can appear to be the antitheses of where we want to be and anathema to life and hope when the reality is, of course, that these states are intrinsic to all lives. Perhaps this is why many are finding they are attracted to kenosis because it tells a more real story of God in the suffering, empty Son. However, we are denied an either/or approach to the Christian life, and we have a more uneasy calling of having to accommodate both states at once, but this is where the persons of Christ and the Spirit lead us.

The Spirit indwells the Son throughout his life and death. This same Spirit will be in our emptying, our smallness, our sickness, our dying, and our deaths and even, at times, lead us to the very same. We are not always led out of loss, but sometimes we are led through it in the pattern of our Savior. But the story of the self-emptying of the Son does not necessarily and not *always* call for a corresponding self-emptying of humanity except

42. One more extreme example of this would be the "Word of Faith" movement which claims that poverty and sickness have been defeated through the cross of Christ and simply need to be "claimed" by the believer. However, it is not just extreme versions of charismatic and Pentecostal theologies that enshrine triumphalism in some form.

to call us to die to our sinful self, which will only be a setting free and a delimitation in a very real sense. Self-abasement, humiliation, or renunciation is a powerful challenge to the powerful, but it is not always needed for those who are already there. Leo speaks of the Son bending down out of pity, a condescension that does not diminish the divine, but increases the human.[43] Kathryn Tanner develops this theme in what is, in my view, a compelling account of the noncompetitive relation between God and humanity that is often undermined by kenotic accounts. As she explains, the "creature does not decrease so that God may increase."[44] We might say that the Son and the Spirit both, while committed to working in and through the human condition, will necessarily be bound to some form of emptying or limitation, but at the same time, they will be delimiting the confines of sinful existence and setting free that which is subject to loss, decay, and death. At times we will see this delimitation erupt in miracles, signs and wonders, and resurrection life. At other times the loss, decay, and death will be all we see because that is the unrelenting nature of existence on earth, that Jesus also indwelt. At these times, the cross and resurrection tell us that this is not all there is, but we can only hold on to this promise by faith and not by sight, and at these times it is right to grieve both what we have lost and what we do not yet have.

So on the one hand, we have the story of the assumption of humanity by the Son that entails a kenosis. On the other, we have the filling of humanity by the divine in the Son in the hypostatic union and importantly for us, by the Spirit at Pentecost, where the Spirit is poured out on all flesh. This filling is a filling with power—power to proclaim the truth of Jesus as the resurrected Savior, to perform signs and wonders, to prophesy, to heal, to deliver the imprisoned and the oppressed. This is not just an eschatological hope but a concrete manifestation of the renewal and regeneration of creation for the freedom from atrophy that is a work of the Spirit. We see a complex story of the power that flows from the incarnation, the crucifixion,

43. "Nor, because He partook of man's weaknesses, did He therefore share our faults. He took the form of a slave without stain of sin, increasing the human and not diminishing the divine: because that emptying of Himself whereby the Invisible made Himself visible and, Creator and LORD of all things though He be, wished to be a mortal, was the bending down of pity, not the failing of power. Accordingly He who while remaining in the form of GOD made man, was also made man in the form of a slave. For both natures retain their own proper character without loss: and as the form of GOD did not do away with the form of a slave, so the form of a slave did not impair the form of GOD." Leo's Tome §3, in *Nicene and Post-Nicene Fathers*, vol. 12, ed. Philip Schaff and Henry Wace (New York: Christian Literature, 1985).

44. Kathryn Tanner, *Jesus, Humanity and the Trinity: A Brief Systematic Theology* (Minneapolis: Fortress, 2001), 2.

the resurrection, the ascension, and the exaltation of Christ as shaping and acting as interpretive lenses for the Christian life.

CONCLUSION

I began this paper by suggesting the church should continue to reflect on what it means to be filled with the Spirit: to walk in the Spirit, to pray in the Spirit, and to follow the leading of the Spirit if this is, indeed, the Spirit of Christ. I have attempted to think through what shape our theology of the Spirit might take if we begin with Christology with particular reference to kenotic Christology and cruciformity. Despite having some reservations regarding kenosis, I would suggest that a christomorphic pneumatology means embracing some form of kenotic and cruciform perspective alongside the language of filling and empowerment that is associated with the Pentecostal Spirit. I want to resist seeing one as a means to the other in this life (apart from the baptismal progression of dying with Christ in order to be raised with him to new life). By which I mean viewing weakness as a means of power, suffering as a means of healing, and so on. Instead, I suggest that we simply have to acknowledge that both can be true in the same moment. We experience emptying and filling, weakness and power, absence and presence, suffering and healing, death and life all at one and the same time.

What is Christomorphic pneumatology? I suggest it means first, understanding the work of the Spirit as a work of God that cannot be described apart from the incarnation and the crucifixion, and which refuses to see the cross and the death of Christ as merely the gateway to new life. Paul says to the Corinthians, "I decided to know nothing among you except Jesus Christ, and him crucified" (1 Cor 2:2). We are faced with the task of working out our pneumatology in the light of the incarnate Christ, the crucified Christ, the risen Christ, and the ascended Christ. This will mean accommodating both a kenotic and cruciform vision. So in part it will mean understanding the Spirit-filled life as including the inevitability of every aspect of human existence including suffering, disappointment, pain, and death. But it will also mean knowing that there are possibilities in this life for healing, renewal, deliverance, restoration, and justice that we see enacted in the life of Christ and his disciples and throughout the church through the ages as the content of the Spirit's work. Maintaining the unity and distinction of Christ and the Spirit means we see God at work in both and cannot collapse one into the other.

This puts us into an uncomfortable position. Nothing allows us to progress beyond the cross in this life. Charismatics and Pentecostals cannot just scoot past or through the cross to the filling or baptism of the Spirit that is supposedly full of promise for life, joy, and peace from that point on. The incarnation and the cross remind us that the Spirit might well lead us to or through our own emptying, desolation, weakness, and death. But there is also a world of the Spirit that is full of life, and we charismatics and Pentecostals tell stories about this world and the possibilities within it: the sick might be healed, the blind might see, the lame might walk, the oppressed might be delivered of evil once and for all. A Christomorphic pneumatology challenges us to relinquish a singular lens. It at once confronts the people of the kenotic and the cruciform Christ and the Spirit-people to accommodate a narrative that questions our precious dogma. Finally, a Christomorphic pneumatology requires us to exercise discernment that comes from dwelling on the nature of God in Christ and the leading of the Spirit. There are no rules that tell us how to respond to the conditions of this life as it confronts us in all its forms. We are not given a blueprint in the face of hardship, suffering, or even evil that instructs us when we are to submit and when we are called to resist, when we might need to protest whatever that might cost us, and when we surrender. These are only discerned in the moment, flowing out of the spiritual gift of wisdom, embodied in Christ and given by the Spirit, and I would suggest, as much as I would like to be able to do so, that there is no way of resolving this tension.

CHAPTER 10

WE BELIEVE IN THE HOLY SPIRIT . . . THE HOLY CATHOLIC CHURCH

JOSHUA COCKAYNE

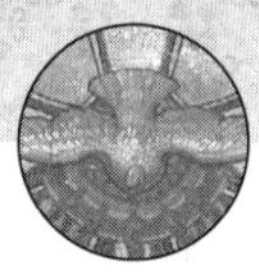

AS THE TITLE OF THIS PAPER SUGGESTS, in reciting the Nicene Creed, we do not claim to believe in God the Father, God the Son, God the Spirit *and* the church. Rather, as T. F. Torrance's puts it, "The clauses on the Church . . . follow from belief in the Holy Spirit, for the *holy* church is the fruit of the *Holy Spirit*. . . . If we believe in the Holy Spirit, we also believe in the existence of one Church in the one Spirit."[1] Put another way, the church is not an organisation instituted and maintained by human beings striving to act as one body (even if the majority of its members are human beings). Rather, the church is a body instituted and directed by the one Spirit, through whom all its members are united.[2]

This paper seeks to develop a social ontology of the church which emphasises the primacy of the Spirit's agency. In doing so, it seeks to utilize "the tools and methods of contemporary analytic philosophy for the purposes of constructive Christian theology."[3] More specifically, I will borrow from the tools and methods of contemporary social ontology to

1. T. F. Torrance, *The Trinitarian Faith: The Evangelical Theology of the Ancient Catholic Church* (London: T&T Clark, 2016), 252.

2. I would like to thank David Efird† and Koert Verhagen for their comments and feedback on earlier drafts of this material, as well as the members of the audience at the LA Theology Conference for their excellent questions.

3. Oliver Crisp, "Analytic Theology as Systematic Theology," *Open Theology* 3, no. 1 (2018): 165.

give a model for thinking about the Spirit's work in uniting the church; to borrow Dietrich Bonhoeffer's words, in this paper "social philosophy and sociology are employed in the service of theology."[4]

The discussion proceeds as follows: I begin by considering the close relationship between ecclesiology and pneumonology in 1 Corinthians. As Paul describes in 1 Corinthians, the church is a social body that is similar in many ways to other social bodies. Borrowing from the language of the political thought of his time, Paul makes clear that the church is united in spite of its apparent diversity. Yet unlike any other social body, 1 Corinthians makes clear that the church's unity comes not from humanly imposed political structures but rather from the work of the one Spirit. Thus, unless the work of the one Spirit is emphasised, the church can only be understood as a human organisation, fractured and broken with little true unity. Instead, I argue, pneumatology and ecclesiology must come hand in hand. Expanding the pneumatological ecclesiology in 1 Corinthians, I turn to consider recent work in social ontology to give an account of the church's unity in the one Spirit. Mirroring Paul's use of political philosophy, I consider how far contemporary social ontology can take us in the endeavour of ecclesiology and emphasise some points of distinction between the church and social bodies more generally.[5]

ONE GOD, ONE SPIRIT, ONE CHURCH

There are a number of places where something like a social ontology is offered in the New Testament in explaining the nature of the church and the relation between members and its whole. Typically, these explanations proceed by way of metaphor—the church is described as a temple of the Holy Spirit constituted by individual bricks,[6] a household constituted by

---

4. In a recent paper, "Analytic Ecclesiology," *Journal of Analytic Theology* (2019): 100–123, I argued that the oneness of the church might be understood by appealing to work in contemporary social ontology. There, I gestured toward two models of thinking about the church's unity; a terrorist cell constituted by ignorant agents united through a top-down organisational structure, and a honeybee colony, which is able to make decisions about its environment as a group which seemingly surpass its capacities to make decisions as individual honeybees. I suggested that appealing to the work of the Holy Spirit, we might say similar things about the church's unity. However, what was left unclear was just how the Holy Spirit might act in uniting the one church. This paper attempts to further develop this model, paying closer attention to the pneumatology at work in the one church.

5. It is worth noting that for the sake of scope my focus will be on the Holy Spirit. This narrowing of focus should not, however, be taken as a tacit denial of the work of the Father and the Son in constituting the church, which I take to be essential.

6. 1 Cor 3:10–17; 6:18–20; 2 Cor 6:14–18.

many stones,[7] as a nation or city comprised of many citizens, [8] and as the body of Christ, in which its members are body parts.[9] This paper focuses on the last of these images and the discussion of ecclesiology in 1 Corinthians in which the body metaphor is used to describe the unity of the church, despite the obvious diversity in practice, behaviour, and worship.

In providing an account of social unity, throughout the epistle, Paul borrows from political philosophical arguments and terminology to make theological points. First, the term *ekklēsia*, translated in English as church, has political resonances. The term was commonly used in Greek to refer to an "assembly of the free-men of a city who were entitled to vote. In a more general sense, it describes any public assembly."[10] Thus when Paul uses the term *church of God* (*ekklēsia tou theou*) in 1:2, he is using an overtly political term to refer to the church. As both Margaret M. Mitchell and Dale Martin have argued in detail, throughout 1 Corinthians, Paul is drawing from the political philosophical thought of ancient Greek literature. In chapter 1 verse 10, for instance, there is evidence that the language of unity and diversity, as well as the command to be of the "same mind" and "same purpose," can be found put to similar rhetorical uses in contexts of political disagreement. The pairing of "same mind" and "same purpose" is sometimes paired in political texts; Mitchell argues that 1:10 "is filled with terms which have a long history in speeches, political treatises and historical works dealing with political unity and factionalism."[11]

Thus in reaching the image of the body of Christ in chapter 12, where Paul's account of unity is filled out in most detail, the readers have already become familiar with thinking of the church through this political lens. The metaphor of the society as a body was common in political and philosophical literature, particularly in the Greco-Roman *homonoia* discourses (speeches used at times of political strife to urge the city or state to remain unified and that all members of the polis remained in their proper place). Mitchell writes that there can be "no doubt that 1 Corinthians 12 employs the most common *topos* in ancient literature for unity."[12] The well-known

7. Eph 2:11–20; 1 Tim 3:14–15; 1 Pet 2:3–8.

8. Heb 11:8–16; 13:7–16; 1 Pet 2:9–10; Rev 21:9–27.

9. Rom 12:3–8; 1 Cor 12:12–31; Col 1:18–20; 3:12–17.

10. Eckhard J. Schnabel, "The Community of the Followers of Jesus in 1 Corinthians," in *The New Testament Church: The Challenge of Developing Ecclesiologies*, ed. J. P. Harrison and J. D. Dvorak (Eugene, OR: Wipf & Stock, 2012), 105.

11. Margaret M. Mitchell, *Paul and the Rhetoric of Reconciliation* (Louisville: Westminster John Knox, 1993), 79.

12. Mitchell, *Paul and the Rhetoric of Reconciliation*, 161.

fable of Menenius Agrippa (which may have its origins in Aesop's fables), for instance, "tells of a revolt of the hands, mouth and teeth against the belly, thus weakening the whole body."[13] As Mitchell notes, Paul's use of the metaphor of the body is not just similar in form but also in detail; many of the *homonoia* discourses using this metaphor use the same body parts as Paul (hands, feet, eyes, ears) and employ a similar rhetorical strategy of personification.[14]

So Paul borrows from political philosophy to emphasise the unity of the church in terms very similar to the unity of any other social body. But he is also keen to stress that in other respects, the social ontology of the church is unlike that advocated by political texts. For instance, Martin has argued that, in addition to borrowing from these texts, Paul also subverts the expectations of those familiar with this genre of writing. Whereas the body metaphor was typically used to keep lower class citizens in their places, Paul uses the metaphor to reverse the worldly "attribution of honor and status."[15] Paul repeatedly emphasises that the seemingly lesser parts of the body ought actually to be held in higher esteem (12:23–24)—thus arguing that the perceived hierarchy of political status is only surface level.[16] We can see this contrast between political and ecclesial social ontology starkly in verse 12; the expectation, especially given the use of the political metaphor, might be that this verse should finish, "just as the body is one and has many members . . . so it is with *the church*."[17] Instead Paul finishes this sentence: "so it is with *Christ*." Paul is here borrowing from the metaphor of the body but also pressing us to move beyond metaphor—this is an ontological statement about the relationship between the members of the church and Christ.

Importantly for our purposes, as we see in verse 13, the oneness of the community comes not from any human organisation or structure but rather from the work of the Holy Spirit, whose activity brings about a unity in Christ. Gordon Fee, writing on the application of this passage to the contemporary church, claims that unity does *not* come through human organisational structures, we cannot force our own "brand of 'spiritual unity' on the church as simply another human machination. Our desperate

---

13. Mitchell, *Paul and the Rhetoric of Reconciliation*, 157–58.

14. Mitchell, *Paul and the Rhetoric of Reconciliation*, 159. Those familiar with Plato's *Republic* will see the obvious points of connection—Plato thinks of the structure of *polis* as analogous to the structure of the individual, and of discord in each as the source of injustice.

15. Martin, *The Corinthian Body* (Hartford, CT: Yale University Press, 199), 96.

16. Martin, *The Corinthian Body*, 94.

17. Richard Hays, *First Corinthians*, Interpretation (Louisville: Westminster John Knox, 1997), 213.

need is for a sovereign work of the Spirit to do among us what all our 'programmed unity' cannot."[18]

Moreover, it is important to see that Paul is not only drawing from Greco-Roman political texts here but also providing an "ecclesial application of the [Jewish] Shema" and its emphasis on the oneness of God.[19] There is "one God" and "one Lord, Jesus Christ," Paul tells us in 8:6, and chapter 12 repeats this emphasis on oneness—the "one church" is the work of the "one Spirit" (12:12–13), as we constitute the body of the [one] Christ (12:27). Paul is affirming "the emergence of a new social construct," which, unlike the Greco-Roman polis, is founded on, and united in "the singularity of the one God and Christ (and their one Spirit)."[20] In other words, while there are clear similarities between the community of the church and other kinds of social community, it is important to see that the church's unity comes not from human structures and the externally imposed ideologies of politicians but only through the work of the one Spirit, who unites the one church with Christ, the one Lord. Tom Greggs puts the point succinctly: "Although the church shares in many—if not all—of the characteristics of other organizations, its primary existence is ultimately distinct from every other expression of human sociality. The church comes into being as an event of the act of the lordship of the Holy Spirit of God who gives the church life."[21]

How, then, might we think about nature of the church as a human community that is united in and through the lordship of the Holy Spirit? Just as Paul uses the sociopolitical thought of his time to outline his ecclesiology, we now turn to consider the application of contemporary analytic work on the nature of social groups.

Contemporary Social Ontology and Ecclesiology

In contemporary analytic philosophy there has been a surge of interest in the metaphysics and ethics of social groups and a growing conviction that not all ethical questions can be answered by appealing only to the actions of

18. Gordon D. Fee, *The First Epistle to the Corinthians* (Grand Rapids: Eerdmans, 1987), 607.

19. Andrew Byers, "The One Body of the Shema in 1 Corinthians: An Ecclesiology of Christological Monotheism," *New Testament Studies* 62, no. 4 (2016): 517.

20. Byers, "The One Body of the Shema in 1 Corinthians," 532.

21. Greggs, *Dogmatic Ecclesiology: The Priestly Catholicity of the Church* (Grand Rapids: Baker Academic, 2019), 2.

specific individuals. Groups appear to be responsible for oil spills, financial crashes, and the rise of xenophobia in ways which do not reduce straightforwardly to individual actions. Recent work on the metaphysics of groups has attempted to make sense of these intuitions.[22] There are some helpful points of clarification in this literature, I think, which can help us to see the role of the Spirit in the church more clearly.

One particular point of clarification comes in considering the ways in which *group* attitudes differ from attitudes of group members. Consider the following remark from a sermon on John 17 by Johann Blumhardt, which I think highlights the need for a clear social ontology in theology:

> Do we as Jesus' disciples really want to become one? . . . We must find a way where what you believe I believe and what I believe you believe. For the Lord says in his prayer, "I have given them glory that you gave me, that they may be one as we are one." What is this glory given to him which he passed on to his disciples? . . . Jesus emphatically promises to give his disciples the Holy Spirit: the Comforter, the guide to all truth, and the One who will unite them. Without this Spirit, they could not become one.[23]

While I'm sympathetic with much of what Blumhardt wants to say about the role of the Spirit in the church, there appears to be a flattening of social ontology at work in his remarks. This is illuminated in his description of the church becoming one when *what you believe I believe and what I believe you believe*. The assumption here is that oneness entails a uniformity of belief. More worryingly, the underlying position here appears to assume that unity is located in the actions or beliefs of human members of the church rather than in the unity of the one Spirit or the one body of Christ.

Even if this isn't the most charitable way to read Blumhardt's comments (something I won't consider here), the position described certainly resembles a familiar way of thinking about church unity. The idea seems to be this: Betty comes to faith in Christ and joins the church by participating in a local church congregation. But Betty knows that down the road Jonathan goes to a church that believes different things (perhaps it holds to the ascension of Mary, for instance), and Jonathan's church does things very differently (they use incense in worship, and don't have any guitars). It seems clear to

22. See Deborah Tollefsen, *Groups as Agents* (Cambridge: Polity, 2015), for a good overview of this literature.

23. Johann Blumhardt, *Gospel Sermons* (Walden, NY: Plough, 2019), 86.

Betty that she and Jonathan cannot be part of the *same* church because if they were truly one in the Spirit, they wouldn't have such differences in practice and belief. I am caricaturing of course, but there's a serious point to be made: to understand the church's unity, we cannot start with Betty's beliefs, Betty's practices, or even the beliefs and practices of her church.

To see this point more precisely, allow me to formulate it in terms borrowed from contemporary social ontology. Consider the following taxonomy of social groups:

> *Coalition*: A group with a shared goal, but without a joint decision-making procedure. For example, "environmentalists," "the oil lobby," "democracy-promoting states," "conservatives."[24]
>
> *Combination*: A group "constituted by agents who do not together constitute a coalition or a collective. Examples of combinations include 'men' (since common advantage does not suffice for a common goal), 'humanity,' 'the international community,' 'the people in this pub,' and 'me, you, and Shakespeare.'"[25]
>
> *Collective*: A group "constituted by agents that are united under a rationally operated group-level decision-making procedure that can attend to moral considerations."[26] That is, the British government is constituted by the ministers of the cabinet, who, through a series of group-decision-making procedure, deliberate on the "best" course of action for the country.

The retort to Blumhardt's position (or some caricature of it) can be made more precisely in these terms. On Blumhardt's position, the church is united only when its members share a commitment to a certain set of beliefs, say, the beliefs of Christian orthodoxy. In other words, the church is thought of as a coalition, in which unity comes through a commitment to a shared goal or set of values. This way of thinking about the church is problematic, for in Greggs' words, "The being of the church is not held in the particular contingent phenomena of the church's forms; the being of the church is held in the constancy of the Holy Spirit."[27]

---

24. Stephanie Collins, *Group Duties: Their Existence and Their Implications for Individuals* (Oxford: Oxford University Press, 2019), 16.
25. Collins, *Group Duties*, 20.
26. Collins, *Group Duties*, 12.
27. Collins, *Group Duties*, 19.

A social ontology of the church must give primacy to the Spirit's agency and only an account of the church as a collective can make sense of this. For collectives, unlike combinations and coalitions, are united by their ontology rather than by any shared goals, commitments, or accidental properties of their members. Note that this doesn't mean that there aren't any obligations for members to believe and act in certain ways but that the unity of the group is not dependent on these individual actions. Another important thing to notice about collectives is that they allow us to distinguish between the beliefs of the group and the beliefs of a group's members. A government can hold that some course of action is preferable, even if its members don't unanimously agree, such as the British government's commitment to 'get Brexit done', despite the divergent commitments of individual cabinet ministers. A committee can recommend a policy, even if its votes are split 90–10. More positively, an organisation can act as a single body even if its employees take on vastly different roles—indeed, it might sometimes aim to compensate for too much of one kind of employee by employing someone with vastly different values to better reflect the diversity of the organisation as a whole. In other words, unity is not the same as uniformity. If the church is a collective, then we can be united as one church, even if we don't believe all of the same things.

Where things become more difficult in applying social ontology to ecclesiology is in considering how the work of the Spirit allows us to think of the church as a united collective, especially given the apparent diversity of the outward forms of the church, as Blumhardt attests to. Again, work in social ontology can help us to make important points of clarification here.

Typically, discussions of collective ontology locate the unity of the group in the decision-making procedures of that group. Christian List and Philip Pettit, for instance, hold that a group agent must have the capacity to form "representational states, motivational states, and a capacity to act on their basis."[28] Moreover, it must do so in a way which meets some basic standard of rationality. As List and Pettit attest to, one of the most difficult problems to be overcome in considering a group as a collective (or "group agent," in their terminology) is that of group aggregation; many majority-based voting systems are unable to meet standards of group rationality (we don't need to worry about the details here; if the church meets the conditions for counting as a collective, it certainly isn't through the aggregation of its

28. Christian List and Philip Pettit, *Group Agency: The Possibility, Design, and Status of Corporate Agents* (Oxford: Oxford University Press, 2011), 20.

members' beliefs and attitudes). For List and Pettit, "To count as an agent, a group must exhibit at least a modicum of rationality. And so, its members must find a form of organization that ensures, as far as possible, that the group satisfies attitude-to-fact, attitude-to-action, and attitude-to-attitude standards of rationality."[29]

List and Pettit's primary concern in *Group Agency* is to provide an account of how corporations and other groups could be considered agents and therefore responsible agents, capable of being held to account for their actions. While they hold that these conditions are typically met through group-level aggregation, they admit that it is possible, at least in principle, to meet these conditions without appealing to the agency of members at all. Elsewhere I have argued that this possibility opens up potential for using social ontology for thinking about the church as a group agent, even if its members' decisions and structures are not the ground of its agency and thereby its unity. Here are three examples I've considered, each of which have some application for thinking about the ontology of the church:

> *Honeybees:* "Bees can combine, on the basis of simple signals, so as to perform as a group agent."[30] While no single bee has this complex level of decision making by itself, the swarm as a whole has "impressive powers of decision making, especially with respect to simultaneous-option decisions."[31] "It is harder to imagine, though not conceptually impossible, that nature or culture could work to a similar effect on human beings eliciting, coalescent agents."[32]

> *Terrorist Cells*: Think of the cellular organization by which, so we are told, many terrorist organizations have operated. We can imagine that a cellular network may be established for the promotion of some goals,

29. List and Pettit, *Group Agency*, 36. Similarly, according to Stephanie Collins (*Group Duties*), there are three individually necessary and jointly sufficient conditions for holding a decision-making procedure to be group-level: (1) "Each member is committed (even if only tacitly) to abide by the procedure's results. This commitment can be overridden, but is presumptively decisive in the member's decision-making" (p. 12). (2) "The beliefs and preferences that the procedure takes as inputs, and the way the procedure processes those inputs to form decisions, systematically derive from the behaviour (e.g., deference, votes, meetings, contributions, etc.) of members, while be *operationally distinct* from the inputs and processes that any member uses when deciding for herself" (p. 13). (3) "The enactment of the group's decisions requires actions on the part of its members, where those actions are also properly understood as attributable to the collective" (p. 14).

30. Thomas Seeley, "Decision Making in Superorganisms: How Collective Wisdom Arises from the Poorly Informed Masses," in *Bound Rationality: The Adaptive Toolbox*, ed. Gerd Gigerenzer and Reinhard Selten (Cambridge, MA: MIT Press, 2001).

31. Seeley, "Decision Making in Superorganisms," 249.

32. List and Pettit, *Group Agency*, 33.

> without those recruited to the different cellular tasks being aware of the overall purpose; they may be kept in the dark or even deceived about it. The organization would be composed of a group of people, in perhaps a thin sense of group, and would function as an agent. But it would do so without joint intention among its members, with the possible exception of a few coordinators.[33]

> *Marvel Cinematic Universe (MCU)*: The Marvel "shared universe" consists of a number of films and television series with an overarching plot and character arch. While actors and crewmembers are ignorant of this overarching purpose, they participate in the actions of the group by following scripts and instructions of directors and producers. The MCU acts as a collective despite widespread ignorance from its constituent members.[34]

I've argued these examples can help explain the unity we find in the church despite its apparent diversity. Perhaps, we might think, the Spirit guides and unites the church through certain instructions (as in the terrorist cell and MCU cases). Or perhaps the Spirit's indwelling provides a kind of instinctive response, such that members are united in action (as in the honeybee case) even if they are ignorant of the mechanisms undergirding unity. All of these examples share a common feature: group-level agency can arise even if it is not the result of coordination of individual members. These examples all give some plausible ways of thinking about unity in spite of widespread diversity and ignorance.

But while these examples have some insights for thinking about how individuals relate to the church, the work of the Spirit acts as a kind of black box for unity in these cases. In other words, focusing primarily on the members of the church and their relation to the group pays insufficient attention to precisely what the role of the Spirit in the church *is*. And so more detail is needed if we wish to emphasise the primacy of the Spirit in the church.

THE SOCIAL ONTOLOGY OF DICTATORSHIPS

Returning to the discussion of social ontology will help us to say something more constructive about just how a single person (i.e., the Spirit) might

---

33. List and Pettit, *Group Agency*, 33. I consider these two examples in "Analytic Ecclesiology."
34. I consider this example in an unpublished manuscript, "Baptismal Obligations."

be thought of as the primary agent in a social whole (i.e., the church). However, as soon as we begin to specify the role of the co-opting agent in the previous examples, we are met with the difficulty of explaining how the whole derives its unity from one individual while retaining a truly *social* ontology. Consider List and Pettit's remarks on the nature of dictatorships, for instance:

> Although some group agents may exist by virtue of the authorization of an individual spokesperson, this case is degenerate, since everything the recognition of such a group agent entails is already expressible in an individual-level language. . . . The realism appropriate in relation to this kind of group agent is a thin and relatively redundant one, compared to the non-redundant realism we defend more generally.[35]

Aside from the fact that this comment appears to undermine their example of the terrorist group agent above, the problem, as List and Pettit see it, is that group agency, which is rooted in individual agency, is metaphysically redundant in important ways. If decision making is the result of one individual in a group (such as a dictator), then it becomes difficult to distinguish between the actions of the group and the action of the dictator. In other words, the actions of the dictator *just are* the actions of the group.

This worry looks more severe when applied to the context of the church. For if we affirm that the unity of the church comes through the agency of the Spirit and that members act akin to ignorant terrorists, script following actors, or impulse following honeybees, then we are forced to admit that rather than talking about the mystical unity of the whole body, *we might as well speak of a corporately empowered individual* (to borrow List and Pettit's phrase), namely, the Holy Spirit. Thus the examples used previously risk collapsing the church's ontology into the ontology of the Spirit. Instead, we need a social ontology of the church that takes seriously the primacy of the Spirit's agency but that doesn't collapse into a metaphysically redundant account of the church's social reality. Putting the point theologically, we need to make some distinction between the work of the Holy Spirit and the being of the church; in Gregg's words, "While the Spirit is the sine qua non of the church, the church is not the sine qua non of the Spirit."[36]

One way of meeting this challenge is to think more broadly about what

35. List and Pettit, *Group Agency*, 7–8.
36. Greggs, *Dogmatic Ecclesiology*, 15.

counts as a group agent. While List and Pettit admit that some groups meet the conditions for agency without group-level aggregation, it is clear that their primary concern is to discuss those groups that employ a rational decision-making procedure involving a number of individual agents. What they fail to attend to is that even metaphysically thin group agents, such as dictatorships and tyrannies, have clear differences between group-level decisions and individual-level decisions. Consider an example from Stephanie Collins to help illustrate this:

> *Collective Rescue*: There are six strangers at the beach. One is drowning and the others are sunbathing. Each sunbather has the goal that the swimmer be rescued, each believes that every sunbather has this goal (and each therefore believes each has prudential reason to do what they can towards this), and each is disposed to act responsively to the others (insofar as they encounter one another) to realize the goal. All of this happens via their exchange of concerned expressions. They are a coalition. The swimmer can be reached only with a motorboat. It will take two people to drag the boat to the water and hold it while a third starts it. The boat will take off straight away, so the fourth and fifth, who will pull the swimmer into the boat, must already be in the boat. . . . Each sunbather is wholly unknowledgeable about rescuing swimmers—except Laura. All see the drowning, but only Laura knows what any of the required individual actions are. Thankfully, Laura knows what *all* the required actions are. Laura asks if any of the others know what to do and receives puzzled looks in response. So she starts instructing one to drag the boat, one to pull the starter cord, and so on. At each instruction, Laura checks that the relevant beachgoer is willing and able to follow the instruction. Each commits (if only tacitly) to follow her instructions and each supposes the others have too. Laura's instructions divide the necessary actions among the sunbathers. Each performs the action that Laura instructs him or her to perform, because Laura has instructed it. The swimmer ceases drowning.[37]

According to Collins, the reason that this account does not imply the kind of metaphysical redundancy which List and Pettit describe is that the "the decision-procedure is group-level (and not merely Laura-level) in that the beliefs and desires that Laura takes as inputs when she is deciding for the group are different from the beliefs and desires that she would take

37. Collins, *Group Duties*, 108–9.

as inputs if she were deciding for herself."[38] In other words, the decisions that Laura makes as the leader of the group are different from those she would make if she were acting as an individual. She acts on behalf of the group in structuring the actions of individuals to bring about the rescue. In particular, when acting on behalf of the group, she takes the desires of others into consideration, she makes decisions that are properly sensitive to the capacities and situations to all of the group's members, and she uses the others of the group to achieve the group's ends. Put simply, while "the group's attitudes . . . fully track Laura's attitudes . . . this is only true of Laura's attitudes *qua* leader."[39] So while it's true that the group-level decision making is entirely in Laura's head, it is not true that the decision of the group *collapses* into Laura's decisions, since even in this case Laura must take a role within the group.

On Collins's more permissive account of social ontology, tyrannies and democracies can be collectives, and they can do this in a nonredundant way. As she describes, "A group can have a distinctive decision procedure even if the group has a leader who instructs all the others such that the decision-making procedure is housed in the leader's head."[40] On her account, all that is needed to give a nonredundant group ontology of a dictatorship is that "non-decision making members (i) are committed to the procedure and (ii) have inputs into the procedure, at least in the minimal sense that they could leave if they wanted to."[41] While Collins admits that many actual dictatorships fail to meet (i) and (ii) (e.g. because agency is enforced rather than opted-into), this is not because the ontology of dictatorships must lead to metaphysical redundancy. The difference between List and Pettit's ontology and Collins's, then, is that according to Collins we can distinguish between individual attitudes to beliefs/actions and group attitudes to beliefs/actions, even if these are entirely in the head of one individual. That is, we can distinguish between Laura *qua* individual and Laura *qua* leader.

THE BENEVOLENT DICTATOR: GROUP AGENCY IN THE ONE SPIRIT

Collins's picture of collective ontology in which decision-making is rooted in the decision-making of one individual helps to focus our ontology of

38. Collins, *Group Duties*, 167–69.
39. Collins, *Group Duties*, 167–69.
40. Collins, *Group Duties*, 166.
41. Collins, *Group Duties*, 166.

the church away from the members of the church and onto the agency of the Holy Spirit, but contrary to List and Pettit's concerns, it does so in a way that allows us to distinguish between the agency of the Spirit in the church and the agency of the Spirit more generally.

Collins's example of Laura and the collective rescue has some promise, I think, for thinking about the kind of agency the Spirit employs within the church. Unlike the previous examples we have considered, in Collins's example, agency is rooted not in organisational structures but in relationship. The reason the beach rescuers can act as a collective is because of Laura's interaction with each individual and her coordination in bringing the preferences of all together into group-level actions. And although the *decision-making procedure* that unites the group is located in Laura's head, the inputs and outputs of the groups actions and decisions lie beyond Laura. This example speaks more specifically into the *how* of pneumatological ecclesiology.

Whereas previous examples left unsaid just how the Spirit acted as the primary uniting agent of the church, an ecclesiology drawn from the *Collective Rescue* example stresses that the Spirit, attentive to the particularity of the church's members (including the needs and desires of every individual), seeks to instruct and guide the members of the church to act as the one body of Christ. Yet, as in the collective rescue case, the Spirit's agency is not exhausted by fulfilling the desires and needs of the individual members, but the Spirit also pursues the good of the collective; the church must act as one body of Christ in unity with the will of Christ and not merely for the good of its members. It follows on this picture that the human acts of the church cannot be synonymous with the divine actions in the church.[42] While the Spirit employs and uses the outward manifestations of the church, it is the Spirit's agency and not these human manifestations that are the locus of unity. Put in philosophical terms—the attitudes of the collective are not identical to the attitudes of its members.

42. Greggs makes a similar point: "The Spirit is the *condition* for the event of the church: there is infinitely more to the dynamic self-determining act of the Holy Spirit than the event of the church, and the church cannot simply be identified with the Spirit. Faithful attendance to the Spirit's activity is needed, but overconfidence that human activity is the condition of or even is divine activity must be guarded against. The church's creaturely forms cannot be the basis for such claims, nor can they straightforwardly be identified with the Spirit's presence. Rather, despite the human propensity to sin and idolatry, it comes to pass that, in the Spirit's gracious faithfulness, the Spirit acts faithfully to bring about the event of the church. No form of church—high or low, traditional or modern—can ever be either conceived as the basis for the Spirit's act or identified with the Spirit's act. The forms are merely the events of the creaturely and contextual spatiotemporal conditions in which the Spirit acts to fulfil faithfully and constantly the promise of the presence of Christ where two or three are gathered in Christ's name" (Greggs, *Dogmatic Ecclesiology*, 9–10).

A collective ontology rooted in the will of a single decision-making person, the Holy Spirt, emphasises that unity is not equivalent with shared beliefs or shared actions but only arises through the agency of the Spirit. Drawing the insights of ecclesiology and social ontology together, here is a picture that, perhaps optimistically, considers what a true unity in the church might consist of:

> *Collective Rescue 2*: There are millions of individuals who belong to the one church. Some worship in formalised, institutional churches, others in non-denominational contexts. Each member of the church has the goal that God's kingdom come (broadly construed), each believes that every other member has this goal (and each therefore believes each has prudential reason to do what they can towards this), and each is disposed to act responsively to the others (insofar as they encounter one another) to realize this goal. But no one of them can fully realize this goal or see how to achieve it. Each church member is unknowledgeable about how to bring about the ends of God's kingdom. All see some of the problems the church faces, but only the Holy Spirit knows what any of the required individual actions are. Thankfully, the Holy Spirit knows what *all* the required actions are. Moreover, the Spirit works in the lives of individual members and communities to orientate them towards these required actions. The Spirit starts guiding one to serve the needs of local community estate, one to write profound and beautiful liturgies, and so on. At each instruction, the Spirit checks that the relevant member is willing and able to follow the instruction. Each commits (if only tacitly) to follow her instructions and each supposes the others have too. The Spirit's instructions divide the necessary actions among the members of the church. Each performs the action that the Spirit instructs him or her to perform, because the Sprit has instructed it. The kingdom of God comes.[43]

This picture paints an image of how true unity in the church might come about, namely, by discerning the will of the one Spirit and acting in accordance with the will of the Spirit in union with Christ.

However, it might be argued that this picture of ecclesiology dispenses with community and the gathered worship of the institutional church and her sacraments altogether. If the unity of the church is found not in some particular method or tradition but in the Spirit, then perhaps unity

43. My adaptation of Collins's "Collective Rescue" case in *Group Duties*, 108–9.

is best found in private meditation in which one encounters the Spirit and discerns the Spirit's presence and guidance. The picture I have been painting admits the possibility—indeed, it is surely possible for the Spirit to use religious hermits and those far from the communities of the gathered church in enacting the will of Christ in the world. Possibility does not admit normativity, however. For it is important to note that one further question concerns precisely how the Spirit instructs the members of the church. While the church must be thought of as grounded in the work of the Spirit, we must still note that it is a community in which the Spirit is primarily revealed. The community is vital for revealing the will of the Spirit to the church.[44] As Greggs puts it, "The church is that community in which the other is given as *a gift in her otherness* by the event of the Spirit's act in creating the particular church in a particular time in its creaturely contingency. The otherness is not an otherness like any in the world: this otherness is based not on utility or attraction but on the very givenness of the other person."[45]

Before concluding, it is worth reflecting a little on why the community of the church might be especially helpful in revealing the will of the Spirit. As I've argued elsewhere (with David Efird), there are good reasons for thinking that an engagement with God in community has potential to provide a richer and deeper experience of God's presence than one might encounter alone. To show why, we draw on the psychological notion of "joint attention." Joint attention, broadly construed, occurs when two or more individuals are aware of one another's awareness of some object of attention. This ability to jointly attend with others plays a crucial role in infant development; infants learn to navigate the world, to develop a sense of self, and are able to imitate the actions of caregivers through joint attention. An important feature of joint attention is that our experiences of the world are shaped by the attention of others. Philosopher of mind John Campbell writes,

> The individual experiential state you are in, when you and another are jointly attending to something, is an experiential state that you could not be in were it not for the other person attending to the object. The other

---

44. Greggs continues, "This community is so vital, since, 'the individual is not already free; sin continues in the life of the church as in all creation. . . . But in the concrete givenness of the other is the gift of the Spirit of God—a gift which leads us to our true identity in God." Greggs, *Dogmatic Ecclesiology*, 44.

45. Greggs, *Dogmatic Ecclesiology*, 40.

> person enters into your experience as a constituent of it, as co-attender, and the other person could not play that role in your experience except by being co-attender.[46]

Consider driving in the car with another passenger (an example given by Campbell); in pointing to a feature of the road (perhaps by telling the driver to watch out for the upcoming speed-camera), the passenger shapes and alters the driver's experience of the road in important ways. Even though the passenger might not be a feature of the driver's direct experience, the driver is aware of the passenger as a co-attender to the object of the road.

The same might be true of participating in acts of liturgy in community. Just as a driver's attention to the road is shaped by a passenger, our experience of God's presence in the context of communal worship can allow others to point or direct our attention to God in ways that would simply not be possible alone. Encountering God in community importantly shapes our experiences and can potentially help overcome blind spots or biases that we were previously unaware of.[47] While it is at least possible for the unity of the Spirit to be achieved through individual prayer and devotion, there are good reasons for thinking that this is not the primary means by which the Spirit communicates, and there are some good explanations for why this might be the case. The discernment of the Spirit's will for the community and by the community is therefore crucial for the unity of the church.

CONCLUSION

While clearly the church has many similarities with other social collectives—it is constituted by diverse groups of people with diverse beliefs and backgrounds yet united to act as one—it is a form of community that is radically distinct from any social or political body. In Bonhoeffer's words,

---

46. John Campbell, "Joint Attention and Common Knowledge," in *Joint Attention: Communication and Other Minds*, ed. Naomi Elian, Christoph Hoerl, Teresa McCormack, and Johannes Roessler (Oxford: Clarendon), 287.

47. We put it as follows: "In allowing others to shape and guide our perception of God in the worship . . . one of the results is that our own biases and impairments can be corrected by sharing attention with others. When alone, we might have the tendency to focus on certain aspects of God's character, and thereby build up a biased picture of God, in worship, it is possible to be guided by the focus of another's attention. This change in our focus might simply be by means of the emphasis another person places on certain words, the shape and posture of their body, or even the focus of their gaze (on, say, the altar, or the cross, for example). All these ways might serve as pointers to redirect our own attention and thereby to experience some different aspect of God, thereby removing our biases in important ways." Cockayne and Efird, "Common Worship," *Faith and Philosophy* 35, no. 3 (2018): 320.

the church is a "form of community *sui generis*."[48] While Paul clearly sees the relevance of political language and metaphor to describe the church, he also roots this ecclesiology in the oneness of God. The church's unity comes not from any human social endeavour but from the work of the one Spirit. I've argued that contemporary social ontology can help give precise language to some of these distinctions and to affirm the doctrine of the church asserted by Paul and many others in the theological tradition. Thus the task of ecclesiology on the ground, so to speak, is that of discernment. That is, the church must discern the will and instructions of the Spirit as they relate to the will of Christ and seek to live faithfully in light of this discernment. This must ultimately be done in the community and for the community.

48. Dietrich Bonhoeffer, *Sanctorum Communio* (Minneapolis: Fortress, 1998), 266.

CHAPTER 11

THE HOLY SPIRIT AS LIBERATOR

An Exploration of a Black American Pneumatology of Freedom

LEON HARRIS

THE DOCTRINE OF THE HOLY SPIRIT has been part of the black experience in America at least since 1619. The black church in many forms speaks of the presence of the Holy Ghost as an experiential reality that determines salvation, their humanity, and their social reality. On May 18, 1952, Dr. Martin Luther King Jr. preached a sermon titled "The Relevance of the Holy Spirit" at Ebenezer Baptist Church; unfortunately, no extant text of this sermon remains. The point here is that although King did not originate the relevance of the Holy Spirit for the black church community, he was aware of what was already important to the survival of the black community. To this end, my goal is to demonstrate that in the experience of black people during American slavery, the activity of the Holy Spirit provided the language, knowledge, and impetus for the liberation of the slaves. I will do this primarily using a phenomenological approach through the voices of the slaves themselves. I will also demonstrate through three representatives of black theology that liberation is a central part of the black theological enterprise. Then, finally, I will outline liberation as an essential element of pneumatology.

THE HOLY SPIRIT AS LIBERATOR OF (AFRICAN) AMERICAN SLAVES

It is not uncommon for evangelical Christians to credit evangelical Christianity for the abolition of African slavery in America, with the primary credit given to William Wilberforce. Regarding the abolishment of slavery in England in 1807, one writer says that "it was a victory for Wilberforce and his friends, but more importantly it was a victory for humanity, accomplished in the name of Christianity."[1] Throughout this author's discussion of the abolition of slavery in England and America, very little—if any—responsibility or credit is given to the slaves. And when the abolition of slavery is viewed through a theological lens by North American Christians, the credit is usually given to Christianity as a world shaping ideology. An ideology that has inherent properties to re-create humanity by overcoming sin when individuals assent to the propositional truth claims of the gospel. Typically, what is missing in this theological retelling of the abolition of slavery is the Trinity. Specifically, the possibility that the Holy Spirit was already working on behalf of the slaves apart from evangelical Christians, who were the slaveowners, is neglected: "Where the Spirit of the Lord is, there is freedom" (2 Cor 3:17). It should be no surprise that when the slaves cried out to God for deliverance, God heard and answered their prayers. In light of the liberating Spirit, I will propose that it was the Holy Spirit who liberated the slaves. It was the slaves' prayers to God the Father and their belief in Jesus Christ that moved the Spirit to act on their behalf.

In order to organize this section thematically, I will use the tradition's psychological model of faith, that is, the intellect (*notitia*), affection (*assensus*), and volition (*fiducia*) in order to demonstrate how the Holy Spirit flamed the African slaves' imagination toward liberation, which, in the face of evangelical Christian opposition, illuminated the slaves' intellect, warmed their affections to be free, and empowered them with a holy call to resist slavery by any means necessary. What is missing in many evangelical accounts of the abolitionist movement is the witness of the slaves themselves. So I will make use of slave narratives, testimonies, and interviews in order to allow the slaves to speak. The slave narratives are not without problems due to the duress that many of the slaves experienced when retelling their experiences. Yet, even when under the scrutiny of hostile white authority, "the volumes of slave narratives provide a theological abundance of religious

1. Paul Backholer, *How Christianity Made the Modern World* (Poole: ByFaith Media, 2009).

experience from non-Christian bearers of God's freeing spirit."[2] Therefore, I will assume the slave narratives are as truthful as most other documents during this time period. It is the theological lessons about the Holy Spirit that are of interest—that is, how did the Holy Spirit, who delivered Israel, also demonstrate the same divine action of liberation within the life of the slaves.

Epistemological Liberation

Regeneration as an aspect of soteriology is attributed to the work of the Holy Spirit who regenerates and renews through the washing of rebirth (Titus 3:5). Calvin puts it this way, "Therefore, as we cannot come to Christ unless we be drawn by the Spirit of God, so when we are drawn we are lifted up in mind and heart above our understanding."[3] For Calvin, the Holy Spirit regenerates our mind in such a way that the believer is illuminated to the truth and grace of Jesus Christ. Without taking away from the tradition, I would like to expand this epistemological arena of the Holy Spirit. The Holy Spirit, as the perfecting cause within the Trinity, perfects the understanding of the oppressed by illuminating their minds to the truth that they are divinely made for freedom. Where the Spirit of the Lord is, there is freedom from the oppressive brainwashing that binds people to the belief that they are inherently and divinely created to be slaves. The Puritans, who served as chaplains on slave ships, who served as slave owners, masters, and overseers, taught the slaves a theological anthropology that situated the African—or any black body—as less than human by divine *fiat*. But the Holy Spirit taught the slaves a radically different theological anthropology. It was under these circumstances that the former slave James Curry realized that God did not create him or any other African to be a slave. Curry says,

> When my master's family were going away on the Sabbath, I used to go into the house and get down the great Bible, and lie down in the Piazza, and read, taking care, however, to put it back before they returned. There I learned that it was contrary to the revealed will of God, that one man should hold another as a slave. I had always heard it talked among the slaves, that we ought not to be held as slaves; that our forefathers and mothers

---

2. Dwight N. Hopkins and George C. L. Cummings, *Cut Loose your Stammering Tongue: Black Theology in the Slave Narratives* (Maryknoll, NY: Orbis, 1992), xvii.

3. John Calvin, *Institutes of the Christian Religion*, 2 vols., trans. Ford Lewis Battles, ed. John T. McNeill (Louisville: Westminster John Knox, 2011), 1:3.2.34.

> were stolen from Africa, where they were free men and free women. But in the Bible I learned that "God hath made of one blood all nations of men to dwell on all the face of the earth."[4]

Notice that for Curry, slavery is against the revealed will of God. At this point, it might be a leap to attribute this to the work of the Holy Spirit, but when this episode is approached theologically, the conclusion seems plausible. First, if the Spirit illuminates the mind to the truth of the Word, it seems reasonable to assume the Spirit is at work. Curry was not instructed by his slave owners, for he was careful "to put it back before they returned." In order to supervise the slaves' Bible reading, Christian masters kept their slaves under strict orders not to read the Bible outside their masters' watch. Curry probably was taught that slaves should obey their masters as recorded by the apostle Paul. Curry probably was taught the curse of Ham theory, that slavery is actually proper to God's will for Africans. Yet Curry states that this is against the revealed will of God. Again, Curry admits that he was familiar with the rumors or tales that the slaves originated as free people from Africa, but those stories do not seem to persuade him of his right to be free. It was the liberating work of the Holy Spirit through the Scriptures that illuminated Curry's imagination that the God who created the white slave owners also created the black slaves—freedom is given to all people by the same God.

THE HOLY SPIRIT WHO LIBERATES DIGNITY

To be a bearer of the *imago Dei* is to be granted the dignity afforded to human creatures by our Creator, a dignity that was corrupted but has been restored through Jesus's life of obedience, his death on the cross, and his resurrection, culminating in his ascension to the right hand of the Father. Jesus, who was baptized with the Spirit, now restores God-given dignity by baptizing humanity with the Holy Spirit. During times of slavery, American Christianity espoused a theology that privileged immaterial nature over material. This meant that white Christians eventually acquiesced by allowing slaves to be baptized and converted as Christians, though their status as slaves remained unchanged. Black Christians were taught

---

4. John W. Blassingame, "Narrative of James Curry," in *Slave Testimony: Two Centuries of Letters, Speeches, Interviews, and Autobiographies*, ed. John W. Blassingame (Baton Rouge: Louisiana State University Press, 1977), 131. Note: I paraphrased this quote in respect to the slaves and the biased reporting by many white interviewers who tended to dumb down the language in order to present the free blacks as uneducated and unintelligent; I will do this for the remainder of this paper.

that their souls were worthy of redemption, but their bodies—their status in society—were established by divine *fiat* for servitude, with less value and status than white bodies. So the Holy Spirit used the gospel of Jesus Christ to restore the *imago Dei* to the slaves, even if white American society failed to recognize it; black Christians knew, believed, and responded in word and action in a new restored manner. Dwight Hopkins says,

> To know oneself as both an object of and co-laborer with divine initiative emboldened one to act in a self-initiating manner. Because one's ultimate authority was greater than the plantation hegemony, black chattel could seize space and time of self-assertion in some of the most least expected instances. To know oneself as belonging to the divine, in a word, empowered one to claim opportunities for life.[5]

The divine grace of the Holy Spirit freed the mind and affections of enslaved black Christians to recognize in the cross of Christ their restoration in a holistic manner. Jesus died in an embodied state, so the slaves surmised that he died for their bodies as well. This way, liberation is a holistic act that includes immaterial and material existence because the black body is worth just as much as the white body. One way this image was restored was during the slaves' secret church meetings, where they would encounter the presence of the Holy Spirit, who in turn liberated their humanity from the hegemonic theology of slavery.

The divine action of the Holy Spirit restored humanity to the slaves because they no longer saw themselves as alone; there is a God in Jesus Christ who is concerned with their struggle. This gave black Christians a sense of agency to cooperate with the Spirit in order to codetermine their own being in the world. Enslaved black Christians now felt a sense of agency and the divine right to resist the physical oppression; the theological hegemonic teaching that defined their life was now considered demonic; the slave masters' worship time designed to control was replaced by secret meetings controlled by the Holy Spirit. Cummings says that for the slaves "their religious independence became a means of defying the dominant powers and creating their own means of coping with the reality of their exploitation and suffering. This defiance, born of the Spirit, was poignantly expressed when the ex-slaves talked about the prayers of the

5. Dwight N. Hopkins, *Down, Up, and Over: Slave Religion and Black Theology* (Minneapolis: Fortress, 2000), 115.

slave community."[6] For the slaves, it was the Spirit who gave them their songs; it was the Spirit who formed their community of love; it was the Spirit who empowered them to defy the direct orders of their slaveowners and interpret the Bible as liberated black Christians. This secret community constituted by the Holy Spirit became a community of hope for the slaves; an expression of the Spirit's work of liberation. The hope became action in which the enslaved black Christians interpreted sanctification as an individual purification of sins which now also include the community's deliverance from the sin of slavery. Just like Israel, enslaved black Christians learned the lessons of Joshua and Caleb that they are coworkers with the Spirit, meaning that they now have the right and obligation to resist and destroy oppression. Now that their dignity has been restored through independence of thought, worship, and action, they also have a right to the same promised land as white people. This way, the Holy Spirit transformed the affections of enslaved black people to accept, embrace, and reorder their existence based on human dignity and freedom—the slaves have hope that one day all slaves everywhere will be free as a result of the redemptive work of the eschatological cosmic Spirit of Christ.

The Holy Spirit Who Liberates the Volition

In Philippians 2:13, Paul says that "for it is God who works in you, both to will and to work for his good pleasure." We also read in Acts 10:38 that Peter preached saying, "God anointed Jesus of Nazareth with the Holy Spirit and with power. He went about doing good and healing all who were oppressed by the devil, for God was with him." Therefore, it seems reasonable to conclude that the empowering presence of the Holy Spirit will result in the desire to do the Father's will. Prior to the empowering of the Holy Spirit, the individual lives in a state of ruptured humanity, which is manifested in a variety of ways depending on the social location of the individual. In regard to the enslaved black Christian, the rupture in humanity was so severe that resisting slavery was unthinkable—to actively campaign for freedom was not an option. There is a sense that the Holy Spirit's love was and is displayed within the individual and communal life of the slaves when both aspects were "born again" with a renewed desire to be free. When viewed strictly biologically, healthy organisms have a

6. George C. L. Cummings, "The Slave Narratives as a Source of Black Theological Discourse: The Spirit and Eschatology," in *Cut Loose your Stammering Tongue: Black Theology in the Slave Narratives*, ed. Dwight N. Hopkins and George C. L. Cummings (Maryknoll, NY: Orbis, 1992), 50.

drive for survival; a drive to be a particular organism free from external constraints to be otherwise. The Holy Spirit liberated enslaved black Christians by restoring the drive to be *that* particular human being and human community; the *will* to obtain the necessary component of being human—freedom—is transformed from an imagination to reality.

The Holy Spirit transformed the theological anthropology that was grounded in the authority of the white master to the rightful authority of God in Jesus Christ—black people have the divine right to resist oppression. Hopkins states that "a divine right to resist, along with the method of co-creating the black self by seizing sacred domains, also fueled black folk's struggle to reconstitute and regenerate their own new reality."[7] This reconstitution is realized when black Christians participate in their self-definition and self-determination, which begins at their secret church meetings. This way, enslaved black people leave their old relationship based on the interrelationship between white master and black slave and enter a new relationship based on the interrelationship between Jesus Christ and black bodies. The slaves are now constituted as a new creation with the corresponding drive to experience and participate in the freedom—materially and immaterially—that each Christian has because of the cross of Christ.

The desire to actively fight for freedom is theologically grounded in the notion that black Christians saw themselves as partners with God to deliver them from white Christian oppression. Harriet Tubman will serve as an example of a black slave freedom fighter who used her belief in Jesus Christ as the theological and philosophical impetus to act, which in turn demonstrates the role the Spirit had in moving these heroes to act. She sang the following song to alert enslaved black people to get prepared to flee:

> When that old chariot comes,
> I'm going to leave you.
> I'm bound for the promised land.
> Friends, I'm going to leave you.
> I'll meet you in the morning
> When you reach the promised land
> On the other side of Jordan,
> For I'm bound for the promised land.[8]

7. Hopkins, *Down, Up, and Over*, 128.
8. Sarah H. Bradford, *Harriet Tubman: The Moses of Her People* (Mineola, NY: Dover, 2004), 16.

When Tubman sang this song, she was using biblical imagery of God's deliverance of Israel to encourage her fellow freedom fighters, and it was a signal that the time to leave the plantation was now. Hopkins says that "the use of liberation language indicated that the coast was finally clear for one more soul's journey to freedom. And it was a joyful song symbolic of praising the power of God's grace over oppression."[9] It was Tubman's belief that the same Spirit who liberated Israel will now liberate enslaved blacks.

Admittedly, this is not an exhaustive treatment of the history of the black church during slavery. What I attempted to briefly demonstrate is that theologically speaking, we can see that the Holy Spirit was moving the slaves toward freedom through the psychological framework of mind, affection, and volition. The enslaved black people encountered the Holy Spirit through the witness of the Word, and in the face of opposition they were moved to resist and partner with the triune God to create a new humanity of free people in Jesus Christ. This same Spirit, through partnering with black Christians, then moved white Christians to partner with them toward the abolishment of slavery. This way, both black and white Christians owe the responsibility for liberating slaves to the grace of God in Christ by the empowering presence of the Holy Spirit.

Pneumatology in Black Theology

On June 13, 1969, the National Committee of Black Churchmen issued a statement regarding black theology. The statement explicated that black theology is not an expression of the theology given by white slave masters but an *appropriation* and interpretation of the gospel *by* and *for* black Christians. The Black Churchmen described black theology as "a theology of black liberation. It seeks to plumb the black condition in the light of God's revelation in Jesus Christ, so that the black community can see that the gospel is commensurate with the achievement of black humanity."[10] The Churchmen delineated that black liberation does not mean the oppression or violence against whites; black liberation means freedom for black people and freedom for whites to stop their racism against black people. The Churchmen conclude with, "the demand that Christ the Liberator imposes on all men requires all blacks to affirm their full dignity as persons

9. Hopkins, *Down, Up, and Over*, 130.

10. Milton C. Sernett, *African American Religious History: A Documentary Witness*, 2nd ed. (Durham: Duke University Press, 1999), 564.

and all whites to surrender their presumptions of superiority and abuses of power."[11] This is the driving force of pneumatology within black theology. By reviewing three representatives of black theology in the persons of Dwight Hopkins, James H. Evans Jr., and J. Deotis Roberts, a pattern will emerge that gives a general agreement to a pneumatology that reflects the experience of enslaved black Christians as rehearsed earlier.

DWIGHT HOPKINS: PNEUMATOLOGY AS COWORKER WITH THE SPIRIT OF LIBERATION

Dwight Hopkins formulates his pneumatology within an encompassing theology of liberation that is the framework for the doctrine of God, Christology, and the redemption of humanity toward freedom. In other words, liberation becomes an overarching metaphor that shapes his theology through the experience of the Holy Spirit beyond mere doctrinal presentations. The Holy Spirit is construed as God *for* us because God is the Spirit of total liberation. God acts for our freedom because in the Holy Spirit God is freedom. This means that instead of revelation being a revelation of the reality of Jesus Christ, revelation is the freedom received in Jesus Christ: revelation is the knowledge by the Holy Spirit that God is freedom for *us*. Jesus Christ is the Spirit of total liberation with us, he is with us in the presence of the Holy Spirit co-constituting the African American self—as well as the poor and oppressed—toward a total liberation in social, economic, and cultural terms. So, faith in Jesus means that "faith lets the poor know that trouble does not last always."[12] Jesus's blood alone is the final arbiter and authority on liberation because the Spirit of liberation rests on Jesus as the one who gives the Spirit. Ultimately, black identity and black culture is given validation, that is, the dignity to exist, because of Jesus and no other. It is the experience of Jesus as the Spirit of total liberation where the eschatological purpose of humanity is conceived as the Spirit of total liberation *in* us.

The Holy Spirit is not relegated to personal sanctification for Hopkins, the Holy Spirit is the Spirit of liberation *in* us, that is, in the individual black body and the black community. The Spirit does this through co-constituting the identity and the ontology of the black person through politico-economics, daily social interactions, linguistics, and racial cultural identity levels. Hopkins says, "These disciplines entail what we have also

11. Sernett, *African American Religious History*, 565.
12. Hopkins, *Down, Up, and Over*, 201.

called methods of the self—that is, knowing oneself and taking care of oneself. In other words, implementing disciplines of creativity is to work with the Spirit to constitute the self through methods of self."[13] This way, salvation is when the Spirit liberates the black community—and also the poor and marginalized—toward a self-determination and self-definition of their existence apart from external hegemonic evils. The ontology of the oppressed is now a new creation, or a re-creation, because their existence is grounded in the freedom of God in the presence of the Holy Spirit. Hopkins does not limit the work of the Holy Spirit only in the oppressed or marginalize, but he does not venture far from liberation as the defining framework. Hopkins states, "To be a human is to work with the Spirit of liberation within us on behalf of the oppressed, in contrast to working with the legion of demonic spirits within us that would turn us away from God's new humanity and new Common Wealth and toward selfishness."[14] In summary, Hopkins defines the work of the Spirit through creation, re-creation, sanctification, and the eschaton as an event of restoring the freedom that is ontologically God for us, incarnationally God with us, and eschatologically God in us.

JAMES H. EVANS JR.: A PNEUMATOLOGY OF BELIEF AND PRACTICE

James Evans Jr. recognizes the interconnection between the doctrine and experience of the Holy Spirit within African American theology as a nexus that shapes the individual and the community. There is no theology of the Holy Spirit apart from a thorough consideration and exploration of the diachronic and synchronic historical experiences of the black church. Evans says, "The theological understanding of the Holy Spirit, or pneumatology, among African Americans, has taken into account the essence and existence of black religious life."[15] This frames pneumatology in a way that guards against the tendencies of some theologians to associate the Holy Spirit primarily with ecstatic emotional experiences, for the Spirit also provides counsel and guidance for the sociological development of the black church. It is in the experience *of* and *in* the black church where the work of the Holy Spirit is nurtured, received, and experienced.

Evans locates pneumatology in the black church within three models in

13. Hopkins, *Down, Up, and Over*, 238.
14. Hopkins, *Down, Up, and Over*, 238.
15. James Evans Jr., "The Holy Spirit in African American Theology," in *Oxford Handbook of African American Theology*, ed. Katie G. Cannon (New York: Oxford University Press, 2014), 166.

relation to black religious belief and practice: radicalism, liberation, and survival. Belief and practice are the links that maintain a coherent pneumatology for Evans. Black radicalism is not a description of subversive activity but a recognition that blacks were meant to live in freedom and with dignity—the black community is precious in God's sight. Instead of subversive activity, black radicalism is grounded in the Spirit's empowerment and right to protest and struggle for freedom in the here and now—the right for life abundantly. Black radicalism is grounded in the belief that God the Spirit is the Creator and Redeemer for them just as the God liberated the oppressed in the Bible. In other words, black radicalism is not social deviance; it is a spiritual way of life, grounded in the Holy Spirit, toward an affirmation of black life. Evans says, "The assertion here is that this radicalism is at the heart of the understanding of the Holy Spirit as Creator in black theology."[16]

There is a pneumatological freedom that takes the form of liberation and survival—theologically speaking, redemption and providence. The Holy Spirit brings joy in the morning because Jesus is the Anointed One who liberates the oppressed. The Spirit liberates from individual and institutional sins; the strictures in social levels, brought about by sin, are abolished. The new community is a community of freedom because the Holy Spirit has redeemed the black community so that it can order its existence apart from the strictures of a fallen reality toward the freedom in the redeemed community. The Spirit sustains the black community through the gifts of the Spirit, which sustain the church through God's providential care. The wilderness becomes a place of transformation, just as it was for Israel, through the sustaining presence of God in the black community, as well as the communities of the poor and marginalized. Ultimately this means that black Christians' dignity, sense of liberation, and actual life of freedom are sustained by the continuing work of the Holy Spirit. Therefore, belief and practice shapes African American pneumatology in a way that impacts the historical reality of the black religious experience through the creation of black identity, the liberation of the black community, and the maintenance of the identity and freedom of the black community due to the providence of the Spirit.

J. Deotis Roberts

J. Deotis Roberts develops a pneumatology that has a structure similar to that of Evans. For Roberts, there must be a realization that Black theology

16. Evans, "The Holy Spirit in African American Theology," 169.

"does not endorse the Western-oriented division between the personal and the social or the physical and the spiritual." When discussing pneumatology in a black theological context, the orthodoxy-orthopraxy scheme must not give priority to one over the other; both necessarily inform pneumatology. So, for Roberts, the Holy Spirit means that God is a vital, acting God; God is that which gives life in creation and re-creation—God is active in human life: "The *pneuma* of God is God acting in Creation, providence and redemption."[17] Roberts desires to remain faithful to the evangelical tradition by maintaining the indissoluble relationship between Christology and pneumatology. He is concerned that some black Pentecostals have been criticized for being too pneumatically oriented and minimizing the christological relationship.

It is interesting that in critiquing Pentecostalism Roberts explicates a robust black pneumatology. For Roberts, liberation becomes the focal point for praising and criticizing Pentecostalism. Roberts explains that black Pentecostalism includes an element of liberation, namely, liberation from the authoritative structures of early Pentecostalism that attempted to deny black members leadership and ministerial roles. On the other hand, Roberts says, "With all of its fervent claims to the outpouring of the Spirit in the individual soul, there is so little evidence of concerns for making life more human for the oppressed."[18] As we saw with Hopkins and Evans, liberation becomes an overarching ruling metaphor for determining a proper pneumatology in Black theology. The Spirit for Roberts works within the church as an institution and an event. As an institution, the Spirit liberates the structures and social order in the historical situatedness of the black church toward creating freedom of the black individual and community. As an event, the Spirit liberates the affections of the black community through an empowering presence that energizes the community to action. Evans finds that the black church is moved by the Spirit's empowerment in such a way that it is concerned with individual relationships with God, but equally the relationship between individuals constitutes a Spirit-filled life. The "fruit of the Spirit" is considered an inherent part of the gospel proclamation, as well as *the* outcome of the gospel: the fruits of the Spirit create a community that co-creates with the Spirit of liberation. This way, the fruits of the Spirit are now defined as having a proper concern and

17. J. Deotis Roberts, "The Holy Spirit and Liberation: A Black Perspective," *Mid-Stream* 24, no. 4 (1985): 398.

18. Roberts, "The Holy Spirit and Liberation: A Black Perspective," 407.

action for the oppressed and poor as an essential aspect of a Spirit-filled empowered gospel of Jesus Christ.

A Pneumatology of Liberation

Where the Spirit of the Lord is, there is liberty. If we consider the experience of the Holy Spirit within the context of the African slaves and then later enslaved black Christians, as well as the theological explication of pneumatology from the three representatives of black theology, it is clear that liberation is a primary aspect that is common to black theology. At this point, I will assume that black Christians' voices are just as valid as any other voice, and their contributions are not merely as black Christians but as Christians. Therefore, for a pneumatology to be complete, it must engage with a robust account of liberation that does not privilege the immaterial over the material. Liberation must include an ontological freedom *to be* that is constituted relationally so that the individual, as well as those social structures that constitute individuals within a given set of relationships, is liberated. In other words, as the individual emerges through a complex series of relationships, which themselves emerge from lower into higher social realities, each social stratification is interrelated so that the individual needs the community, and the community needs the individual. The Holy Spirit is the Spirit who perfects *koinonia* and freedom. Karl Barth says that "God's being consists in the fact that He is the One who loves in freedom. In this He is the perfect being: the being which is itself perfection and so the standard of all perfection. . . . The one perfection of God, His loving in freedom, is lived out by Him, and therefore identical with a multitude of various and distinct types of perfection."[19] Therefore, liberation is that which is lived out in our created reality in a way that alters the structures of reality that determine the ontology of the individual; our particularity is determined by relationships in our social reality, so our freedom is a work of the Holy Spirit to create a community of freedom.

In a sense, the divine action of liberation as witnessed in the economic life of God must be the same divine action that is in God's immanent life: God reveals as he is. The Holy Spirit liberates creation to be itself because God relates to creation out of free love, not necessity. In this way, because the Spirit's action is that of perfecting in love, creation is free to relate to

19. Karl Barth, *Church Dogmatics*, ed. G. W. Bromiley and T. F. Torrance (Peabody, MA: Hendrickson, 2010), II.1, 322.

the Creator, but as a creature. The perfect love between the Father and the Son, which is shared by the Holy Spirit, is now turned toward creation by the same action within the triune God. The Holy Spirit prepared Christ a body so that Christ can share God's love with creation—an action of perfection by the Spirit. The Holy Spirit anointed Jesus Christ at his baptism to inaugurate Christ as the head of a new community that shares in God's love. At the resurrection, the Holy Spirit created a new spiritual existence that demonstrated the Father's love, which was given to the Son, and which through the action of the Spirit was also shared with creation. Creation is liberated from fulfilling some lack in the Creator because the Spirit is continually perfecting the love that was given from the Father through the incarnated Christ—God is complete in himself. Creation is not necessary for God to demonstrate love, for God is co-love in his eternal being: creation is free to respond to God in an appropriate manner without becoming God to do so because God does not rely on creation to experience love. Freedom is shaped by God's love, which means that freedom in creation is conceived as a gift from God that is ultimately *for* and *to* God. Freedom is not to be conceived as the freedom to be away from God or other creatures. The Father's two hands, the Son as redeemer and the Spirit as liberator, actualize freedom in creation so that creation is free to be in a relationship with God and with other creatures.

There is an active element of liberation in pneumatology in that the Holy Spirit liberates the Father and the Son to be *that* Father and *that* Son. Colin Gunton states that "we may say that the Spirit's function in the Godhead is to particularize the *hypostases* . . . to liberate them to be themselves, to be particular persons in community and as communion."[20] This means that this particularizing act is an act of the Holy Spirit whereby the Father and the Son attain perfection and retain their distinctions. The Father's perfection is actualized when his relationship with the Son is perfected *when* it is shared with the Holy Spirit. The Son's perfection is likewise only truly actualized when the love he received from the Father is shared with the Holy Spirit. The distinctions of the Father and the Son are maintained because the Father is ever the source of this reciprocal love, and the Son's love is begotten by the Father's love. The Father is the originator and the Son is originated eternally in love. The personhood of the Father and the Son are each perfected because the Holy Spirit takes this divine reciprocal

20. Colin E. Gunton, *The One, the Three, and the Many: God, Creation, and the Culture of Modernity* (Cambridge: Cambridge University Press, 1993), 190.

love they share and completes it by allowing it to become a perfected charity-love per Richard of St. Victor. The Holy Spirit's distinction is also maintained because the Spirit receives love from the Father and the Son. There is a logical *taxis* but not a temporal one; the activity of love between the Father, Son, and Holy Spirit is an eternal activity.

This active liberation of the Holy Spirit in the immanent life of God is translated into an active liberation within creation, within our creaturely reality. The Spirit liberated Christ's humanity to be free to be the Son of God in relation to the Father and free to be the Son of Man in relation to humanity. Jesus announces that the Spirit of the Lord is upon him. For Jesus, this anointing with the Spirit is realized in that he gave good news to the poor, released the captives, gave sight to the blind, and freed those who were oppressed. The year of Jubilee was not simply a release of moral guilt, it was a material release from socio-economic oppression. Jesus is announcing a radical shift in the sociological existence of the world, a shift that is now determined by liberation, by the freedom that is God and is given by Jesus's empowerment with the Holy Spirit, who perfects freedom. Jesus liberated those oppressed spiritually as well as socioeconomically and politically. Jesus consistently crossed sociological boundaries in order to invite outsiders inside; he established a church that was commanded to be a different type of sociological existence, an existence of sharing resources and existing as a community of persons-in-relation. Just as the Holy Spirit actively participates in the freedom of the Father and the Son, the Spirit liberates believers toward a Spirit-filled Christlike existence of dying to the world's strictures and living for the other to free them from oppression, poverty, captivity, and blindness—materially and spiritually. The Holy Spirit demonstrated this active liberation in the book of Acts when the church freely shared their resources in Acts chapters 2, 4, 5, and 6. In the dispute between the Hellenistic and the Hebraic Jews, the Spirit reordered the social reality of the early church in Acts 6 to liberate the widows among the Hellenistic Jews from the denial of their daily resources to live. So pneumatology must include an element of active liberation of those who are afflicted by the sinful structures and strictures of this fallen world. In concrete terms, the active side of pneumatology liberates believers from an active participation in the oppressive structures and strictures of our fallen world toward an active participation in working against those same oppressive structures and strictures toward the liberation of those powerless in our world. The Spirit of liberation transforms individuals' fallen nature of selfishness into a self-giving to others in order to fight alongside with the Spirit to destroy all forms of socio-economic-political oppression—as a form of sin—that has fallen upon others.

There is also a passive element to pneumatology that allows those who are suffering from oppressive elements in this fallen world to embrace the hope of the liberating Spirit. Frank Macchia uses the root metaphor of Spirit baptism to ground his theology in the work of the third person of the Trinity. Macchia explains,

> Central to the Trinitarian structure of the story of Jesus is the Father's loving bestowal of the Spirit lavishly ("without limit," John 3:34) on Jesus at his baptism as the sign of divine love and favor and to declare Christ's sonship (Matt. 3:17), an anointing that begins at Christ's conception (Luke 1:35), is found at his crucifixion (Heb. 9:14), and culminates in his resurrection (Rom. 1:4).[21]

In Macchia's scheme, the Father "baptizes" the Son with the Holy Spirit; the Son returns the love of the Father by "baptizing" the Father with the Holy Spirit. Here baptizing is a metaphor for the action of love between the Father and Son in the person of the Holy Spirit. This divine action of love, which culminates in the Son being baptized with the Spirit and becoming the one who gives the Spirit, is the same action which God displays as love for his creation. The Spirit is the bond of love because the Father pours out the Spirit on his Son and through his Son on creation. Elsewhere, Macchia says that "we need to exercise caution here so that we do not de-personalize the Spirit by eliminating the Spirit's participation as person in the *koinonia* of Father and Son, relating to them in ways appropriate to the Spirit."[22] In this way, the Spirit is the third person of the Godhead who opens God's communion and mutual indwelling beyond God's self to the other; the Father-Son relationship moves to the other, the Holy Spirit, who in turn opens communion to the many of creation. The experience of God's love is located in the presence of the Holy Spirit when creation, especially the church of Christ, is baptized with the Holy Spirit who liberates.

This way, pneumatology must include a passive element in which the Father's love and Jesus's grace are experienced in the liberating work of the Holy Spirit. The Holy Spirit who is given by the Father and the Son,

---

21. Frank D. Macchia, *Baptized in the Spirit: A Global Pentecostal Theology* (Grand Rapids: Zondervan, 2006), 118.

22. Frank D. Macchia, *Justified in the Spirit: Creation, Redemption, and the Triune God* (Grand Rapids: Eerdmans, 2010), 302.

or through the Son (this is not the place for the *filioque* debate), in order to liberate those who are oppressed by the sins of this fallen world. The divine action of liberating Israel from societal slavery is that same action we rehearsed in the African slaves. The Spirit is working not just to open our hearts to the reality of Jesus Christ but also to re-create the social structures and strictures in our churches and society at large. It is in the church where we should develop a pneumatology of liberation that works on behalf of those who are powerless in this world to extricate them from those demonic forces working toward slavery instead of the freedom that is given to every human being by God. Concretely speaking, the passive side of pneumatology means that some will receive liberation from participating in the selfishness of this fallen world, and others will receive the liberation of having their dignity restored through the Spirit's work. The outcome will be an ecclesiology that is giving to others in need (the active) and restoring the dignity and self-determination *to be* for the oppressed and marginalized (the passive).

CONCLUSION

I attempted to demonstrate that the Holy Spirit is responsible for granting freedom to the slaves. First, by actively giving enslaved black Christians the drive to participate as a partner with the Spirit to resist slavery and fight for freedom. Second, the Holy Spirit worked passively on the slaves' behalf through the structures of society to move key figures to fight on behalf of the slaves (who were already resisting slavery by various means). I also briefly introduced three representatives of black theology to demonstrate that liberty is a common theme in their projects. Finally, I attempted briefly to develop a pneumatology that requires freedom as a perfection of God through the active and passive work of the Holy Spirit. Hopefully, this will create an ecclesiology that is pneumatologically grounded, one that constitutes a community that gives of itself to work for the liberation of those who are oppressed and treated as less than human, a church that realizes that all members have equal access to the table of our Father through Christ, meaning that each community has a voice that should be heard and not dismissed. The Spirit liberated each community to be *that* community in Christ in our historical reality, so they deserve to experience a life of freedom in the Spirit. Where the Spirit of the Lord is, there is liberty.

CHAPTER 12

RUNNING AWAY FROM SORROW

Pneumatology and Some Modern Discontents

EPHRAIM RADNER

THE HOLY SPIRIT TEACHES US to die faithfully. Let me begin to unpack this unprepossessing claim with the aid of Schopenhauer's distinction between "natural" and "artificial" education or teaching. It is a distinction that we can perhaps apply to pneumatic education as well and will open up my concerns.

Schopenhauer, as many of us know, was a great early nineteenth century German philosopher, the self-styled rival of Hegel. Unlike Hegel's vision of an ever-developing and perfecting Spirit realizing itself through history, Schopenhauer saw reality as one big purposeless and impersonal movement of striving, undetermined "will." Everything, human beings included, is an instance of this striving, and the press for survival, reproduction, and the rest is the particular form of this aimless drive that constitutes what "is." Obviously, this is a rather bleak view of things, and Schopenhauer himself granted that to be the case. Human life, through this ceaseless press, is a concatenation of directionless suffering. But we can mitigate this, at least, by facing the facts and not constantly resisting them. Schopenhauer was one of the first Westerners to latch on to Eastern religions, and here aspects of early Hinduism and Buddhism come into play: go with the flow of things, and do not try to manipulate them according to some scheme that must, in any case, eventually be crushed by the brute power of the universal Will.

There is the carcass of an expansive pneumatology here, but that's not my purpose in bringing Schopenhauer up. Rather, I am interested in his concern that young people, especially, be properly trained to live in this brutal world. They need to be educated.[1] And education is, in the end, about learning the "truth." This is, of course, a Christian concern too: we must come to know the world as it is; God as God is; and the world as God's. How does this learning happen? Schopenhauer, who was *not* a Christian, railed against what he called "artificial" education, one that fills young people's heads with "abstract ideas," theories, principles, fantasies. These abstract ideas, Schopenhauer argued, constrain a young person's mind to see reality a certain way that, when they actually encounter the world over time, proves simply false. The world is not subject to our theories; it is brute force on its way to nowhere. *This* is what young people need to learn, so that they can figure out how to navigate reality. Schopenhauer raged against reading novels, for instance, and we can easily suppose what he might think of the whole onslaught of other media narratives and claims now swirling about young people's imaginations. "Anxiety" and "false confidence," he says, are what "theoretical" education trains young people into. And that is a recipe for deepening pain because suffering will inevitably come and explode your pitiable expectations. Instead, with his somewhat Romantic notion of the peasant classes, Schopenhauer argued for the superiority of "natural" education, as he put it: just living and observing the world and people. Inductive learning with a vengeance, you might say. Only after time, a long time, of such observation might one figure something out—tentative, *ad hoc*, determined, who knows? But it will hardly resemble the world of earnest philosophers, calculating politicians, and glib moralists. What about day-dreaming theologians? Not theirs either. I will come back to this.

In any case, the Holy Spirit is a "natural"—a *divinely* natural—educator, not an artificial one. For the Holy Spirit teaches us to die faithfully, as I said. Above all! This chapter will, in a circuitous way, meditate on this claim. And the claim is not meant in a limited way, as if, among the many things the Holy Spirit does, there is also the interesting task of helping us to die faithfully. Or even that, what the Holy Spirit *does* is but a shadow

1. Arthur Schopenhauer, "On Education," in *Parerga and Paralipomena: Short Philosophical Essays*, trans. E. F. J. Payne, vol. 2 (Oxford: Clarendon, 1974), 627–33.

of who the Holy Spirit *is*, his actions being a set of assignments after the accomplishment of which he can go home and do his own thing. It is more than this. The early twentieth-century Jewish philosopher Franz Rosenzweig began his great work *The Star of Redemption* with the following sentence: "From Death . . . arises all knowledge of the All."[2] Rosenzweig understood, before Heidegger, the mysterious form of our opening to God as being located in our mortality. And I will be suggesting that the Holy Spirit is the very divine condition for a reality that places death and faith as the limit of creaturely existence, beyond which we ourselves cannot go, at least as we are currently framed.

The Holy Spirit *is* this very reality, divinely construed. To say "Holy Spirit" is to say that we are made by God to die and, in dying and moving to such a death, to turn in faith and hope and even love to the one who has so made us, the maker who remakes as well. That is the "whirl of the world," *anima mundi*, the Spirit that sustains, that is at the root of all things. I am pointing to the need, as it were, to engage the economic-immanent relationship in terms of Spirit in a particular way. A little bit of Schopenhauer, but then something quite different.

Still, if the Spirit "animates" the world, then a little Schopenhaurian natural and inductive learning can be not only useful but also essential. What is a human life? What is a human death? The Spirit is itself when it is showing us just such lives and deaths.

This line of reasoning—and its challenge—has pressed itself on me recently in the discovery of a modern theologian I had not known before, Ulrich Simon. Since, in the perspective of inquiry I am suggesting, biography is always a pneumatic affair—the Spirit shows itself in showing us the world as it is—let me tell you something about Simon. For if biography and thus memory *are* pneumatic affairs, the task of not forgetting is perhaps a special pneumatic virtue above all. I came across Simon when I found his name in a list of Jewish-Christian theologians, a category I had been rummaging around in. I began to look into his writings. Born in 1913 in Berlin, he died in 1997 in Britain, having moved there at the age of twenty, became an Anglican priest, and then taught theology at Kings College, London, for thirty-five years. Simon was not a great theologian, but he was remarkable, and through this pneumatic reality that is a particular life,

2. Franz Rosenzweig, "Vom Tode, von der Furcht des Todes, hebt alles Erkennen des All an," in *Der Stern der Erlösung* (Frankfurt: Kauffmann, 1921), 7. Cf. *The Star of Redemption*, trans. William W. Hallo (Notre Dame: Notre Dame Press, 1971).

a real life, his experiential insights are unique and deserve reflection. What follows, then, is a little something about Ulrich Simon.[3]

Simon's Jewish family, like many German Jews of the time, was "assimilated"—that is to say, it had given up particular Jewish practices and melded into the general Christian forms of life given in the surrounding environment. Although his father would attend synagogue twice a year, Simon went to the vaguely Christian schools every cultured German did in his context. Indeed, German high culture is what formed him. His father, James Simon, was a fine musician—a performer and a composer who knew everyone famous from the era. Young Ulrich grew up amid the celebrities of a now vanished world of art and ideas: Klemperer, Kleiber, Walter, and Horowitz all crossed the Simon home's threshold, along with literary luminaries like Thomas Mann and Max Scheler, joining in parties or small recitals. Down the street lived the Bonhoeffer family, and Ulrich remembered their warm home with fleeting images of welcome and benevolence. Ulrich's father, James, however, was not much of a success for all his connections. In the economic crisis after World War I, the family was driven into horrendous penury, like so many thousands of other Germans. Ulrich later recounted wandering about in the winter through the rural outskirts of Berlin with his mother and being sent into farms, past vicious dogs, a gaunt child capable of eliciting sympathy, to beg for potatoes or eggs from peasants.

Meanwhile, Germany had begun its confused but energized descent into political chaos and finally hell. Ulrich managed to get back to school, to learn his philosophy, read his literature, and even begin to wonder about God, with figures like Harnack and Barth pushing into his young consciousness. Everything fell apart, of course. In the early '30s, the family understood its precarious position, their quasi-Christianized and German veneer mocked and then stripped off by political passions whipped up by the suddenly powerful forces of fascism that saw non-Aryan ethnicity, particularly Jewish ethnicity, as ineradicably filthy. Ulrich's father, in any case, was barely making a living as it was. The family scattered. Ulrich was sent to England, his older brother had left for the Soviet Union, and his parents went in two directions, his mother to Switzerland, his father to Holland. Cut off from his family, Ulrich made his way, with help from groups assisting refugees, through British school and then, drawn to the

3. The details of his life are drawn mostly from Ulrich Simon, *Sitting in Judgement, 1913–1963: An Interpretation of History* (London: SPCK, 1978).

Christian faith in a deep way, he entered the Anglican ministry, first working in parochial settings, then returning to graduate school and a career teaching theology, marrying, and raising a family.

In a way, it was a smooth life. But of course, it was nothing of the kind. Though his mother was finally able to join him, Ulrich mostly struggled on his own for many years. He lived and ministered amid the rubble and dead bodies of the Blitz. And when the war was over, after much difficulty he discovered that his brother had been killed several years before in Stalinist purges and that his father, rounded up in Holland, had disappeared in the German camps, first in the strange musical culture of the Theresienstadt concentration camp—part of a lively group of prisoners who gave concerts and lectures to one another—and then finally to Auschwitz. The last sight survivors had of Ulrich's father, apparently, was of him sitting on a suitcase at the train station, waiting to be taken away to his end, scribbling out some notes on a sheet of music paper, oblivious of the sad winds swirling around him. Most of James Simon's music is completely lost, although there is a small collection of unpublished pieces, mostly from the '30s in manuscript, that he sent to a friend in New York before he was arrested, and that is preserved in the Leo Baeck Institute. One can hear a couple of performances of the few existing works, including a moving "Lament for Cello," clearly drawn out from a deep biblical well—it is on a Dutch internet site devoted to "forbidden music" from World War II, the fluttering detritus of mostly murdered Jewish and resistance composers.[4]

Ulrich Simon, the theologian, had to try to make sense of all this. His 1978 quasi-autobiography, *Standing in Judgment, 1913–1963: An Interpretation of History*, from which I extracted these signposts, is an attempt to do so. In this book, he is mostly interested in ideas, failed ones: Chesterton's and Belloc's blindness and antisemitism; the cowardice of most religious leaders in the face of cultural and political madness and rot; the indulgent silliness of what emerged in the '60s among Christian writers—he doesn't hesitate to call them sentimental Gnostics trying to play footsie with a rapidly atheizing culture and so on. His heroes (Bonhoeffer, Barth, and others) had the virtues of not being fooled about the world and its peoples. Simon's bitterness and anger are directed most forcefully at "appeasing" Christianity, obviously in its political forms before World War II, but more broadly still

4. Biography, references, and links at https://www.forbiddenmusicregained.org/search/composer/id/102025; the "Lament" can be found at https://www.forbiddenmusicregained.org/search/composition/id/102050.

at the whole attempt to make the world seem morally livable on its own terms. What were these people thinking? he wonders.

Although he wrote about a number of topics, in the end it is "tragedy" that, in a way, orders his mature focus. Simon wrote a short book on the topic entitled *Pity and Terror: Christianity and Tragedy*,[5] but the theme winds its way through all of his last works. Simon is not the most supple thinker here, and as I said, his work as a whole does not rise to the level of greatness. He tends to write in short rapid bursts, densely and without elaboration and sometimes without visible coherence, as if ideas and impressions flow out of his imagination and simply fall upon the page in succession, leaving readers to pick their way through the littered field. In a way, however, this makes his writing all the more descriptive of his own frame of mind, a kind of unintegrated search for "something"—the divine thread, as if it weren't at all obvious. Tragedy, in any case, has been a topic of much debate and study over the last few decades, especially in literary scholarship and has received some substantive theological reflection, in particular in the work of Donald MacKinnon and, most recently, following him quite closely, of Rowan Williams.[6] Simon was, in this case, part of a growing movement of thought.

Most writers today agree that it is difficult to pin down exactly the "what" of tragedy, and that Aristotle's classic definitions are of limited usefulness as one passes through the self-styled tragic works of Shakespeare and his contemporaries or of German or Spanish baroque drama or French classical plays and on and on. That there is no "best" answer and approach to tragedy, even definitionally, is perhaps intrinsic to the elements that tragedy engages: not just human suffering but suffering bound up with forces—whether divine or natural—beyond a human being's control, the struggle with which constantly defies simple moral analysis. Simon grappled with a steady fixture of modern analysis of tragedy, linked in part with the seminal work of the critic George Steiner:[7] Can there be such a

5. Ulrich Simon, *Pity and Terror: Christianity and Tragedy* (Basingstoke: Macmillan, 1989).

6. Among numerous writings, see D. M. MacKinnon, "Theology and Tragedy," *Religious Studies* 2, no. 2 (April 1967), 163–69; MacKinnon, "Atonement and Tragedy," in *Borderlands of Theology* (London: Lutterworth Press, 1968), 97–104; Rowan Williams, *The Tragic Imagination* (Oxford: Oxford University Press, 2016). For recent rethinking of some of these questions and their presuppositions, see the collection, *The Transformations of Tragedy: Christian influences from Early Modern to Modern*, ed. Fionnuala O'Neill Tonning, Erik Tonning, and Joylon Mitchell (Leiden: Brill, 2019).

7. See George Steiner, *The Death of Tragedy* (London: Faber and Faber, 1961); Steiner, "A Note on Absolute Tragedy," *Journal of Literature & Theology* 4, no. 2 (1990): 147–56; Steiner, "Tragedy, Pure and Simple," in *Tragedy and the Tragic: Greek Theatre and Beyond*, ed. M. Silk (Oxford: Oxford University Press, 1996), 534–46; and Steiner, "'Tragedy,' Reconsidered," *New Literary History* 35, no. 1 (2004): 1–15. On Steiner and MacKinnon as common learners, see Graham Ward, "Tragedy as Subclause: George Steiner's dialogue with Donald MacKinnon," *Heythrop Journal* 34 (1993): 274–87.

thing, he wondered, as "Christian" or even "biblical" tragedy? Is Samson a tragic figure? What of Jacob? And, most especially, Jesus Christ? Does the resurrection, the resolving act of the creator God of Judeo-Christianity, simply vacate the problem that informs a tragic view of the world, as it seemed to do for one thousand years before the literary innovations of early modernity? Did Christianity, as Simon partially accepts, demote tragedy as an accurate descriptor of the world, both out of a profound insight and with profound negative costs?

For both MacKinnon and Williams, tragedy involves aspects of suffering and moral questioning that are, as they say, "intractable" or "nonnegotiable." The world will not give away its burdens, and individuals cannot escape them, however much and however nobly they resist. But unlike Steiner, who is not quite an atheist, Williams cannot agree that the world is constituted by a tragedy that could ever be characterized as "absolute." There *is*, after all, the resurrection! And Simon agrees, but he somehow cannot put it all together. In an earlier book, one of the first Christian books ever written on the topic, entitled *A Theology of Auschwitz* from 1967, Simon battles with the two sides of the experience of the tragic: suffering and the morally destructive realities of evil that are immovably real.[8] Yet, in his reading, they are all really and concretely taken up in the passion of Jesus such that this immovability is somehow transformed into the passage into and, as a result, of the transcendent truth and goodness of God. Auschwitz only makes sense, Simon seems to say, through the real existence of not just resisters but *faithful* resisters, such as Bonhoeffer, whose grasp of or by the transcendent God effectively transfigures the reality of Auschwitz.

Simon's book on Auschwitz, however innovative, had little influence and has been quickly forgotten. Around the same time as it appeared, another book by the Jewish rabbi Richard Rubenstein came out, *After Auschwitz: Radical Theology and Contemporary Judaism*, whose overt argument for the "death" of any traditional notion of God caught on and to this day has kept hold of public attention.[9] Rubenstein's argument that the Holocaust "killed off," in a way, any potent vision of God's existence seemed much clearer than Simon's ambiguous swimming about in the waters of the tragic, which, intrinsically, reaches out for some grasp of divine absolutes in the form of Christ. The contrast between Simon's perplexing survival and the

---

8. Ulrich Simon, *A Theology of Auschwitz: The Christian Faith and the Problem of Evil* (London: Gollancz, 1967).

9. Richard Rubenstein, *After Auschwitz: Radical Theology and Contemporary Judaism* (Indianapolis: Bobbs-Merrill, 1966).

utter loss of his beautiful father, family, and home—standing in the midst of incalculably extending rubble—is simply hard to maintain as a place of life.

How does the Holy Spirit enter into any of this? In two ways for now: First, the Spirit, as it turns out, is Simon's theological category of choice to deploy in describing this strange place of standing in the midst of tragedy. Second, to the degree that Simon's usage not only makes argumentative sense but in fact illuminates his own struggle, there is something for us to glean here, pneumatically in particular.

At the end of his autobiography, Simon turns to the figure of Samson, which Milton had made so central to his much debated poem *Samson Agonistes*. The Israelite judge dies in the ruins of the Philistine palace he pulls down upon himself and his enemies, and he does so, no one doubts, in some form of "triumph." It is not, however, a victory, Simon notes, achieved through some "*deus ex machina*" who whisks Samson away from danger. Rather, the hero's "tragic history owes . . . everything to the spirit inside the man, who exchanges life for death, so that death may cease its hold on life."[10] Simon then argues that the "future . . . must assume the supremacy of the Spirit," just in the way it builds upon and transcends tragedy.[11] This is it: the Holy Spirit is the revelation within the tragic of the transcendent God, who has taken the reality of tragedy—intractable, immovable—to himself in Christ, but who goes and exists beyond it. The Holy Spirit holds together, somehow, this divine truth of tragic hope, keeps it from being wishful thinking, foolishness, fantasy; even while keeping it strictly within the bounds of faith in the unseen.

I want to be clear in my presentation: Simon intuited rather than explained this somehow. He rarely makes an open pneumatological argument. He is constantly dodging back and forth on the page, letting his literary notes and vignettes pile up without often an obvious current and direction. But the intuition is there, and it is an intuition that many other theologians have rarely achieved. His deeper insistence is that one must always say "this *and* this": this difficult and often crushing reality of human life *and* this God. Both and. What marks the pneumatic character of existence is that "this" life—such as it is from 1913 Berlin through winding and often dead-ended byways of Moscow, Zurich, Amsterdam, Theresienstadt, Auschwitz, and London—is ordered to and by "this God," who has followed the order of his making. The pneumatic character of "this and this," then,

10. Simon, *Pity and Terror*, 161.
11. Simon, *Pity and Terror*, 161.

does not indicate so much an ontological *break* in human existence, between horror and light or struggle and redemption, but simply the apprehending rather than fracturing reality of God. The difference is important: only God holds it all together. Only God.

I dwell at length on this now obscure theologian, Ulrich Simon, because the Holy Spirit is, straightforwardly but in explicit theological terms, about human lives like his, lived in this way and oriented to this straddling of contrasts. It is not about the abstracted categories of the systematicians. The theological challenge of tragedy, into which lives like Simon's are embedded, is to speak of living with contingent vulnerability not so much as something real but as something that the acknowledgement of and faith in God does not simply wave away to the side of things. The challenge of any theological claim to the truth of the "transcendent" God is that this God be able to offer a framework *for*, not an alternative to, the realities of life as it is lived by many. Such a divine framework must provide a hope that is foundational to yet never expropriative of existence as it is received. My simple argument is that a proper theology of the Holy Spirit, then, is one that provides both the descriptive object and its character expressed in Job's exclamation of thanks, "The Lord gave and the Lord hath taken away; blessed be the name of the Lord" (Job 1:21).[12] It is a thanks concretized in the first part of his praise, "naked came I out of my mother's womb; naked shall I return thither." Yet "blessed be the name of the Lord."

I have recently written about pneumatology as an early modern invention, beginning in the late sixteenth and early seventeenth centuries, that then only developed over the past 300 years into the contemporary technical theological discipline related to the Holy Spirit that we know today.[13] For a long time pneumatology, so-called, was a "science" that dealt with universal physical properties, vapors, and ether; mental or psychological arenas of divine illumination or craven fantasies; powers that could move across space and time; metaphysical patterns of invulnerability; the march of history; the embrace of infinity; and the experience of cosmic union. In all of this—examined at Scottish universities, within the laboratories of Anglican and Methodist adepts, or in the surgeries of Continental and then American armies, in the public spaces of futuristic oracles—the Holy Spirit was often mentioned, but in ways that thoroughly confused it with

---

12. Here and elsewhere my biblical quotations are from the King James Version.

13. Ephraim Radner, *A Profound Ignorance: Modern Pneumatology and its Anti-Modern Redemption* (Waco, TX: Baylor University Press, 2019).

the hopes for some humanly grasped "spirit" somehow connected to God, from vacuums to electricity to simple and deep perception and human transfiguration. Only by the 1970s did something called *pneumatology* get established in our divinity faculties, tied exclusively to the third person of the Trinity. But by this point, the theologians—mostly subconsciously—had swept up all these previous elements into the Trinitarian toolbox, along with the existential presuppositions that fueled their appearance in the first place.

For behind pneumatology's early modern development was the deep press of bewilderment and pained amazement at a world and society that had simply expanded beyond the breaking point: new peoples, vast distances, divided churches, uncontrollable wars, and now the ever-communicated realities of disease and its dissolving powers. *Spirit* was to be the gateway out of or at least the resolving tonic within such a world. But to this degree, the Holy Spirit—even as its pneumatological elaboration was often bound up with the intolerable experiences of suffering and confusion—was an almost deliberate way to run away from tragedy. The notion was, of course, that God could not be found in such a place as this, where the scope of challenge and with it suffering had exceeded human calculation and easy manipulation. There was nowhere to run to, so the Spirit offered the means to run away in another direction altogether. Modern pneumatology, such as it has been bequeathed us in its specifically theological form, trades on these dynamics, however much it is often clothed in the tropes of orthodoxy.

Why is this wrong? Why should the Holy Spirit *not* be the means by which to escape this fallen world? There is a simple theological answer: if the Holy Spirit is our exit strategy, the human experience of "intolerability" becomes literally apotheosized. Since the universal Spirit, in modern perspective, is precisely that by which pneumatic forms have populated the world as a whole, Christian and non-Christian, to imagine the Spirit as the moving walkway through the door that leads away from this life is to imagine the whole world as it is now, as the place God would have us curse, silently or aloud, *for the sake of knowing God.*

To be sure, the intolerability of the world that modern pneumatology trades upon is rarely consciously asserted. Its masks include the blind Pollyannas, the crude dispensationalists, and the master-commandants ruling over their progressivist minions in the work of social amelioration. All of these flourish in a world divided from the Spirit's establishing force. Simon was right that sentimentalized Gnosticism is one form of this era's religious orientations, but so is the grim insistence on constructivist fantasies that give rise to the kinds of Orwellian dystopias that populate the so-called "globalized" civilization, where benignity and benevolence become the tyrants meant to tame our creatureliness. To all is common the repeated refrain that "this is not our world; we are meant for something better." If this is what Paul meant when he rejected a resurrectionless existence as "pitiable" (1 Cor 15:19), then I have misunderstood him. For Paul's worries were not about the world but were aimed at those who did not know "the power of God," in Jesus's terms (Mark 12:24)—the God who, after all, made and governs *this* world, not another. Hence, just this world, intolerable as it might seem for some, is the realm of the Spirit purely and utterly.

Let me return to the category of tragedy. Whatever its proper literary definition, I would agree with recent theologians like MacKinnon and Williams that a central aspect of the tragic is its facing into the "intractability" of worldly burdens. There are simply things we cannot run from or make right: when your spouse gets incurable cancer, when you hit a pedestrian while driving under the influence, when every choice you are offered, like Bonhoeffer, violates your conscience. Just here we need to rethink, among other things, our notions of the Holy Spirit. There is in fact an area of contemporary study known as *intractability theory*, bound up mostly with computational science and logic—what kinds of problems are solvable given the time and space of computational limits, even imagined ones.[14] And this goes to that fascinating, if sometimes frightening, border of science that lies between psychology and computers, located in the workings of the human brain: there are things, even within our own selves and thoughts, that we are incapable of explaining, let alone even setting straight. The point, more broadly, is this: some things simply cannot be solved. Applied to the lived world of social relations and interior perception rather than logic, the unsolvable, the intractable, and the inevitable turn out to embrace much of our experience. Why don't we teach people about any of this?

For, truth to tell, we are all simply stuck with much that constitutes our lives and the lives of others: ability and disability, disease and contingent strength, mental illness, personalities and their limits, when and where one is born, with whom one is raised in terms of parents and siblings and others. I, along with everyone else, at some point or another and probably at numerous points, will have to face the almost overwhelming reality of something I simply cannot fix, resolve, or change. Every person will have

---

14. The "classic" textbook on this is M. R. Garey, M. and D. S. Johnson, *Computers and Intractability: A Guide to the Theory of NP-Completeness* (New York: W. H. Freeman, 1979).

to learn to live with this basic existential *aporia*, or else exhaust themselves in futile rebellion, or disappear into a life of willful fantasy.

The philosopher and mathematician Leibniz, inventor with Newton of the "infinitesimal" calculus, may have thought these intractables were all divinely explainable, precisely in real, if complexly transcendent, computational terms.[15] But just this hope turned out only to be a kind metaphysical transposition of intractability: the best of all possible worlds, in God's terms—as he labeled the framework of his *theodicy*—still seemed not only filled with terrors, but inescapably so. Whatever Leibniz really thought he was doing—and I think he was far more savvy than Voltaire, his bitterest critic, could grasp, and perhaps less mathematically reductive than some today believe—I emphasize the prime "intractable" that stands as the base of his system. That is, of course, God himself: the world *is* the "best of all possible words" because we cannot, by definition, get away from God, nor can we comprehend him who is the inescapable, immovable, unresolvable, limit upon all limitations. To be sure, there is a category difference that may subvert the analogy: God is not intractable in the way that human stupidity, malice, and mortality may be. Yet if contingency and finitude, as well the vulnerability that derives from these, are intractable aspects of human existence, what makes these constraints the fundamental elements of tragedy, at least for Christians, is their bondedness to, even genetic linkage to, God's own being as our creator. Because *God* has made us, we are limited, and this fact cannot be gotten around, but it must somehow in the end be faced. MacKinnon called tragedy a kind of "negative natural theology" in that it unveils the irreducible difficulty of God but nonetheless displays this absolute intractability as a divine revelation.

That is to say, our unsolicited births and our inescapable deaths, with all their attendant challenges to love and loss, are themselves divine revelations, the earthly intractables that ascend and descend to the Great Intractable, such that the exclamation "The Lord gave and the Lord hath taken away; blessed be the name of the Lord" is an apocalyptic truth, giving form to the praise of something like Psalm 139 ("Whither shall I go from thy Spirit?" v. 7). And if the Holy Spirit—the Spirit of truth, as Jesus calls him (John 14:17; 15:26; 16:13)—somehow suffuses the world's existence as modern pneumatology tends to emphasize, then the Holy Spirit is not only "the

---

15. Cf. the mathematician Gregory Chaitin's conclusion, based on his reading of Leibniz, that "God is a computer programmer" in his essay, "Leibniz, Information, Math & Physics," in *Thinking about Gödel and Turing: Essays on Complexity, 1970–2007*, ed. Gregory J. Chaitin (Singapore: World Scientific, 2007), 235.

Spirit of life" (as the creed insists) but also in a real way the Spirit of death, of dying. He is the Spirit, that is, of just *this* life that comes and goes from the hand of God. "Who knoweth the spirit of man that goeth upward, and the spirit of the beast that goeth downward to the earth?" (Eccl 3:21), asks Solomon the Preacher. The Christian knows that this spirit (his or her own), through the Holy Spirit, goes, finally, to the Father, and for whatever final revelation there may be of him who made us from nothing. "It is appointed for men to die once, and after that comes judgement" (Heb 9:27). But the passage from one to the other, from death to the appearance of God, is the same for man and beast both: "As the one dieth, so dieth the other; yea, they have all one breath [or *ruach*]; so that a man hath no preeminence above a beast" (Eccl 3:19). With St. Paul, the Preacher here might well say, "And I think that I too have the Spirit of God" (1 Cor. 7:40). Is not the book of Ecclesiastes a pneumatic text, telling us about the truth that "suffuses" all things?

To die, then, is a pneumatic event, just as to be born, which ought to place the Holy Spirit at the center of Christian tragedy, where I believe he *is*. Whether Jesus himself is rightly considered a tragic figure—and few critics, either religious or literary, except the most kenotically driven, would say he is—Jesus's followers most certainly are. That includes the apostles; that includes Christians of today. Caught within the intractability not only of this world's press but of our own divinely granted bodies and souls and their constraining networks of difficult relations, we Christians, quite frankly, *struggle*. Paul talks repeatedly of "toiling" and "striving" (cf. Col. 1:29; 1 Tim 4:10; 6:12; 2 Tim 4:7), with its rooted sense of the *agōn*, and Hebrews grounds this in the endurance of suffering (Heb. 10:32; 12:4), with blood and martyrdom literally standing as its summit and end. The struggle, the literal "agony" of the Christian's life, is ingredient to its character. One strains ahead, as Paul puts it; one "endures," as Jesus puts it (Mark 13:13); and one does this "to the end," the final place where, of course, all is "finished," as Christ describes his last breath (John 19:30), as a kind of "fulfilment."

On the one hand, this side of existence that runs into the "end" is one that every human being is fixed within, believer or not. What the Christian does, following Jesus, however, is not to escape it but to *hope* in face of it. It is this hope alone that stands as the bridge to the other side of "finishedness," to the vision of God's intractable life and power that we can only intuit at this time. Chapter 1 of 1 Peter lays it all out well: suffering now for the sake of one whom we do not now see, we endure by faith in the hope of his revelation. We do this, furthermore, precisely as grass that withers in a day, in the shadow of a living Word that abides forever. Paul is right: if there is no resurrection, we Christians, of all people, are to be most pitied. But why? Not because we have suffered, for in this we are no different than all creatures. Rather, because we have *hoped* in vain. And to the world, who sees no more than we, nothing could be more tragic than straining after the invisible.

I want to emphasize the direction I am indicating here. I am not trying to encourage, as a strand of especially Old Testament scholarship has in the past few years, that we rediscover the centrality of "lament," for instance, as a vehicle of divine revelation and response. Nor even, on a more metaphysical level, that we should take Romans 8 as the defining lens for pneumatic reality, such that the Spirit's groaning with the world says all there is to say. It says something, but not enough. A more traditional pneumatic charism, the so-called "gift of tears," certainly underscores the important role lament and creational yearning may have in understanding the Spirit and living with the Spirit. But even in this case of "tears," the charism's originating monastic ascetic category of *penthos*, often translated as "compunction," indicates that pneumatic mourning is tied as much to the sorrow of repentance as to anything.[16] And repentance, in turn presses in the direction of faith, not simply of sorrowful dissatisfaction. My point, then, is broader than valorizing lament as a Christian category. Instead, what I am trying to indicate is how we must not *oppose* the Spirit to the world of created existence and struggle. Because of the Spirit's creation of this world, this world's struggling existence as pneumatic truth and revelation is ultimately the only way that faithful witness can be pursued or enabled. Only *because* the world's struggle is the Spirit's self-giving is "faith" a reality of creaturely blessing. Only dying in faith can reveal that and what the Holy Spirit is, at least for us human beings.

I began this essay by asserting that "the Holy Spirit teaches us to die faithfully." That faith, of course, is not simply a sorrowing or a yearning. Nor, for that matter, does sorrow and yearning constitute the "tragic" in a specifically Christian perspective. As St. Peter writes in his first epistle, a faith that faces into death, or a faithful death simply, is one filled with holiness, with love, with grace, with a sustaining power, and even with joy, though of a particular kind, which Peter calls an "joy unspeakable,"

16. Irénée Hausherr, *Penthos: The Doctrine of Compunction in the Christian East* (1944; repr., Kalamazoo, MI: Cistercian, 1982).

a *chara aneclaletos* (1 Peter 1:8). St. Peter's outline provides all the traditional elements of pneumatic anointing, whether according to the charismata or the virtues. But what keeps these elements in Peter's description honest, if you will, is the fact that the Holy Spirit takes them all—his listeners and their pneumatically charged existences—to their deaths, consigning their ultimate value to a resurrection that has not yet come, nor that we can yet conceive clearly. The epistle of 1 Peter, after all, is a call to martyrdom, which is nothing else than a faithful death crystallized as such.

This was Ulrich Simon's insistence in his *Theology of Auschwitz*. His heroes, as it were, were people like Walter Rathenau, a courageous political leader in post–World War I Germany who was gunned down by antisemitic protofascists; Edith Stein, the Jewish philosopher and convert to the Christian conventual life who died at Auschwitz; and Bonhoeffer, of course. They were indeed tragic heroes, whose existences could not escape the intractable assaults of their times, their neighbors, or their coreligionists even. Their resistance, to keep to the plot of tragedy, was given in the fact that they lived and died in hope—faithfully. To quote 1 Peter again, "Wherefore let them that suffer according to the will of God commit the keeping of their souls [to him] in well doing, as unto a faithful Creator" (1 Pet 4:19). Just this, this faithful hope, transformed their Christian (and Jewish) tragedy into a witness to the transcendent good of God in the face of all chaos and evil, even and especially in their dying, "The Spirit seals their transitory lot with the stamp of eternal purpose," Simon wrote.[17]

As Simon laid out in his book on Auschwitz, the form of this pneumatic "seal"—the faithful death that transfigured all existence, all creation, all relationships between Creator and creature, or at least revealed their truth utterly—was Jesus Christ. Just *this* death in faith, a pneumatic death, in a substantive sense, given over to God, is that of Jesus's final self-commendation, etched in the Psalms and announced in the Scriptures: "How much more, then, will the blood of Christ, who *through the eternal Spirit offered himself unblemished to God*, cleanse our consciences from acts that lead to death, so that we may serve the living God!" (Heb 9:14 NIV). From this perspective, the Spirit gives us a saving death, the consummation of faithful death, the death of Christ, as the great education to life.

But this education, the pneumatic education of the faithful death of Christ, is etched in the shape of the natural world. It is only because the world is God's that we are his also even in our deaths. There is no relation

17. Simon, *Theology of Auschwitz*, 83.

to God apart from this world, just as it comes to us, a world in which Christ dies faithfully. But this world, given to us, *is* our relation to God, not to something else or something less. And the constitution of this gift of the world is the Holy Spirit, who, as Augustine most emphatically insisted, is "Gift" itself. There is no world or life without the Holy Spirit, but conversely, from the subjective vantage of the creature, there is no Holy Spirit without the world. The conjunction is what is redemptively creative, and thus hopeful. To be born, to breathe and grow, to weaken and finally die in just the way the world is so constituted, that is, as creatures of God's gracious creation, to be spiritually taught—this is faith. In this teaching, all the charismata and beatitudes we rightly identify with the Holy Spirit—wisdom, meekness, courage, poverty of spirit, gentleness, joy, charity—inductively form the breath of such a movement from birth to death, not as something extraneous to the world, but as that which most fully expresses the world as God's. Such a pneumatically educated life must, and does in fact, include children, the elderly, the peaceably protected, but also—perhaps most pointedly, and most commonly too, as Simon suggested—the brutally dispossessed and stymied, for whom, in all cases, the commending of one's life to a "faithful creator" displays the cosmic stamp of God's goodness, the Christic stamp, which marks created being as just that, God's making, the very meaning of the "natural."

My worry is that modern pneumatology, by contrast, has developed into an "artificial education" for Christians. It is a theoretical extravaganza that ends up listing all the mistakes of existence that it purports can be rectified, cancelled out, and forgotten: sex, vulnerability, weakness, stymiedness, dispossession, death itself. The artificial education of Christians leads to a similar defeat as Schopenhauer's atheistic version: anxiety, false confidence, crashing disappointments, and despair. The same concern drove Simon's protest on behalf of tragedy in the face of the theologian's facile sentimentalizing of created existence, dancing around the eucharistic table holding hands and mouthing banal songs (as he put it).[18] Instead, the body and blood of our Lord is properly consumed in following his path through the world. It is a path, the form of which the Gospels trace in quiet detail, all the way to his death and self-commendation in faith. Where he has gone, we will go. But one goes this way, the way of faith, in descriptive honesty and remembered exactitude. Of all the sciences, the most pneumatically endowed is history. For there, in the infinite

18. Simon, *Pity and Terror*, 137.

complexity and possibility of the world's stored reality, lies the stuff of God's making, his incarnation, and his redemption. Only the Spirit could leave Ulrich Simon with the rescued image of his father, sitting on a suitcase at the Theresienstadt train station, creating music only God would ever hear. Such a faith as this.

Scripture Index

Scripture Index

Scripture Index

SUBJECT INDEX

Subject Index

Subject Index

AUTHOR INDEX